WHEATON PUBLIC LIBRARY
225 N. CROSS
WHEATON, IL 60187
(630) 668-1374

THE
CHAIN

Farm, Factory,
and the Fate of
Our Food

TED GENOWAYS

HARPER

An Imprint of HarperCollins*Publishers*

HarperCollins books may be purchased for educational, business, or sales promotional use. For information, please e-mail the Special Markets Department at SPsales@harpercollins.com.

FIRST EDITION

Photographs by Mary Anne Andrei

Library of Congress Cataloging-in-Publication Data

Genoways, Ted.
  The chain : farm factory / Ted Genoways.—First edition.
    pages cm
  Farm factory
  Includes bibliographical references.
  ISBN 978-0-06-228875-2
  1. Meat industry and trade—United States. 2. Food processing plants—United States. 3. Factory farms. 4. Industrial safety. 5. Hormel Foods Corporation. I. Title. II. Title: Farm factory.
  HD9415.G46 2014
  338.7'664920973--dc23
                                                                2014019018

14 15 16 17 18   OV/RRD   10 9 8 7 6 5 4 3 2 1

For Jack

The speeding-up seemed to be growing more savage all the time.

—Upton Sinclair, *The Jungle*

CONTENTS

PART FOUR

PART FIVE

PART SIX

PROLOGUE

Maria Lopez will never forget that day.

It was 2004, the middle of an ordinary shift on the line at Hormel Foods—a sprawling brick-and-concrete complex, just across the Union Pacific tracks on the southern edge of Fremont, Nebraska. The worker beside her fed pork shoulders one after another into a spinning saw, just as he did every other day of the week, while Lopez gathered and bagged the trimmed fat to go into Spam. The facility in Fremont was just one of two plants in the world where Hormel made its signature product, so the pace of work had always been steady. But the speed of the line had jumped recently, from 1,000 hogs per hour to more than 1,100, and Lopez was having trouble keeping up. As her coworker reached for another shoulder, she rushed to clear the cutting area—and her fingers slipped toward the saw blade. Lopez snatched her hand back, but it was too late. Her index finger dangled by a flap of skin, the bone cut clean through. She screamed as blood spurted and covered her workstation.

Later, a surgeon was able to shorten both ends of the bone and stabilize it with a screw before delicately repairing the tendons and reattaching the nerves and blood vessels. A month after that, Lopez needed another surgery to insert a second pin to straighten a crook in the bone. In the end, she lost all feeling in her finger—

but missed just two months of work. It was only after she returned to Hormel that Lopez discovered a stomach-turning truth: that while she sprinted to the nurse's station and was taken to the Fremont Area Medical Center, while she waited, finger wrapped, in the emergency room for the surgeon to drive in from Omaha, the cut line at Hormel continued to run. That hour, like virtually every working hour, without interruption, the plant processed 1,100 hogs—their carcasses butchered into parts and marketed as Cure 81 hams or Black Label bacon, the scraps collected and ground up to make Spam and Little Sizzlers breakfast sausages. Her coworkers were instructed by floor supervisors to wash the station of her blood, but the line never stopped.

Maria remembered all this while she fried *papas* in the kitchen of her home on the outskirts of Fremont, her index finger pointed straight as she gripped the spatula. She told me that her numb finger made her clumsy at her job at Hormel, and she grew worried that her fumbling might lead to a more serious injury. In 2006, when the speed increased yet again—this time to more than 1,200 hogs per hour—Maria quit. Her husband, Fernando, who still worked at the plant, told me that the line was now moving at more than 1,300 head per hour, and the injuries were increasing and becoming worse. He had a friend who was a "gut snatcher," tasked with pulling innards from swinging carcasses. One day, when he took too long clearing an abdominal cavity, the backsaw cut through the spine and sliced off four of his fingers. "I think he lose two of these," Fernando said, pointing to his middle and ring finger. Then, as if an afterthought, Fernando added that he too had lost part of a finger—the tip of his left pinkie to a rib cutter. In every case, he said, "they washed it up but never stopped production. It's terrible to work on the line."

Workers' rights advocates agree. In September 2013, a coalition of civil rights groups, led by the Southern Poverty Law Center and the Nebraska Appleseed Center for Law in the Public Interest, called on the U.S. Occupational Safety and Health Administration (OSHA) and the U.S. Department of Agriculture (USDA) to "reduce the speed of the processing line to minimize the severe and systemic risks" faced by American meatpackers, such as repetitive stress injuries and cuts and amputations, which affect meatpacking workers at "alarming rates." They pointed to an extensive study of packinghouse employees conducted by Nebraska Appleseed in 2009, which found that 52 percent of all workers felt that conditions had become less safe in the last twelve months, with "the vast majority" citing line speed as the cause. Despite the report, all of the plants studied had seen further speedups in the intervening years.

But only a handful of packinghouses in the entire country have been permitted to run as fast as the Hormel plant in Fremont. Thanks to a special program piloted by the USDA more than a decade ago to test the effects of reduced inspection on food safety, five pork processing facilities nationwide have been allowed to set their own line speeds. And Hormel managed to get all three of the slaughter operations that it owns or operates into that select handful. This increase in work speed positioned Hormel to capitalize on the coming economic crisis and the demand it created for budget-friendly meat like Spam. But this seemingly minor change in plant operation—upping the speed of slaughter on just three kill floors and speeding butchering and processing in just the two plants where Hormel manufactures Spam—also set off a wide-ranging and sometimes disastrous series of events.

What follows, then, is not just the tale of what happened when Hormel decided to speed up production but also an examination of the knock-on effects of that decision, over a period of years, up and down the supply chain—from the confinement facilities where high-density hog farming increasingly threatens environmental quality and animal welfare to the packinghouses where workers face some of the most dangerous working conditions in the country and hostility from the communities where they live to the butcher counter at the supermarket, where the safety and wholesomeness of the food supply have been jeopardized. It is a portrait of American industry pushed to its breaking point by the drive for increased output but also a cracked mirror in which to see our own complicity, every time we choose low-cost and convenience over quality. It is, in short, an attempt to calculate the true price of cheap meat.

Part One

Chapter 1

THE BRAIN MACHINE

On the kill floor of Quality Pork Processors Inc., the wind always blows: from the open doors at the docks where drivers unload massive trailers of screeching pigs, through the overheated room where the hogs are butchered, to the plastic-draped breezeway where the parts are handed over to Hormel Foods for packaging. The air gusts and swirls, whistling through the plant like the current in a canyon. In the first week of December 2006, Matthew Garcia felt feverish and chilled on the blustery production floor. He fought stabbing back pains and vomiting, but he figured it was just the flu. El Niño had touched the prairies of southern Minnesota with unusually warm air that fall, and public health officials were warning that powerful strains of influenza might sweep the state. But he was still in his teens and strong—and he was determined to tough it out.

Garcia had gotten on at QPP in Austin, just two hours south of Minneapolis–St. Paul, only twelve weeks before and had been stuck with one of the worst spots on the line: running a device known simply as the "brain machine"—the last stop on a conveyor snaking down the middle of a J-shaped, steel-encased bench called the "head table." Every hour, more than 1,300 severed pork heads went sliding along the belt. Workers sliced off the ears, clipped the snouts, chiseled the cheek meat. They scooped out the eyes, carved out the tongues, and scraped the palate meat from the roofs of mouths. Because, famously, all parts of a pig are edible ("everything but the squeal," wisdom goes), nothing was wasted, not even the brains. A few years before Garcia started on the line, someone up the chain of command, someone at Hormel, had found a buyer in Korea, where liquid pork brains are used as a thickener in stir-fry.

So all week long a woman next to Garcia would carve meat off the back of each head then let the denuded skull slide down the conveyor and through an opening in a Plexiglas shield. On the other side, Garcia inserted the metal nozzle of a 90-pounds-per-square-inch compressed-air hose into the opening at the back of each skull, tripping a trigger that blasted the pig's brains into a pink slurry. One head every three seconds. A high-pressure burst, a fine rosy mist, and the slosh of brains slipping through a drain hole into a catch bucket. (Some workers told me the goo looked like Pepto-Bismol; others described it as more like a lumpy strawberry milk shake.) When the ten-pound barrel was filled, another worker would come to take the brains for packaging and shipping. And the hollow skulls were dropped down a chute, where yet another worker, one Garcia never saw, gathered heads to be ground into bone meal. Most days that fall, production was so fast that the air never cleared between blasts of the brain machine, and the fine mist would drift, coating workers at the head table in a grisly mix of tissue and blood.

No one thought much of it. On the slaughtering side—the so-called hot side or warm room—temperatures were kept artificially high to stop blood from clotting and clogging drains, to prevent fat from hardening and gumming up the machinery. Everyone's bare arms and faces were covered with gore, their white smocks

gone red and slicked with grease. And the thick air was made
even more choking by the Whizard knives—spinning circular
blades, powered by a roaring pneumatic compressor. Sooner or
later, the steady hum of the Whizards and the brutal repetition
of line jobs—some duplicating the same cut as many as 30,000
times per shift—gave everyone carpal tunnel syndrome or ten-
donitis. And all you have to do is wait in the QPP parking lot at
shift change to see the shambling gait that comes from standing
in one spot all day on the plant floor. Eight hours straight, Garcia
stood, many days without so much as a lunch or bathroom break,
slipping heads onto the brain machine's brass nozzle, pouring the
glop into the drain, then dropping the empty skulls down the
chute—fighting his way through headaches and waves of nausea.
"It was like a flu," he told me later, "fever, vomit, weakness—the
kind of weakness that I just don't get work done fast enough." But
if he wanted to move up, he couldn't afford to miss any days, not
when the bosses were pushing for more and more overtime.

That fall, rampant defaults on subprime mortgage loans had
sent the housing market into a nationwide tailspin, and, with the
looming threat of recession, demand for Spam was climbing. The
line ran faster and longer—two shifts each weekday, most Saturdays, even some Sundays, and still Hormel couldn't keep up.
There was talk of adding a third shift. By Thanksgiving, Garcia
would return home spent, his back and head throbbing. But he
soon realized that this was more than just exhaustion from over-
work or some winter virus.

On December 11, Garcia awoke to find he couldn't walk. His
legs felt dead, paralyzed. His family rushed him to the Austin
Medical Center, not far from the subdivided Victorian they rented
on Third Street. Doctors there sent Garcia for a complete exam at
St. Mary's Hospital, part of the Mayo Clinic in Rochester, about
an hour away. By the time he arrived, he was running a high fever
and complaining of piercing headaches. He was immediately ad-

mitted and put through a battery of tests—including MRIs of
his head and his cervical and thoracic spine. Every one indicated
neurological abnormalities, most importantly a severe spinal cord
inflammation, apparently caused by an autoimmune response. It
was as if his body were attacking his own nerves.

In the coming days, as his condition spiraled downward, baf-
fled doctors struggled to understand what was happening to
Garcia. He was transferred to the clinic's Mary Brigh Building
for extended inpatient care. By Christmas, he had been bedridden
for two weeks, and his physicians feared he might be suicidal.
Garcia was diagnosed with "acute adjustment disorder"—the
medical term for severe depression brought on by a sudden and
unexplained illness or injury. They sent a psychiatrist to counsel
Garcia. He needed to prepare himself for a different kind of life,
they said—one in a wheelchair.

There is no Matthew Garcia.

Or, rather, Matthew Garcia is not his name. It's the name I've
given him to shield him from Immigration and Customs Enforcement, but I don't know his real name anyway. All I know is
the name on his driver's license, his I-9s and ITINs, his medical
records and workers' comp claims. All I know is the name on
his Social Security card. But that name belongs to someone else,
someone in Texas, in prison or worse, someone with a suitably
Hispanic name who sold his information or had it stolen from
him. There is no Matthew Garcia in Austin, Minnesota, and if
you go looking, you won't find him.

But then there's also no Emiliano Ballesta or Miriam Angeles
or any of the other Hispanic workers who stood side by side with
Garcia at the head table, because seemingly everyone working at
QPP in the first decade of the new century had a fake name and
false papers with a phony address. And not just the people on

the kill floor. Quality Pork Processors is simply another way of saying Hormel, and QPP's corporate headquarters in Dallas is just an accounting firm, a mailing address, and a tax shelter in a poured-concrete office park along the LBJ Freeway. And if you leaf through a phone book in Austin, Minnesota, you can find a listing for Kelly Wadding, the CEO of QPP, but if you drive there, you'll find no house, no such address.

In Austin, such half-truths and agreed-upon lies are as much a part of the landscape as the slow-moving Cedar River, which divides the two sides of town. On one bank stands the Hormel plant, with its towering six-story hydrostatic Spam cooker and sprawling fenced compound, encompassing QPP and shielded from view by a fifteen-foot privacy wall. When I asked for a look inside, I got a chipper email from Julie H. Craven, the company spokeswoman: "They are state-of-the-art facilities (nothing to be squeamish about!) but media tours are not available." On the other bank is the Spam Museum, where a patois of aw-shucks midwesternisms and corporate double talk are spoken like a second language. Former plant workers serve as Spambassadors, while Monty Python's "Spam Song" is piped in on an endless loop ("Spamity, Spam! Spamity, Spam!"), and the sanitized history of Hormel unfolds in more than sixteen thousand square feet of exhibits, artifacts, and tchotchkes. There's even a booth with a digital countdown to see if you could pack Spam fast enough to keep up with the speed of the factory line.

One room is done up as the Provision Market, the original storefront opened by George A. Hormel (pronounced HOR-mel to rhyme with "normal") in the Litchfield Building on Mill Street in November 1891. What the exhibit labels won't tell you is that on Thanksgiving Day of that year, Hormel took his sweetheart, Lillian Gleason, skating on the frozen river, then walked her to the old creamery tucked amid a grove of scrub oaks on the east bank where he had set up his meatpacking plant. He wanted Lillian to see the new two-horsepower engine he had just bought along with a power chopper and stuffer to make sausage. This was going to be the beginning of big business for Hormel. Lillian must have been impressed; when she married George three months later, she was three months pregnant with their son, Jay.

From the earliest days of the business, George Hormel understood economies of scale. In the first year, he and his sole employee could slaughter three animals on a good day. By the next year, better tools and divided labor allowed them to more than quadruple their output. But their greatest expansion came during an unlikely time: in 1893, railroad overbuilding, combined with a severe drought on the western plains, caused a bank panic and the deepest depression in American history. Hormel, instead of cutting back, concocted a risky plan. First, he saw that failing railroads meant cheaper shipping, so he started importing hogs from all over Minnesota and Iowa and sending the butchered meat to retailers as far away as St. Louis and Chicago. Second, the arrival of the refrigeration car had allowed eastern competitors to elbow into the midwestern market for fresh meat, but Hormel banked on the assumption that empty pockets meant that people would be willing to eat more smoked and cured meat. Among his new ideas was thinly slicing and sugar-curing back meat, which he marketed as a novelty breakfast item he called Canadian bacon.

Even a fire that destroyed the creamery in 1896 became an opportunity. Hormel built a new facility in its place with high volume in mind and expanded his staff to twenty men. By the time the country began to emerge from the panic, Hormel's—as locals called it—was processing 60 hogs a day and had persuaded the Great Western to lay a rail line directly to their door. By the turn of the century, the plant was processing 120 hogs per day. By the time the United States entered into World War I, they were up to 2,000. At the brink of the Great Depression, when George handed the business over to Jay, the plant was processing 4,000 hogs per day.

In one corner of the Spam Museum, George and Jay, portrayed as full-size, ghostly white figures (like corporate George Segal sculptures), reenact the moment in 1929 when the family business was passed down. "I'm getting too old to run this company," George says in the stilted recording. "It's time for you to take over." When the real Jay C. Hormel ascended to president, the company, for all its increased production, faced serious economic crisis. But Jay was a masterful manager—and, like his father, a gambler in the true capitalist sense. Remembering the expansion that Hormel's had achieved in 1893, Jay bet that Americans, once again with little money in their pockets, would buy into the idea of low-cost canned dinners. He developed two of the country's first meat-based canned soups: Hormel chili and Dinty Moore stew. To distinguish them from condensed Campbell's Soups, they were marketed as "the big meals in the big cans."

Strong sales of Hormel's new product lines kept the company afloat—but workers were dissatisfied that their wages had not risen along with profits. In 1932, Joe Ollman and John Winkels on the hog kill teamed up with Frank Ellis, the foreman of the hog-casing department, to begin organizing plant employees under the International Union of All Workers. About the same time, Jay Hormel made a rare miscalculation. Seeking to reduce turnover on the line, he instituted a progressive pension plan, something he regarded as an incentive to stay with Hormel. After all, the company would contribute $1 every week toward retirement and life insurance, against just 20 cents deducted from each worker's paycheck. But Jay didn't bother pitching the plan to employees; he simply instructed foremen to strong-arm workers into signing membership cards—a style of leadership he later rued as "benevolent dictatorship." When the supervisor on the hog kill buttonholed one worker and forced him to sign, labor organizers incited a ten-minute work stoppage until the foreman tore up the man's membership card.

When rumor of the incident spread through the plant, it was enough to spur enormous turnout for a union rally in Sutton Park. Impassioned speeches from Ellis and Ollman convinced six hundred Hormel workers to sign up on the spot, and talk arose of organizing workers throughout Austin. Local business leaders panicked. Jay Hormel urged them to accept union labor. "I am not going to get mixed up in a fight in my hometown," he declared. But other businesses refused to allow their workers to organize, and Hormel was reluctant to put himself at a competitive disadvantage. "He suggested that we go out and organize the other packing plants first," Frank Ellis later remembered. "We told Mr. Hormel that we would organize the other plants, but needed more money now; higher wages was our problem and competition was his."

In November 1933, Ellis and other union organizers, armed with pipes and clubs, escorted Hormel from the general offices and shut down the plant's refrigeration system—threatening to spoil $3.6 million of meat. For three straight days, Hormel went to the picket line to meet with union leaders and address workers from an improvised platform. He brought the strike to a quick end by accepting a series of forward-looking incentives, including profit sharing, merit pay, and the "Annual Wage Plan," an unheard-of salary system in an industry dominated by piecework and hourly rates. Hormel also agreed that increases in output would result in more pay for workers, and he even guaranteed them fifty-two weeks' notice prior to termination.

Perhaps most importantly, Hormel recognized the newly formed union. "I couldn't lick you, so I joined you," he told them. The concessions earned him a matchless period of management-labor harmony, but *Fortune* derided Hormel as the "red capitalist"— and the Depression was cutting deeper and deeper into fresh and cured meat sales. Paying high wages for slow-selling products was eating up Hormel's profit, and lower sales meant less money to pay workers. When Jay attempted layoffs, he was met with a sit-down strike in 1934. To keep workers on the line and improve his margins by reducing waste, he devised yet another canned product, this one made from ground-up scrap meat.

But like everything in Austin, it first needed a new name. He called it Spam.

Just as Emiliano Ballesta's shift at QPP was ending on February 12, 2007, a massive blizzard came sweeping down from Canada. Snow shifted and swirled across Interstate 90. By the time Ballesta reached his mobile home west of the highway on the outskirts of Austin, drifts were starting to pile up, and he entered to find that the pipes had frozen solid. Worried about his wife and five children—most of all, his five-year-old son, who had recently been diagnosed with leukemia—Ballesta shimmied into the crawl space with a pair of small kerosene heaters. Instead of thawing the pipes, he ignited the wispy insulation hanging from the floorboards, and, in no time, flames engulfed the trailer. When police and firefighters responded to the call, they found thick smoke rolling from under the eaves, Ballesta and his family unharmed but watching helplessly as everything they owned burned. By morning, nothing remained but a blackened hull.

The family bounced around after that, crashing with friends and family, sleeping on couches and floors for weeks at a stretch. Ballesta's most pressing concern was making sure that his oldest son, a senior at Austin High School, graduated on time and that the rest of his children had a place to sleep. To save up enough to make rent on an apartment of their own and replace some of their belongings, Ballesta started taking extra overtime hours at QPP. He had been working at the plant since 1994, most of that time at the head table, chiseling meat from the cheeks and jowls of hogs' heads. Despite his experience and despite the fact that recent immigrants on the line regarded him as something of a father figure, Ballesta was only making $12.75 an hour—barely a $26,500 base salary. But he had worked Saturdays to pick up overtime for as long as he could remember, and lately there was plenty available.

As the recession took hold, both Hormel and QPP offered more and more hours to workers. Hormel employees told the *New York Times* that they'd never seen so much overtime. One worker boasted that he'd been able to buy a new TV and refrigerator with his additional pay. Though head meat goes into sausage, not Spam, the increased production of one item increases output of everything else. So as Hormel increased production of ham and shoulder for Spam, Ballesta was racking up overtime hours at the head table, too—so many hours, in fact, that he could afford to move his family into a rented house not far from the plant. And his son graduated right on schedule.

In May 2007, Ballesta was at the commencement ceremony when he noticed his legs starting to feel tight and numb. Within days, his right hip and thigh were throbbing, and it was as if the soles of his feet were on fire. At first, he chalked it up to fatigue, so many extra hours standing, but soon he was having trouble walking from the QPP parking lot to the plant door. He could barely make it to the locker rooms on the top floor, dragging up the staircase by pulling himself on the steel handrail.

Ballesta didn't know it, but he wasn't alone. Miriam Angeles, who worked near the head table removing remnants of spinal cords, had started having burning pain in her lower legs, too, and now her right arm had begun falling asleep—both at work and at home, when she tried to nurse her infant daughter. Mariana Martinez, who floated from station to station filling in for sick workers, had been spending most of her days at the head table since March, and now she too was suffering from headaches, backaches, weak legs, and burning feet. Susan Kruse, the woman who stood on the other side of the Plexiglas shield from Matthew Garcia, clearing neck meat from the aperture where the spinal cord enters the skull, had a knot in her left calf that wouldn't go away. When the cramps spread to her right leg, and stiffness in her hands turned to tingling, Kruse finally went to the doctor.

In the meantime, Mayo doctors had prescribed Garcia a steroid to calm his nerve inflammation, and he'd improved enough to lift himself from his wheelchair and get around without a walker. He still hadn't regained pelvic floor function, robbing him of bowel control and forcing him to insert a urinary catheter each morning, but he managed to return to work at QPP. Garcia was sent to the box room, where he unloaded pallets of cardboard to be assembled for shipping, but he could only stomach half shifts before the pain was too much and he had to go home to bed. While he was out, the harvesting of brains continued. Some days his spot was filled by Mariana Martinez, but usually another worker, a young woman named Santa Zapata, took over threading twenty skulls per minute onto the brass nozzle of the brain machine.

From its conception in 1937, Spam served a business function, not a market demand. If Hormel was going to pay workers guaranteed wages and promise to make no seasonal layoffs, then Jay Hormel reasoned that those workers should be assigned to tasks previously considered too time-consuming to be cost-effective. For decades, the company had discarded thousands of pounds of pork shoulder deemed unworthy of the effort it required to cut it off the bone. But now, Jay surmised that the cost of additional wages would be offset if Hormel could simply convince customers to buy that scrap meat. The company already had established a thriving market for canned hams, first developed by Hormel in 1926. But Jay understood that consumers had gone for that product because, once removed from the tin, the ham inside looked like what they could buy at their local meat counter. No one went to the butcher shop to buy loose pork shoulder and fat trimmings. So Hormel's meat scientists came up with the idea of spicing the shoulder and cooking it into a loaf.

The technical team made two early decisions. First, to appeal to pennywise housewives, the loaf would be twelve ounces—enough to feed a family of five for dinner, with leftovers for sandwiches the next day. Second, to create the impression that the product was a modern innovation, not just an attempt to repackage waste, it would come in a rectangular block, made to fit on a slice of square sandwich bread like that first nationally marketed by Wonder Bread in 1930. According to legend, Julius A. Zillgitt went to the Square Deal Grocery on Main Street in Austin and found a square can of Mazola. He filled the tin with meat, sealed it, and cooked it. But when he opened the can, he found eight ounces of rock-hard meat and four ounces of water. This was only the first of countless setbacks. The Hormel newsletter later itemized the litany of troubles that plagued early development: "the can, the solder, the seam, the fill, the mix, the cure, the age of the pig, the feed of the pig, the cast of the moon." The eventual solution is still a tightly held secret, but it involved vacuum mixing, quick sealing, and pressure-cooking. Zillgitt was ultimately awarded share of a patent for a new process and specially designed machine devised "for browning and forming solid meat."

Now all Jay Hormel had to do was convince the public to eat it. So on New Year's Eve 1936, he threw a party at his twenty-six-bedroom mansion on the eastern edge of Austin. Each guest was greeted at the door with a clutch of blank cards and then offered a new, nameless pork shoulder loaf, prepared in several ways—chopped into squares and poked with toothpicks, diced up into salad, sliced and fried. To get a cocktail, everyone first had to write an idea for the product's name on one of their cards. The first ideas were too literal. But Jay later joked that "along about the fourth or fifth drink they began showing some imagination." Kenneth Daigneau, a New York actor in town for the holidays to visit his brother, Hormel's vice president, hit upon "Spam"—a play on the spiced meat loaf and its hamlike appearance. The name was officially registered as a trademark on May 11, 1937.

To launch the product, Hormel's marketing team took out four-color ads in all the ladies' and home magazines. They sent out groups of young sales executives, dubbed "Spam Crews," to promote their new product to wholesalers and local markets across the country. They launched the Dollar Bill Campaign, going town to town offering one dollar for opinions of Spam, then publishing the most positive comments in the next day's newspaper. They even arranged for George Burns and Gracie Allen to promote Hormel on their popular radio show. By 1940, Spam was being eaten in 70 percent of the urban homes in America.

And after the Japanese bombed Pearl Harbor, Hormel secured a contract with the military to supply Spam to every hungry GI around the world. With the government go-ahead to substitute potent sodium nitrite for traditional sodium chloride, Hormel could crank out a product that would keep indefinitely. The company sent K-rations up supply lines across the Pacific and secured Spam acclaim as the "meat that won the war." Never mind that GIs hated the stuff and flooded Jay with hate mail, which he kept in a drawer he called the Scurrilous File. "If they think Spam is terrible," he told the *New Yorker* in 1945, "they ought to have eaten the bully beef we had during the last war." When peace arrived, Dwight D. Eisenhower wrote Hormel: "I ate my share of Spam along with millions of other soldiers. I'll even confess to a few unkind remarks about it—uttered during the strain of battle, you understand. But as former Commander in Chief, I believe I can still forgive you your only sin: sending us so much of it."

Hormel won the forgiveness of other veterans when the company created a special workers program, in which up to 15 percent of the workforce could be given light duty if disabled. And there was plenty of work. Spam's unflagging production sustained war-crippled Europe in the 1950s. More than that, it cemented Spam's place in the popular imagination of Blitz babies. Monty Python's famed skit (the one playing on an infinite loop at the Spam Museum), in which Spam is cooked into every menu item at a London greasy spoon, was a riff on the inescapability of the canned meat in the British diet under food rationing. For American baby boomers, too, Spam became a symbol of America's postwar love affair with processed food—and an emblem of how America's industrial might meant that workers enjoyed a stable, middle-class existence.

But all that started to change when Jay Hormel died in 1954 and the company passed out of family hands and came under new corporate leadership that wasn't interested in continuing his progressive benefits. In 1975, future president Richard Knowlton began to negotiate a new contract with the union on the promise that Hormel would build a new plant that would reduce workloads. In fact, the new plant allowed Knowlton to gut long-standing incentive programs and increase line speeds. That led to a bitter strike—and completed the transition from George A. HOR-mel & Company, the family business, to Hor-MEL, the corporation where a new pronunciation was embraced as part of a new identity. But that era was about more than rebranding. It was the start of false identities meant to duck standing contracts and future responsibilities; this was when everyone learned to speak the local dialect of truth, when the cut-and-kill side of the operation became Quality Pork Processors and the workforce became populated with undocumented immigrants working under fake names.

In September 2007, Richard Schindler, a family care physician at the Austin Medical Center branch of the Mayo Clinic, sent a group email to four colleagues in neurology in Rochester, outlining the details of an emerging case. "There are several disturbing facts involved," Schindler wrote. Nearly a dozen patients had come to him in the last year with symptoms consistent with something like the rare disorder chronic inflammatory demyelinating polyneuropathy (CIDP)—death of the peripheral nerves caused by damage to the fatty neural covering known as the myelin sheath. None of the patients had previous histories of serious illness, and all were young and (with only one exception) Hispanic.

Most troubling, he wrote, the patients all worked on the cut line at Quality Pork Processors—a detail that had just recently been discovered and then only by chance. Nearly all of the patients were too weak to drive and were getting to their doctor's appointments using a car service run by Colombian-born Walter Schwartz, and in the doctor's office they were relying on translation services offered by the medical center's Spanish interpreter, Carol Hidalgo. Schwartz and Hidalgo noticed the similarity of symptoms, and when Schwartz told her that he had been scheduling appointments for all of these patients around their work schedules at QPP, Hidalgo decided to bring it to the attention of Dr. Schindler.

Schindler interviewed the patients and discovered that they not only worked at QPP but very near one another; many were posted at the head table or nearby. He contacted Carole Bower, the plant's occupational nurse, who reported that she had been noticing workers whose feet were so tender that they struggled with the stairs to the top-floor locker rooms, high above the roar of the factory line. She referred six workers to Schindler. Among them was Matthew Garcia, who, after a few weeks working in the box room, had returned to his station running the brain machine—first working four-hour half shifts, then building up to six-hour days—but his symptoms soon returned. He began falling on the plant floor, his legs numb and motionless under him. Schindler found that Garcia and Santa Zapata, the woman who replaced him on the brain machine, were the most advanced cases. "Sounds like this needs more investigation," Schindler concluded in his email. "Suggestions on how to proceed with this?"

Daniel Lachance, one of the neurologists Schindler contacted, was intrigued by the case histories the email described. Schindler's account reminded Lachance of a case in 2005, when he had treated a woman for carpal tunnel syndrome. After reviewing her electromyogram and other tests, Lachance had suspected something more—that her carpal tunnel was not compressing her median nerve but rather that the nerves of her hands themselves were inflamed. But her test results didn't match any known disorders. Like the patients Schindler was treating, that woman had been young, Hispanic, and previously healthy—but she had returned to Mexico before her spinal fluid could be tested. Lachance remembered Garcia, too, from his hospitalization the year before. Steroids had helped reduce the swelling of his nerves, but doctors could never identify the cause of his spinal inflammation. Lachance hadn't considered employment history during his initial treatment for either patient, but on checking the medical files, he discovered that both had worked at QPP.

Lachance had been doing neurology consults in Austin, so he had access to the records for these new patients and decided to dig deeper. He discovered that Garcia was among this new group of patients and that the others, just as Schindler described, also appeared to be suffering from similar symptoms. But the diagnosis of CIDP struck Lachance as a mathematical impossibility. "Those types of illness seem to, statistically, come up in the population at a rate of two per hundred thousand," Lachance told me later. "So here, over the course of a couple of months, I was aware of up to a dozen individuals from one town of twenty-two thousand who all happened to work in one place."

Lachance consulted several neurologists at Mayo and developed a battery of tests to rule out known illnesses. He brought the affected workers in, one by one, and crossed off items from a laundry list of diseases and disorders. It wasn't mad cow or trichinosis, the two most common slaughterhouse illnesses. It wasn't a simple muscular disorder like carpal tunnel syndrome or any known autoimmune response like rheumatoid arthritis or lupus. It wasn't cancer or a virus. It wasn't bacteria or a parasite. Lachance concluded that the slaughterhouse illness was likely some kind of autoimmune disorder, but he couldn't identify the exact vector— and couldn't yet rule out the possibility that it was food-borne and transmissible to anyone who was eating Hormel products. All he could say for certain was that the illness was somehow triggered by recent increases in the speed of the chain on QPP's production line.

"The line speed, the line speed," Lachance said when recounting those patient interviews later. "That's what we heard over and over again."

Chapter 2

HAVE A CUP OF COFFEE AND PRAY

When Upton Sinclair published his novel *The Jungle* at the end of February 1906, he hoped to shock readers with his account of the mistreatment of immigrant workers in Chicago's slaughterhouses. Instead, his book created instant public outcry over the unsanitary conditions it described—how workers put out poison for rats, then swept their carcasses into the sausage grinders; how tripe and cartilage were dyed and flavored with spices, then sold as deviled ham; how men in the cook room occasionally fell into open vats and sometimes went undiscovered for days, their flesh mixed into cans of lard. Sinclair groused that the book became a bestseller "not because the public cared anything about the workers, but simply because the public did not want to eat tubercular beef."

For regulators, however, the horror felt by Sinclair's readers couldn't have come at a better time. At that very moment, there was legislation before Congress calling for the establishment of federal meat inspection by the USDA. President Theodore Roosevelt, who had supported the bill as part of his reelection platform, wrote to Sinclair, promising that "the specific evils you point out shall, if their existence be proved, and if I have power, be eradicated." He appointed labor commissioner Charles P. Neill and social worker James Bronson Reynolds to carry out a government probe. When the Neill-Reynolds Report turned out to be even more damning of industry practices than *The Jungle*, Roosevelt pressured Congress into passing sweeping reforms. The Federal Meat Inspection Act of 1906 mandated individual examination of all livestock before slaughter, postmortem rechecks of each carcass to ensure health before processing, compliance with new sanitary standards, and agreement to submit to constant monitoring by federal inspectors. Most important, the act authorized the USDA to condemn any meat determined to be unfit for human consumption—and even empowered the department to close down the operations of repeat violators.

Sinclair, for his part, was unimpressed by the new legislation. He saw the federal inspectors, with their blue uniforms and shining brass buttons, as nothing more than political cover for a corrupt industry, claiming that "the laws regulating the inspection of meat were written by the packers" and "paid for by the people of the United States for the benefit of the packers." He warned that federal meat inspection laws were a diversion and anticipated that the industry would make sure that inspection addressed only the barest concerns about the deadliness of a product. There would be no supervision, he predicted, of chemicals used to color meat or harsh additives used to preserve it; there would be no regulation against cooking adulterated meat to make it safe for consumption or tests for trace amounts of contamination. Nothing, in short, would slow down the line.

Sinclair knew firsthand the unstoppable momentum of production. He had seen the hog-killing floors of the Armour and Swift packinghouses adjoining the great Union Stock Yards in Chicago. Each room had a supervisor with a watch, and work there was "determined by clockwork." Another man was paid to press the gang to move faster, to slaughter more hogs. But then, each day, the expected speed was slightly higher—and cutters farther along the line, paid as pieceworkers, suffered regular reductions in wages, because, the bosses observed, their jobs took less and less time to perform. Sinclair knew that the industry would make up the extra costs in establishing sanitary conditions in exactly this way—and the public, so long as they were assured that their meat was safe, would care little for the welfare of the workers in the packing-houses. Later in life, Sinclair would famously lament, "I aimed at the public's heart, but by accident I hit it in the stomach."

Still, for the better part of a century, the Federal Meat Inspection Act formed the basis for Washington's authority to supervise and regulate the meat industry under the USDA—and later the USDA's Food Safety and Inspection Service (FSIS). It was a commonsense system in which an increased number of carcasses dictated an increased number of inspectors, and the time needed to carry out proper examination created an unofficial throttle on line speed—as production could go only as fast as inspection would allow. But then there arose an opportunity to reduce the number of hands prodding and squeezing the glands and lymph nodes of each carcass. All it took was a nationwide panic—and the right man to make the most of it.

"I grew up in a Hormel family," Richard Knowlton wrote more than a decade after he had retired as the company's chief executive in 1995. His father had worked at the Austin plant, scaling and weighing livestock as it arrived by rail. Knowlton grew up just a few blocks away with six brothers and sisters in a four-room house. His blue-collar neighborhood was a cluster of tiny clapboard houses built in the 1920s to accommodate the swelling ranks of Hormel workers and their growing families. George A. Hormel's brother, John, personally paid to build the Crane Community Chapel so that the neighborhood kids would have a place to attend Sunday school. And the plant was close enough that Knowlton's father could walk. "Especially in the fall of the year, I remember him going back to work after dinner and after having already put in a full day beginning at 6 a.m. Every other Sunday, he would also do full-day shifts, and I remember him taking me along to watch him weighing the hogs. He did this to earn $11 to $12 a week. With seven children, my dad was desperate for work and considered himself lucky to have a job. Believe me, at a tender age, I understood the reasoning of unions."

In June 1948, when he turned sixteen, Knowlton hoped to follow in his father's footsteps. He went to the plant before the start of the morning shift and put in his name for a summer job. But he was turned away—so he went back the next day and then the next. "I showed up at 5 a.m. at the employment office for three weeks hoping to land an opening," he remembered. Finally, one morning, the employment manager took pity on him. "Knowlton, I'm sick and tired of looking at you," he said. "Go out and go to work." After a brief training period, Knowlton landed on second shift in the gelatin department, dipping hog skins into acid baths to extract aspic as a thickener for commercial ice cream and cake frosting.

One day, Knowlton came barreling into the plant. "I was rushing through the side door," he wrote, "trying to get an early punch on the time clock for the afternoon shift. Jay Hormel was coming out. I didn't see him and knocked him back into a corner of the entryway. I quickly brushed off his clothes. When I realized who he was, I was sure I would be fired. He said, 'Why don't you lift up your head and watch where you're going, kid?'" In later years, Knowlton made clear what reverence he held for Jay Hormel, often pointing out that they were the only two company CEOs to have been born and raised in Austin. But as Knowlton went away to college, returned to a sales job, and steadily rose through the management ranks, he eventually came to regard many of Jay

Hormel's worker incentive programs as outdated. When Hormel died of a heart attack at age sixty-one in 1954, the presidents who immediately followed him regarded it as their responsibility to caretake his vision for the company, but Knowlton had other ideas.

"Hormel's labor practices continued pretty much as he established them for the next fifteen years after his death," Knowlton remembered. "What Jay Hormel couldn't foresee . . . was that technology would also be a major factor to change the meat sector and the entire food sector just as it has the automotive industry." Knowlton first came around to this belief after taking over as plant manager in 1959. Determined to reexamine line operations from top to bottom, he decided to seek out a solution to a long-standing problem in the production of Spam.

For more than two decades, removing carpal bones and connective tissue from the pork shoulders had been the most time-consuming part of the process, because it required careful knife work by numerous skilled meatcutters. Knowlton was determined to automate this step of production. He found a Dutch manufacturer at the annual convention of the American Meat Institute to build a prototype deboner and then spent more than a year working with Hormel engineers adjusting the apparatus. The technical challenge was significant, but once they had conquered it, Knowlton wrote, the "resulting bone-free pork shoulder along with boneless ham made a nice can of Spam, with substantial labor savings." In no time, it was possible to reduce one of the most heavily staffed portions of the plant to a crew of just twenty workers.

When Knowlton was promoted to vice president of operations in 1974, he reasoned that the entire plant could be reconceived in exactly this way. He went before the board and made the case that $100 million for a new factory was a worthwhile investment. Not only would profits rise but the initial cost could be recouped in just three years by adjusting worker wages to match the downward slide of their competitors. Knowlton knew the union would fight

the maneuver, but he told the board that a "wholesale retrenchment in hourly wages" was now "an indisputable fact of life in the
meat-processing industry." If the company bought out the contracts of senior workers, they could slash Jay Hormel's incentive
programs and offer lower wages to new employees, who would be
low-skill machine operators, rather than skilled meatcutters. This
would drastically reduce the number of workers needed to operate
the new plant (from 2,950 to 1,150) while still upping output.
All they would need to do "to meaningfully increase production
volume" was run the line at much higher speeds. To make this
dream reality, Knowlton would first have to contend with one of
the strongest labor unions in the country. And even if he could
beat them, he would have to convince the USDA's Food Safety
and Inspection Service that faster lines did not necessarily equal
a threat to food safety. He would have to wait nearly two decades
for the right opportunity.

In 1993, Knowlton finally got the crisis he needed. Over the
course of that January, 623 Americans, most of them in the state
of Washington, were sickened by a rare strain of *E. coli*. Four of
those affected, all children, died as a result of their infections. The
outbreak was soon traced back to tainted hamburgers sold at Jack
in the Box restaurants, touching off questions about the safety
of ground beef and calls for stricter meat inspection. Amid this
heightened concern about microbial contamination, the American Meat Institute (AMI) proposed implementation of microbiological testing as part of what they termed Hazard Analysis and
Critical Control Points (HACCP) inspection. J. Patrick Boyle,
longtime president of AMI, touted the program by explaining
that it was based on the inspection system developed by NASA
and Pillsbury for assuring food safety aboard American-manned
spaceflights going back to the 1950s. Within months of the Jack

in the Box outbreak, Boyle petitioned the Department of Agriculture to implement an HACCP-based inspection models program (HIMP). The argument was that meat inspection needed to rely on microbiological testing, rather than traditional organoleptic inspection, which producers derided as "poke and sniff."

The idea for the program sounded convincing enough: if plants hired their own quality assurance officers to sort out diseased animals in the livestock area and carcasses in the kill room before they ever reached government inspectors, then, in theory, there would be improved inspection. That weeding-out process would reduce the chance of cross-contamination, and inspectors could focus on likeliest problem spots along the line, where they would conduct random scientific testing. Meanwhile, plant supervisors would have the flexibility to devise their own inspection processes, rather than being forced to adhere to rigid cookie-cutter requirements. Best of all, these efficiencies would streamline production, reducing the cost of meat for consumers without sacrificing food safety. At the heart of the American Meat Institute's campaign in support of HACCP was the axiom that microbiological testing of carcasses is always superior to merely inspecting carcasses by hand.

But doubters pointed out that the AMI is a lobbying organization for large meat producers. It was founded as the American Meat Packers Association in 1906, after the publication of *The Jungle*, for the purpose of resisting implementation of Theodore Roosevelt's meat inspection reforms. Food safety advocates and the meat inspectors' union alike worried that HACCP was just a newer, more sophisticated way of reducing "friction points"— the industry term for anything that slows production, including inspection. They cited a requirement in the Federal Meat Inspection Act mandating manual inspections of *all* carcasses by trained federal inspectors, while the HACCP model would rely on spot-checking *select* carcasses. (That's why inspectors joked sardonically

CCP stood for "Have a Cup of Coffee and Pray.") More
nt, this nonstandard model meant that producers would
e lead on inspection, while the USDA was relegated to
double-checking. Therefore, the question was not whether microbiological testing was superior to physical inspection but whether
self-regulation with occasional spot-checking was superior to universally applied government inspection. In 1997, the USDA decided to find out; for the pork industry, they agreed to allow a test
in five processing plants.

Instrumental in that victory was a man named Joel W. Johnson.
Hired as the executive vice president of Hormel in 1992, Johnson
had a well-earned reputation as smart and hard-charging. A Harvard MBA, he had also taken a one-year leave from General Foods
in 1967 for a tour in Vietnam, where he had served as a captain in
the U.S. Army and been awarded a Bronze Star. At Oscar Mayer,
he rose to the top on his belief in ready-to-eat, prepared dinners
(so-called value-added lines). After Kraft Foods bought the company in 1988, he had launched the hugely successful Lunchables
line—a clever repackaging of Oscar Mayer bologna with Kraft
cheese and Kraft-owned Ritz Crackers.

Richard Knowlton hoped that Johnson could work similar
magic with the Spam line, which had seen downward trending
sales figures for years. In the early 1980s, American Can, the principal supplier of Hormel's metal containers, had even conducted
an internal study, concluding that the public's growing concerns
over eating foods high in fat and sodium meant that Spam would
be dead within a decade. Knowlton remembered thinking, "Like
heck it will." He believed that Johnson's brash style could reimag-
ine and revitalize the brand, but even Knowlton was a bit taken
aback by Johnson at first. "I was interviewing Joel," he remembered
years later. "It had gone on all day, so I finally said, 'Why don't
we go shoot a quick nine holes?' Well, he shot a perfect thirty-six
at me. I thought, 'This is a guy who plays too much golf—when

does he work?' I also thought, 'He must have a lot of gumption to come here and shoot a thirty-six at his future employer—and take my money for it!'"

Johnson quickly applied that audacity by suggesting that the Jack in the Box scare presented a marketing opportunity for Hormel. He wanted to create what he called a "novel usage occasion"—a fun new way of eating Spam that also exploited people's doubts about ground beef. He proposed encouraging consumers to slice Spam blocks longways into a trio of quarter-pound squares that they could grill and eat on a bun. Pitched as the perfect alternative to "messy" ground beef, the Spamburger was given a $14 million print and television ad campaign as "the only hamburger made with ham." At the same time, Johnson made a major push to get Spam into state fairs and grocery displays; he held a recipe contest through the *Minneapolis Star-Tribune*, and even negotiated a deal to get Spam on the shelves at Kmarts nationwide. Still recovering from the early 1990s recession, blue-light shoppers happily chose precooked Spam over more expensive hamburger that they worried might be tainted. Sales of Spam rose by nearly 35 percent in less than two years.

For his efforts, Johnson was appointed to succeed Knowlton as CEO in October 1993—and the company name was officially changed from George A. Hormel to Hormel Foods, signaling the end of the company's transition from family-owned business to corporate entity. At the same time, Johnson was climbing the ranks of the American Meat Institute. "Once he joined the executive committee," AMI president Boyle later remembered, "he was quickly recognized for his leadership." Johnson was elected treasurer in 1994, secretary in 1995, vice chairman in 1996, and chairman in 1997. All the while, he was becoming convinced of the value that reduced manual inspection and higher line speeds would have for keeping up with production of Spam. Boyle later remembered that Johnson was "among the first" to support the

HACCP-based inspection models program—and enrolled Quality Pork Processors, the in-house cut-and-kill operator for Hormel in Austin, Minnesota, and the Hormel plant in Fremont, Nebraska, as two of the first three HIMP plants for pork. "Joel was fully behind it," Boyle said.

Under the program proposal unveiled in 1997, the number of on-line USDA inspectors in each pilot plant would be reduced from seven to four, and participating companies could increase line speeds beyond the limits otherwise imposed. In addition to the two Hormel plants, the model was scheduled for testing at Excel Corporation in Beardstown, Illinois; Hatfield Quality Meats in Hatfield, Pennsylvania; and Farmer John in Vernon, California. But before it could be fully put into place, the meat inspectors union sued, arguing that the program violated the Federal Meat Inspection Act. After five years of legal battles, the U.S. Court of Appeals for the District of Columbia Circuit agreed, ruling that delegating the task of inspecting carcasses to private employees did, in fact, violate the legal requirement that determination of meat safety be carried out by trained federal inspectors.

Participating companies responded angrily. The National Joint Council of Food Inspection Locals filed a complaint with the Federal Labor Relations Authority, alleging that Kelly Wadding, CEO of Quality Pork Processors, had even pressured the local union in Minnesota to lobby upper-level officials to withdraw their objections to the reduced inspection model. (Had the charge stuck, it would have been a violation of fair labor laws.) The FLRA dismissed the complaint on a split vote in 2002. And eventually all parties reached an unexpected deal. If the meat inspectors' union would not object to just three on-line inspectors in each of the five pilot plants—even fewer than the original proposal—then the USDA would fund additional relief inspectors who would work away from the line. More jobs for the inspectors' union, less inspection for the packers: everyone was happy—except food safety advocates, who worried that consumers were being placed at risk. Nevertheless, the agreement was approved, and Hormel began training new quality-control managers right away.

Nick Rinaker vowed never to work at Hormel Foods. His father had spent decades, forty-three years in the end, as a forklift driver at the plant in Fremont, starting before what Rinaker called "the big wage change" and staying on after, because he needed the money to take care of Nick's mother, who suffered from lupus. But the younger Rinaker could never forgive the wage cut exacted by Hormel in the 1980s and instead started his own contracting firm, eventually persuading his father to leave the plant and join in the business.

But in 1992, Nick injured his back on the job and needed a series of expensive surgeries. "The only company with halfway decent insurance in town was Hormel Foods," he told me, "and they were hiring new cleanup people." He took the job reluctantly at first, but hosing down equipment was easy enough, and the nighttime hours allowed him to continue picking up some cabinetry work during the day. Everything seemed to be going well, until the day another employee accidentally released a herd of hogs from a pen in the livestock area, badly trampling Rinaker's foot. Nick was reassigned to tagging carcasses, considered light duty, but he sustained a fall there that left him with a shattered heel. He filed a grievance against the company, claiming an unsafe workplace. In return for dropping his complaint, Rinaker was offered one of the newly opened positions in quality control. He was given a six-week course in what he called "the basic can-and-can't-do" on the line and trained on the HIMP directives.

Under the new system, inspections started in the holding pens—with sick hogs, whenever possible, separated out before reaching the kill area. Inevitably, though, some hogs that should have been condemned slipped by. They were slaughtered and sent through the normal series of baths, shaves, and cuts. With reduced government inspection to identify them as they entered the cut line, it was now the job of quality-control auditors like Rinaker to assure that those sick hogs weren't butchered and sent to market. The auditors stood at brightly lit viewing stations, where they could check viscera and glands in the head and throat for any signs of abnormality, even while the corresponding carcasses were being cut. If there was a problem identified in a bin of lymph nodes, the corresponding carcass was moved from the chain to a side rail (or "railed out"), where it was tagged and condemned. The pace was fast and the pressures were high, Rinaker told me, but at first, the system worked okay. The line was running 900 hogs per hour, and it was possible to conduct adequate inspections in the time allowed.

But, little by little, the work grew faster. The line speeds were changed on Mondays, Rinaker said, and the mood before weekly pre-work meetings, when the new chain speed would be announced, grew tense as workers waited to see if they would be issued another increase. One week, the company would order a slight speedup, Rinaker explained, and then see what parts of the process began to break down under the strain. The speed would hold steady while new systems or equipment were developed, and then another increase would be ordered.

Throughout every shift, a union-hired industrial engineer would walk the plant floor with a stopwatch around his neck, counting the cogs in the chain to make sure that Hormel wasn't exceeding the allowable number of carcasses per minute. But Joseph Rezac, the chief shop steward in Fremont at the time, later explained, "There's more to this than just getting the numbers." Often when workers were objecting to line speed, he said, a time study would show the line in technical compliance; the real problem was dull knives or an undermanned workstation.

To address each particular workflow problem, Hormel developed, patented, and installed new automated equipment designed to speed up cutting off heads, removing viscera, and halving carcasses. Hormel even patented a process for splitting skulls and harvesting brains and glands (noting on the patent application that "all animal tissue has some commercial value"). To allow workers making skilled cuts to keep pace, the company installed a conveyor system and humming automatic knives throughout the plant, and they broke up complicated tasks into single, repetitive motions. Union leadership rarely objected, because increased speeds provided a ready argument for additional hires, which in turn expanded membership and filled union coffers.

And from that point forward, the chain virtually never stopped. "Before HIMP," Rinaker said, "USDA had total control. If fecal was spotted, the line stopped while it was removed. After HIMP, Hormel just railed out affected hogs where they could be cleaned or reworked." There was such resistance to stoppages that Hormel began issuing rewards to quality-control auditors if the line was off for less than ten minutes that day. Soon, the only limit on Hormel's daily kill was the number of hogs they could acquire, so the company negotiated an arrangement with the state of Iowa that would allow them to invest in hog farms and further increase production. By the end of 2006, the line speed had risen from 900 heads per hour to as fast as 1,350 heads per hour—not only a 50 percent speedup, but also roughly 20 percent faster than any high-capacity plant under standard USDA supervision. The problem was simple, Rinaker told me: "Your ability to inspect is fine when you are viewing hogs at nine hundred per hour. Anything faster, you miss fecal."

To help keep up, Hormel increased the workforce in Fremont

from roughly 1,000 people to about 1,200—but, without physical expansion of the plant, these new workers actually gave rise
to dangerous crowding along the line. "Accidents happen often
from someone overreaching," Rinaker told me, exactly as had happened to Maria Lopez, when her finger was severed by the saw
blade. But even in instances where workers were injured and meat
had been contaminated by blood, the quality-control auditors
were expected to keep the line moving. "Speeding up the line has
caused all types of operator injuries," Rinaker said. "Part of my
QC duties was cleaning the human blood off surfaces to protect
against blood-borne pathogens."

Rinaker complained to a supervisor that these procedures
were harming the safety and quality of Hormel's product. But
this was no longer the family-owned business that his father
had worked for, he told me; this was now the Hormel Foods
Corporation. (Even in e-mail correspondence, Rinaker always
drew a careful distinction between the old company, "George
A. Hormel," and the new company, "HFC.") When he raised
concerns about compromised quality, Rinaker said a supervisor
told him, "I couldn't care less about quality. Quality slows down
production."

"All the employees are there for one purpose," Rinaker explained, "to help the supervisor realize the dreams of the production manager—and his dreams are directed by Austin."

Thanks to HIMP, those dreams were fast made reality. Almost
from the moment the HIMP program was finally implemented,
the participating meatpackers saw huge benefits; in 2004, Excel
and Hatfield achieved the largest production increases of any two
packers in America. Meanwhile, the other three plants were all
ramping up production for Hormel—not just the official Hormel
plant in Fremont and Quality Pork in Austin, but also the Farmer
John plant in California, which Hormel purchased outright at the
end of 2004. With that acquisition, all three of Hormel's cut-and-

kill operations—the plants that still supply all 9.4 million hogs for its operation worldwide—were authorized by the federal government to run their lines as fast as they could.

Supported by the USDA's experimental program, Hormel's CEO, Joel Johnson, adopted a corporate strategy that emphasized Spam and other value-added products. Asked later why he had pursued this path, Johnson explained, "There are the obvious things we read about over and over—working families, the lack of time for dinner preparation and so forth. But there are other issues that are harder to quantify. There's no question that the cooking skills in American households have deteriorated, and I don't see anything on the horizon that is going to turn that around. Publishers may be selling a lot of cookbooks, but I think consumers are using them like wallpaper—as decoration."

In addition to prepared food lines, Hormel began partnering with other brands, like Famous Dave's, and buying up existing brands, such as Lloyd's Barbeque, in order to get their company's pork into a wider range of readymade products—and reap greater profits. In 2005, Johnson retired as CEO, and Jeffrey M. Ettinger, formerly Hormel's corporate attorney, was appointed to take over. In the two years that followed, the company spent $7 million on a plant expansion in Fremont, $3.5 million on an expansion of Quality Pork in Austin, and another $6 million on building a sister plant to Quality Pork in nearby Albert Lea, Minnesota, under the name Select Foods. The expansion paid off. Ettinger soon announced that Hormel was generating $1 billion in annual sales from new value-added products.

When the subprime mortgage crisis pulled the nation toward recession and other companies scrambled to introduce budget-friendly products, Hormel was already perfectly positioned. They had invested heavily in brands favored by women reentering the workforce. And they were able to produce vast quantities of low-cost meat—including old standbys Spam, Dinty Moore Stew, and Hormel Chili—for families that were suddenly without one income and struggling to make ends meet. In the first years of the recession, sales of Spam climbed by double digits. And those sales, in turn, drove overall profitability. Between 2006 and 2013, Hormel increased sales across the board by more than 43 percent—from $5.75 billion to $8.23 billion. As Hormel touted Spam as a good buy for penny-conscious consumers, they also promoted shares in the company as a recession-proof stock for investors looking for an opportunity in the midst of economic downturn.

But Hormel's cheap meat came at a high cost to its workers.

Pablo Ruiz speaks with a heavy accent, but his English was good enough to make him an asset at Quality Pork, where he could communicate instructions from white supervisors to Hispanic line workers. And he had experience. Ruiz had worked for several years sorting cattle alongside USDA inspectors at the Swift & Company plant in Worthington, Minnesota, so when he moved to Austin and came on at QPP, he was promoted to process-control auditor after just eight months. It was his job, in essence, to stay one step ahead of the plant's on-line USDA inspector, to keep an eye out for potential violations and troubleshoot before a problem got big enough that the inspector might order a line stoppage.

On the processing floor, Ruiz floated between stations. Each hour he did ten checks of incoming carcasses for obvious physical defects, ten checks at the viscera table (looking for kidney abscesses and liver flukes), ten checks at the head table (looking for swollen lymph nodes that might indicate tuberculosis or other infection), and ten checks to approve completed cuts before they were sent to the cold side for packing. And each hour he stuck a thermometer into collected bins of brains and ovaries and pancreases to be sure that they were within approved temperature ranges.

Ruiz told me that, by 2006, the chain was running so fast that QPP's lone government inspector sat in a chair alongside the line, because he only had time to do visual inspections. "We just check at the head," Ruiz told me. "We check the lymph nodes, the glands, the brain to see any type of sickness." Ruiz said that he didn't think it was enough government oversight. Under ordinary USDA guidelines, inspectors are required to check the tail, head and tongue, thymus, and all viscera of each hog. They palpate the lymph nodes of the large intestines and lower abdomen to check for tuberculosis nodules, feel the intestines themselves for parasites, and turn over every set of kidneys to check for hardness due to inflammation or hidden masses. At QPP, Ruiz said, the in-spectors just visually double-checked the work of process-control auditors. "But that's why the line goes so fast. When I was there, it was 1,305 per hour. This means ten thousand hogs achieved every eight hours. That's money in the bank—easy, quick."

But in late 2006, after the latest speedup, the line got going so fast that hog heads started piling up at the opening to the plastic shield that guarded head table workers against spatter from the brain machine, and the force of the conveyor belt pressing the heads forward cracked the Plexiglas. Ruiz recorded the needed repair but, in the meantime, attempted to patch the fracture. "I put up plastic bags to protect the people there," he said, but every day or two, the wind whipping through the plant would rip and fray the bags. So Ruiz would put up new bags, fixed in place with tape. In the midst of all this, he noticed that Matthew Garcia, the scrawny kid who ran the brain machine, was missing days of work, and then was gone altogether.

"I thought, Oh, maybe he's quit or got another job, but then after maybe four months, I saw him back to work." But instead of running the brain machine, Garcia was in the box room, working just four hours, then returning home.

"What's going on with you?" Ruiz remembered asking.

Garcia told him he had been hospitalized at the Mayo Clinic for more than three months. "He said he couldn't walk at all," Ruiz remembered. "He said he's got a special class to do things in a wheelchair—to shower, to get on clothes, to eat." The conversation worried Ruiz; he himself had been having trouble making his auditing rounds lately, moving with such a slow shamble that his supervisor had taken to teasing him about his shuffling gait. Over the next six months, the pain worsened.

Finally, Ruiz went to see the plant nurse, Carole Bower, about the chronic burning in his feet and hands. She suggested that he might be suffering from carpal tunnel syndrome or beginning to develop arthritis, but by October 2007, she must have known it could be something more serious. A half-dozen workers from the kill floor had come to Bower with complaints similar to those listed by Ruiz, and she had referred them to Richard Schindler at the Austin Medical Center, who had then reached out to Mayo Clinic colleagues in neurology. But for some reason, Ruiz was not referred for medical examination.

Instead, Ruiz continued to shuffle from one station to the next, struggling to stay ahead of the relentless pace of the line. Then, on November 20, while going to check the temperature of bins of viscera, he collapsed on the kill floor. One moment he was walking, Ruiz told me; the next he was on the floor, his glasses scattered across the concrete. A coworker rushed to help him stand and limp to the nurse's station. Ruiz could feel blood soaking through his pants and filling his right boot, but, try as he might, he couldn't move his legs.

Chapter 3

ALTER EGOS

In early November 2007, Aaron DeVries, an epidemiologist at the Minnesota Department of Health (MDH) in St. Paul, drove to Austin to review the medical records of workers from Quality Pork Processors reporting a shared set of mysterious symptoms. MDH had received a call from Daniel Lachance, a neurologist at the Mayo Clinic, worrying that these cases might represent a new form of peripheral neuropathy, emanating from the slaughter operation. After initial review, Lachance couldn't rule out the possibility that the illness was food-borne or even transmissible from person to person, so he urged the department to investigate immediately.

DeVries was a young man, just a few years out of medical school with only three months under his belt at MDH, but he had already earned a reputation as a careful and caring medical investigator. After Hurricane Katrina, he had gone to Lafayette, Louisiana, as part of the Medical Reserve Corps, to provide primary care to evacuees, and he had recently begun working with HIV/AIDS patients at the University of Minnesota's Delaware Street Clinic. Upon arriving at the Austin Medical Center, DeVries began reviewing patient health records, going down his checklist, striking out possible sources of the QPP workers' illness. First and foremost, there were no reports that workers' families were suffering from similar symptoms, so the disorder didn't seem to be transmissible by human-to-human contact. But their complaints, DeVries quickly realized, were inconsistent with any known infections. Like Lachance, he concluded that the illness had to be a new kind of autoimmune disorder, most likely triggered by something inside the plant.

When he was done reviewing patient histories, DeVries went directly to QPP, where he was given a quick tour of the line by Carole Bower and then shown to a conference room where he met with owner Kelly Wadding and human resources manager Dale Wicks. Wadding made a rough sketch of the warm room where all of the sick employees worked, and Wicks pulled up each worker's station ID so Wadding could mark his position on the line. The map confirmed what Richard Schindler at the Austin Medical Center had already surmised: almost all of the workers were clustered at or near the head table. DeVries recommended that he return soon with an MDH team to conduct an environmental assessment of that area.

Three weeks later, just after Thanksgiving, the MDH team, led by DeVries and state epidemiologist Ruth Lynfield, returned to QPP. Before entering, they were given plastic aprons, plastic booties and gloves, plastic masks, and plastic hairnets to go under their hard hats. As Wadding guided them along the cut line, the medical team quickly recognized that workers wore almost none of this protective gear, because it was clingy and uncomfortable inside the warm room. Even at the head table, employees were bare-armed, and none of them wore a respirator or goggles. The team progressed down the steel bench, observing each employee's workstation, before eventually reaching the brain machine. They stood silently for a moment, watching the bursts of air rising into a red cloud—a small amount each time but enough, as it drifted and accumulated, to gradually coat workers from one end of the head table to the other. Lynfield, watching each blast of pressurized air raise a small swirl of pink mist, asked Wadding, "Kelly, what do you think is going on?" Wadding reportedly replied, "Let's stop harvesting brains."

Much would be made later of that response, of how Wadding had ordered the brain machine removed from the factory floor immediately, of how he had the apparatus dismantled and brought to the conference room where he sat with the MDH team after the plant tour—to prove that it was out of commission before they even left the premises. Much praise, too, would be voiced for his willingness to speak to reporters in the wake of an MDH press release announcing an outbreak of a neurological disorder in his plant.

What no one knew then was that, in the weeks between Devries's first visit and the arrival of the full MDH team, QPP quietly sold an 80 percent interest in itself—all 800,000 of the available voting shares—for just one cent per share. Control of a company with an exclusive contract to supply the flagship plant of Hormel Foods, with an estimated $280 million in annual revenue, was signed away for just $8,000. The buyer, Blaine Jay Corporation, had incorporated in 2004, but this was its first purchase recorded with the Texas state franchise board (on November 15, 2007). Corporate documents list an accounting firm on the LBJ Freeway in Dallas as Blaine Jay headquarters and Kelly Blaine Wadding as president.

Wadding denies that he knew in advance of the MDH visit that a piece of faulty equipment was causing the illness among his workers, and he responded angrily when I suggested later that it appeared, to me, that he had not only known but quietly arranged for a way for the company to avoid taking a financial hit before inviting health inspectors inside. He insisted that his company would never resort to such a business trick. "That did not happen," he told me. "That simply did not happen."

Dale Chidester, the longtime office coordinator of the United Food and Commercial Workers Local 9, was a bear of a man with unruly hair and a salt-and-pepper goatee, but he spoke in a sweet, soft rasp. His office in the Austin Labor Center, the official name of the local union offices, somehow made Chidester seem older than his years. The building's brickwork and institutional architecture, mostly reserved these days for elementary schools and county lockups, was like a time capsule of Depression-era proletarianism. Each morning, Chidester opened the window at the check counter, pushing up the wooden shutter as if it were a gate on a service elevator, and planted himself in his creaky office chair—a picture of FDR over one shoulder, a picture of Geronimo over the other.

Chidester didn't yet live in Austin during the 1985–86 strike that so harshly divided the town. He was still working at the Hormel plant in Ottumwa, Iowa, but he remembered well the regular four-hour runs up Interstate 35 to deliver supplies to the families struggling through those lean months. Chidester started in meatpacking in the late 1970s, just as the country was sliding toward recession and all of the major meatpacking companies were consolidating and forcing workers to accept lower wages. He told me he had witnessed a lot of dirty tricks meant to double-cross the unions. The Wilson Foods pork-processing plant in neighboring Albert Lea filed for bankruptcy in 1983 in order to nullify existing contracts and cut workers' average pay from $10.69 an hour to $6.50. With improved margins, owners were able to sell the company at a sizable profit.

In Austin, the Packinghouse Workers Local 9 (P-9, as it was then known) bristled at talk of lower wages. Workers had already conceded too much in return for Richard Knowlton's promise to build a state-of-the-art plant and keep Hormel's primary operation in Austin. He had convinced P-9 to give up the incentive pay system, freeze wages until the new plant was complete, and sign away the right to strike until three years after the plant opened. Knowlton had recognized that profit margins were vanishing from butchering and designed the new plant around the concept of highly automated tasks performed by low-skill workers—but he never informed P-9 of his plans. When the new plant did finally open, P-9 workers were shocked by the radical shift toward automation. They had been told that these changes would make their jobs easier, but instead, it simply made the work more monotonous and much faster.

Peter Rachleff, a labor historian at Macalester College in St. Paul, interviewed dozens of workers about revised operations inside the new plant. He described the new technology and new speed with chilling clarity: "There was automated batching in the dry sausage, prepared sausage, and canned meat departments; integrated computer inventory management; flexibility in hog-skinning; automated storage and retrieval systems; forklift robots; and automatic ham deboners, together with faster power saws and knives. Chain speed was so fast that workers often stumbled into one another as they fell behind." Some workers were injured as a result of the breakneck pace, slicing open their arms or mangling fingers in new equipment. More commonly, the new, machine-sharpened knives dulled quickly, and workers overexerted while making cuts, causing a rash of carpal tunnel syndrome.

Worst of all, the so-called "new plant agreement" that did away with the incentive system had replaced it with a union-negotiated standard that all workers were expected to meet. Like a latter-day Jay Hormel, Richard Knowlton had seen the key to improved margins in maintaining a steady pace of work. But, unlike his forebear, Knowlton was reaching for increased profits (as well as a hefty bump in his own compensation) by wresting away worker benefits. In October 1984, after all of these changes had been implemented, Knowlton demanded a 23 percent wage cut, from $10.69 an hour to $8.25, insisting that the new plant had turned the work into unskilled labor. Under the no-strike restriction of the union contract, P-9—which had just been absorbed into the United Food and Commercial Workers—had no recourse until August 1985. Workers were outraged but had only two choices: quit or stay on at the new plant for close to a year.

On the very day the no-strike period expired, P-9 walked out, beginning a thirteen-month standoff that remains among the most notorious and rancorous in American history. But P-9 wasn't just battling Hormel; they were also fighting their new union bosses. Fearing that Hormel couldn't compete against larger companies that had already brought union wages down to $8.25, the UFCW leadership in Washington, D.C., urged P-9 to accept the lower pay, so as to restore the chain bargaining system that had existed for decades, with a common wage scale across all companies and plants. When P-9 refused, and even organized a nationwide boycott of Hormel products, the UFCW sent a letter to every local in the AFL-CIO, declaring the walkout a wildcat strike and asking other plants not to support P-9.

Caught between the international union and the local office, many workers crossed the picket lines—the windows of their cars pounded daily by outraged coworkers. Minnesota governor Rudy Perpich called in the National Guard to protect those workers, along with the scab workers brought in from outside. Finally, after a year of heartbreak and a rift among friends and union brothers that still divides Austin, the UFCW ended the strike by putting P-9 into receivership. They negotiated a one-cent increase over the wages proposed by Hormel, in return for agreeing to allow a lower wage for newly hired workers. To keep Hormel from cleaning house and installing an all-new workforce, they negotiated an agreement that senior workers would retain preference for high-paying jobs inside the plant and former strikers would be given preference for rehiring as scab-occupied positions were vacated. P-9 leadership warned that creating a two-tier wage scale would turn the workforce against itself, but they were powerless to resist the agreement negotiated by UFCW.

"That strike was an unconditional surrender," Chidester told me, knitting his fingers behind his head and creaking backward in his office chair, "because, you know, the company won." But if workers felt sold out by the union, it was nothing compared to the betrayal they soon suffered at the hands of Hormel.

The QPP parking lot is gravel, and on a day like the one when I was first there—the very beginning of March, when the mercury had finally pushed above freezing and the glaciers of plowed snow were starting to drip and calve—the driveway to the security gate turns muddy and rutted and pocked by potholes. At four, the sun hung blindingly bright in the sky, and the entrance to the fenced grounds was alive with workers flowing in and out: the shift change. They were mostly Hispanic but also Somali and African American, all pushing through the narrow turnstile as I waited for the security guard to reemerge from his booth. One man, his dreadlocks wound and tucked under a blue bandanna, swiped his employee ID several times, before he shouted out, "I guess my card not working, man." He spoke with the unmistakable lilt of Jamaica. The guard buzzed him through, then opened the door a crack, apologetically. "They are just ridiculously uptight about things like this," he told me. Indeed, in the years since the outbreak caused by the brain machine, QPP had never allowed a reporter onto its grounds—until I visited.

Finally, Carole Bower arrived and ushered me toward the entrance. She was dressed in hospital white, down to her shoes. Even her manicured nails were tipped in white, and her hair had been frosted with highlights. Her demeanor, too, though not exactly icy, was officious. She passed through the double doors without looking back. She was very sorry to have kept me waiting, she said, but "Quality Pork and Hormel take security very seriously." A stream of workers climbed stairs toward the kill floor. They moved steadily past the laundry room window, taking clean white aprons. But Bower steered me away from their path, gesturing toward the office entrance. Inside, all eyes rose from their computers; heads poked above their cubicle walls as we passed.

Once we had squeezed into a tight, private office borrowed for the occasion, Bower shut the door and closed the blinds. She sat behind the desk and opened a manila folder, revealing a set of talking points. As I asked each question, she scanned the prepared remarks and read the appropriate response. I felt bad for her. She seemed taxed by the dilemma of owning up to QPP's role in the outbreak without accepting culpability. But even when I asked questions that departed from her bullet points, Bower steadfastly defended the speed of QPP's response to the outbreak and reiterated management's deep caring for the affected workers. "When the public health department came on site, we had open meetings with all of the employees in our two big break rooms," she said. "They took them off their work time, paid them for their time, and the president of the company and our HR manager and myself and anyone else that was involved talked to them, had interpreters, explained what was going on. We had weekly meetings just like that with everybody in the plant for the following four, five, six weeks."

I told her that I had interviewed more than ten affected workers and found only one who had attended any of those meetings and noted that it would have taken a dozen such meetings, for each time there was a new development, to inform workers this way. Bower's calm reserve faltered.

"We had multiple meetings," she snapped. "We would have the day hot side, the day cold side, livestock. . . . We probably had four meetings in a row."

She stared across the desk at me, her lips pinched.

"Right," I said. "I just don't see how—"

"Day and night," she interrupted. Then paused again.

"But—" I started.

"For *weeks*," she said. Her face grew flush. "Do you see it now?"

In November 1987, barely a year after the conditions of the strike resolution were made official, Hormel announced a shutdown of nearly half of the new plant. The company said it would continue to operate the packaging operation on the refrigerated side, but the cut-and-kill would be taken over by Quality Pork Processors Inc. QPP then existed only on paper but was headed by Richard C. Knight, a former executive at Swift, the Chicago-based meatpacker that pioneered the conveyor line and had a major plant in nearby Worthington. Knight claimed his new company would be separate from Hormel, though QPP would buy exclusively Hormel contract hogs and sell the butchered meat exclusively back to Hormel. They would use Hormel's space and Hormel-owned equipment, rely on the Hormel mechanics, and drive Hormel forklifts.

Leaders of the wounded and strike-weary P-9, newly re-dubbed UFCW Local 9, felt this was a union-busting tactic and asserted that 550 former strikers still on the preferential recall list were entitled to the new jobs created by the subcontract—and at the wages the union had just agreed to. Hormel denied this and, to make its point, erected a wall in the middle of the plant to divide Hormel from QPP. Eventually it would add a separate entrance and run a chain-link fence through the center of the parking lot. "It's kind of like taking a room in the middle of a house," Dale Chidester told me, "and saying it's not really part of the house."

Local 9's attorney asked the *St. Paul Pioneer Press*: "What good is a union contract if the company can avoid the contract by simply leasing its premises to another company and get the work done at non-union rates?" On the first day of operation in June 1988, an arbitrator agreed to take up that question and ordered QPP closed down. But the union no longer had the strength to engage Hormel in a protracted battle. After a year of legal wrangling, Local 9 eventually conceded. The contract was amended to allow lower pay for subcontractors, and the plant reopened in June 1989. UFCW bosses in Washington, D.C., hailed the deal as a victory, even though they had won a wage of only $9 per hour at QPP after the local had gone on a yearlong strike to protect a $10.69 hourly wage at Hormel just three years earlier. The two-tier pay scale that the old P-9 leadership had warned against was now a permanent reality—but cloaked in double talk. "It's not a two-tiered wage," Chidester told me with an ironic smile. "It's just a subcontractor with a lower wage scale."

With new wages came new workers, and even rumors that QPP recruited laborers in Mexico. Matthew Garcia said he didn't know of formal recruitment, but in his hometown of Magdalena Peñasco, a small village in the state of Oaxaca, nearly every adult male he knew had, at one time or another, worked at QPP. By the early 1990s, Austin had gone from having a united local workforce to having a sharply divided workforce that, while still technically unionized, is, on the QPP side, decidedly less vocal and less powerful. By some estimates, QPP's labor force at the time of the neurological outbreak was 75 percent immigrant. But the anger of former strikers who had been promised preferential rehiring did not fall on QPP for its hard-nosed labor practices; many townspeople instead turned on the immigrants who filled the positions that Hormel had promised. Chidester just shrugged. "It's still leftover bitterness from the strike," he said.

Workers who attended the QPP meetings in late 2007, people like Miriam Angeles, remember the break-room gatherings very differently from Carole Bower. When Angeles spoke to me at Austin's Centro Campesino—with the cultural center's director, Victor Contreras, serving as interpreter—she said management insisted that, although people from QPP had become sick, there was no evidence that the illness originated from inside the plant. The managers instructed workers to keep quiet until the company made a public statement. "We prohibit any comment about this," she remembered being told. "Anyone who comments on this disease, you could lose your job."

Affected workers were instructed not to identify themselves in the group meetings nor ask questions. In one meeting, however, a sick worker rose in a swell of panic to ask Kelly Wadding, "What's going to happen with my health?"

Wadding, according to Angeles, said: "Sit down. We're going to talk to you in the nurse's office."

After that, there were more meetings, but sick workers were afraid to speak out. They whispered in locker rooms. They phoned each other at home. They slowly figured out who some of their suffering coworkers were, but when Wadding called a final meeting to announce that the mystery illness was under control, Angeles said employees who were still on work restrictions were too scared to say anything. And though they were all in the UFCW, neither Local 9 nor the bosses in Washington, D.C., took up their cause.

To this day, there is no agreed-upon number of QPP workers who were affected by the illness. The MDH conducted a survey and found fifteen. In his published study based on rigorous testing, Lachance says he found twenty-one. Thirteen were sufficiently incapacitated to file workers' compensation claims against QPP. The count is further complicated by the revelation that MDH reached out to the two other plants in America where pork brains were being harvested, and some published reports include seven additional cases from the Indiana Packers Corporation plant in Delphi, Indiana, and one more from the Hormel plant in Fremont, Nebraska.

Angeles didn't seek out sick coworkers. She had two daughters, one still a newborn, and she couldn't risk getting into any trouble with her bosses. She resolved to just do her job and keep quiet. She never complained, she told me, even though she said her supervisor never honored her doctor's orders that she sit for fifteen minutes every two hours. When the strong medications that had been prescribed for pain in her arms left her with blurred vision, the supervisor still refused to let her take a break. "No," Angeles said she was told, "you have to keep working."

Many of the most severely incapacitated workers didn't attend the QPP meetings because they were out from work for weeks at a time. They only found out about what was happening to them by chance. Susan Kruse, who was at home and unable to work, didn't learn of the outbreak until she saw it on the evening news. Emiliano Ballesta didn't know how widespread the illness was until he arrived for a steroid treatment at the Austin Medical Center and found the waiting room filled with his coworkers. Upon returning to QPP after another five months out, Matthew Garcia was surprised to discover that Dr. Lachance had referred him, along with a group of fellow employees, for examination by P. James B. Dyck in the neurology department at the Mayo Clinic. Only at the end of the checkup did Dyck explain to Garcia that there was an "epidemic of neuropathy" that was affecting QPP workers—a newly discovered form of demyelinating polyradiculoneuropathy.

After careful study, medical investigators had unanimously concluded that inhaling aerosolized brains had caused workers' immune systems to produce antibodies. Because porcine and human neurological cells are so similar, the antibodies didn't recognize when the foreign cells had been eliminated. Even when Garcia's body had eliminated all of the hog tissue he had inhaled, Dyck explained, the antibodies kept fighting the infection, destroying Garcia's own nerve cells.

The explanation made sense, except that, according to company officials, QPP had been blowing brains, off and on, for more than a decade. So why did workers fall ill now and not earlier? The answer offered by the Mayo Clinic is complex but boils down to one key change: increased line speed. Garcia told me that he had been having trouble keeping up with the breakneck rate of production, making the already grisly job of blasting brains ever messier. To match the pace, the company did what they always do: turn to automation. They switched from a foot-operated trigger to an automatic system tripped by inserting the nozzle into the brain cavity, but sometimes the blower would misfire and spatter. Complaints about this had led to the installation of the Plexiglas shield between the worker manning the brain machine and the rest of the head table. When further increased speed had caused pig heads to pile up at the opening in the shield, and the jammed skulls had cracked the plastic, more mist had been allowed to drift over the head table. And the longer hours worked in 2007 had, quite simply, upped workers' exposure.

But Dyck had some good news for Garcia. The investigators were not in total agreement. He and Lachance diverged from the description of the disorder favored by the Minnesota Department of Health and the U.S. Centers for Disease Control and Prevention in one small but critical way. MDH was calling the disorder progressive inflammatory neuropathy (PIN)—and the designation would catch on with the media, which liked the linguistic rhyme between the tingling, pins-and-needles sensation that signaled the disorder's onset and the acronymic shorthand—but the Mayo team rejected this name because the doctors there didn't believe that the disorder was progressive. Now that QPP had halted harvesting pig brains, Dyck told Garcia, he believed his condition should improve.

But the future for Garcia and other sick workers was much more difficult than that—not only physically but psychologically. After the removal of the brain machine, Garcia was taken to his new workstation, mere feet from his old spot at the end of the head table. Seeing the blood on the floor and the hog parts sliding by on the conveyor, he started to panic. He was afraid that he would again be exposed, that his condition would return and worsen. He couldn't catch his breath; his chest tightened. He begged to leave and called his social worker. She secured Garcia a different job, away from the head table, but even with light duty, he struggled to maintain full-time hours for the better part of 2008.

More than a year after his diagnosis, Garcia still had burning in his feet, his knees clicked when he walked, and his bowel and bladder problems persisted. Not yet twenty years old, he was catheterizing himself four times per day. In a follow-up examination, Lachance found a suspicious spot on a nerve at the base of Garcia's brain and would eventually diagnose it as a nerve-sheath tumor. Soon even Dyck and Lachance would have to concede that several of the most severe cases were showing halted function of the sweat glands, a clear indicator of nerve death. Matthew Garcia and others were suffering from permanent, irreversible damage.

Part Two

Chapter 4

LITTLE MEXICO

Every afternoon, when the last bin of untrimmed hams is emptied out, deboned, injected with a sodium solution, and sent down the line to be cooked, Raul Vazquez walks out of the Hormel plant on the outskirts of Fremont, Nebraska, crosses the abandoned avenue to the employee parking lot, and heads west out of town. He drives for the better part of an hour along Highway 30—a thin ribbon of blacktop, shadowing the Union Pacific tracks and the tortuous Platte River—until he comes to the exit for the town of Schuyler. Vazquez lives there and owns a modest off-sale liquor store, set up in an old shop front along Twelfth Street, one of the brick roads in the historic downtown. His wife, Miguela, works in the store all day and every night has a simple dinner waiting when he arrives. They eat together with their five children in the back room before Raul gathers the kids and drives them back to their house for homework and then bed. Miguela stays at the store until closing, rarely making it home before midnight.

To see them at the store, you wouldn't guess how hard Raul and Miguela work, how little time they have together as a family. When I first visited them one Friday evening, the two oldest boys sat behind the counter, entranced by the Disney Channel—its laugh track nattering from a tiny picture tube atop the refrigerator case. Their wily three-year-old brother teased his baby sister, kicking a balloon around the aisles and snatching it away. Miguela grinned with resignation amid the din but laughed away any suggestion that the chaos ever got to her. Even Raul, fresh from his shift at Hormel and the hour commute, seemed content running the register—ringing up a customer, who was picking up a bottle of Jose Cuervo on his way home from a long week.

It seemed the perfect tableau of immigrant determination and upward mobility, but the liquor store in Schuyler was actually an act of compromise. When Raul first came to Nebraska, his brother had a job at Hormel and said he could get work for Raul and Miguela there, too, until they got on their feet. They already had enough put away to qualify for a loan to buy a house in Fremont and take in renters to cover the mortgage until they established credit for a business loan. Once that happened they expected the booming Hispanic population would provide a steady clientele to support a restaurant, a bakery, maybe even a small grocery store. But six months in, Miguela couldn't take the work at Hormel. She was spending all day cutting meat away from the necks of hogs that had been shackled up and split open; the work left her sickened and exhausted, and she was barely making enough to pay for babysitters for the children. She finally quit to be with the kids full-time, but the family struggled to get by on Raul's salary: only after a year on the kill-floor, hitting hogs with a double-prong prod to stun them for slaughter, was he finally promoted to "sticking"—plunging a sharpened steel blade into each pig's jugular, sending geysers of dark blood coursing over the white tiles of the abattoir. But worse than the hard work and the scant wages was the darkening political climate.

In late 2006, when the housing bubble burst and the economy began to falter, the scarcity of jobs seemed to bring simmering anti-immigrant resentment to a boil. Nebraska's Democratic senator Ben Nelson, who was in the midst of a reelection campaign, saw an opportunity to run to the right of his ultraconservative Republican opponent, Pete Ricketts, former CEO of Omaha-based TD Ameritrade, when Ricketts proclaimed support for the controversial stance that illegal immigrants should "self-deport" and then be allowed to return with temporary worker status. Nelson pounced, telling NPR that the United States needed "a hard barrier" between itself and Mexico. It wasn't enough to apply pressure and expect the flow of immigration to reverse itself, much less grant a path to citizenship; people without proper documentation had to be found and forcibly removed. The coldhearted rhetoric helped Nelson secure reelection in a landslide.

During that same election season, a half dozen local jurisdictions around the country, seeing the Republican hardline anti-immigration platform devolve into just another empty campaign promise, decided to tackle the matter in earnest for themselves. In places as diverse as Riverside, New Jersey, and Escondido, California, municipal measures sought to oust undocumented workers by imposing local penalties on businesses and landlords who employed or rented to people without proper proof of citizenship. Half the cases stalled in the blocks, due to poorly written proposals riddled with plainly unconstitutional language, but the other half, with the aid of the politically ambitious attorney Kris Kobach, who had cut his teeth under U.S. Attorney General John Ashcroft, were more cleverly composed and seemed headed for long court battles. The towns spotlighted in these cases—Hazleton, Pennsylvania; Valley Park, Missouri; and Farmers Branch, Texas—garnered a trickle of negative national press, but they also became rallying points for anti-immigration activists, who soon went looking for other towns with their own rapidly changing demographics.

Outside Raul's liquor store, on the streets of downtown Schuyler, the change in the makeup of that part of Nebraska is apparent everywhere. Each night, the illuminated sign above his store blinks to life, lighting the words: Liquor San Miguel. The store is named in honor of the patron saint of Raul's birthplace, Chichi-hualco, a farming village in the mountains of southern Mexico's state of Guerrero. All of Schuyler has become a haven for immigrants from Raul's hometown, and, drawn by the meatpacking industry's arrival in rural Nebraska, their mass migration has largely accounted for an explosion in the area's Hispanic population— from fewer than 1,000 in 1990 to nearly 16,000 today, roughly 20 percent of the population in the state's northeastern corner. On one block in downtown Schuyler, there's La Paleteria Oasis Mexican ice creams, La Gloria Spanish-language greeting cards, the convenience store Variedades Fredy's, and El Paisano's cell phones and calling cards. The next block over, Los Amigos auto sales is across the street from Chabelos custom detailing and not far from El Pueblo Tires and Corral's Car Repair. The old location for Didier's Grocery, across the street from Raul's liquor store, has been converted into a dance hall called the Latino Club, and on Saturday nights the thumping bass of Tejano tunes throbs through the cinder-block walls. When Clarkson TV & Appliance vacated, Raul's wife's cousin opened a market called La Tienda Chichihualco and packed its tight aisles with Mexican foodstuffs.

No wonder some Nebraskans have taken to calling towns like Schuyler "Little Mexicos." For many older residents of those small towns—who take pride in their Norman Rockwellesque image, where people greet each other in the Wal-Mart parking lot and go to church together on Sunday, and where the streetlights flicker out at midnight—the arrival of this immigrant population is a threat not just to the status quo but to their sense of self and their very way of life. Many remember when a spot on the line at Hormel was the most coveted job around. But ever since the union-busting of the 1980s and the reduced-inspection agreements of the 1990s and 2000s, those jobs have been largely taken over by a workforce of undocumented immigrants willing to work twice as fast for lower pay—a fact that many old-timers blame for the swift decline of Fremont and surrounding communities.

Throughout 2007, as Raul and Miguela worked at Hormel, made mortgage payments on their house, and struggled to put aside money to start a bakery in Fremont, there was a growing rumble among longtime residents that their town, like other small towns across the country, should take matters into their own hands.

Hormel opened its plant in Fremont to meet swelling demand for meat after World War II. During the war years, the company had cranked out so many Spam-filled K-rations that by 1945 fully 90 percent of the output from the facility in Austin, Minnesota, was purchased by the U.S. military. When founder George A. Hormel died in June 1946, he left his son, Jay, with a remarkable challenge: maintaining sales now that Americans GIs were back home. But Jay made a characteristically savvy gamble: he wagered that returning vets, as they reentered the workforce and enjoyed new buying power, would want more meat.

He guessed right. In the first quarter of 1947, meat consumption nationwide rose by more than 20 percent—a real increase of more than 1.7 billion pounds. Prices climbed so high on upsurging demand that New York's mayor called for a congressional investigation. But the *New York Times* concluded that it wasn't price-fixing that was driving prices; it was scarcity of supply. "Americans are meat-hungry," the reporter explained. "There are just more persons consuming more meat than ever before in the history of the country." To ease high prices, the federal government began subsidizing corn as feed and petroleum to cut the expense of getting livestock to market. This allowed Hormel to improve their margins on quality cuts of meat for American dinner tables while showing record profits by exporting canned goods to war-crippled Europe.

The acquisition of the Fremont Packing Company, a small plant thirty-seven miles west of Omaha on the Burlington and Union Pacific railroads, was meant to help Hormel keep pace with the runaway demand—but the move was also more than simple expansion. The nation's largest meatpackers were just beginning their generation-long migration away from urban centers, in favor of setting up shop in small towns. Hormel hoped that establishing rural direct-buying stations would allow them to negotiate lower prices than they paid for animals brought to auction at sprawling stockyards. Also, at the very moment of the Fremont expansion, major packinghouses in Omaha were in the grip of a walkout by striking stockyard workers. Faced with the real possibility of running out of supply, those plants—including Swift, Armour, and Wilson—were forced to negotiate higher wages and better hours with the United Packinghouse Workers of America. By opening their plant outside of Omaha, Hormel was closer to farms and feedlots and farther from union bosses and the solidarity of fellow workers.

But no one in Fremont was worried about such things in 1947—especially after Hormel announced plans, almost immediately upon opening, to expand the production line from roughly one hundred workers to nearly six hundred. At a time when the average farm operator was earning just under $2,000 per year, the arrival of five hundred new jobs (which, on average, paid $3,000 each) was an unbelievable godsend. Overnight, nearly 15 percent of Fremont households saw their income jump by a third. And their increased earnings soon brought shared prosperity to Fremont's Main Street as well.

At the same time, the U.S. government announced the extension of the Bracero Program. Literally meaning "strong arms," the initiative had started as a short-term agreement with Mexico to import seasonal workers after President Franklin Roosevelt's signature on Executive Order 9066, authorizing the establishment of internment camps, emptied fields of Japanese immigrants in 1942. Now, with the program extended to the postwar era, rural families who claimed continued labor shortages were able to keep their farms running cheaply on Mexican labor and then send their sons, newly home from Europe and the South Pacific, from the front lines to the factory lines.

Best of all, company bosses had pioneered what was referred to as the "Hormel experiment"—a salary system that removed seasonal uncertainty for workers, who previously had been given long hours during summer and fall, when fattened animals were brought to market, then laid off during the winter and early spring. For Hormel, paying salaries saved costs on training at the beginning of each season and reduced the transience (and mobility) of its workforce. For workers, the loss of flexibility was an easy trade-off. At the time the Fremont plant opened, the *Los Angeles Times* reported, "Most Hormel workers own their homes and have cars, refrigerators, well-dressed, well-fed, well-educated children." For decades after, wages there held firm at 20 to 30 percent above the average for a manufacturing job, regardless of what was happening in the larger economy, and many in Fremont came to regard the plant set just outside the city limits as the benevolent giant that provided for the community.

Then in 1978, the Fremont chapter of UFCW, Local 22, accepted the same contract—and wage cut—that had been given to workers in Austin as part of the new plant agreement. Within five years, new CEO Richard Knowlton issued his infamous demand for a second pay cut, slashing hourly pay by 23 percent and pushing Hormel's wages below the industry average for the first time in more than ninety years of doing business. You ask anyone in Fremont and they'll tell you the same thing: for all those years, the guys who worked on the meatpacking line had nice houses with boats in the driveway and pools in the backyard. Suddenly, after generations of prosperity and job security, the future for Hormel workers looked uncertain.

Harold Harper was working the night shift on the bacon slice at the Fremont plant when Knowlton first proposed the wage cut, and he remembers exactly how the union responded: "Of course, we said, 'Bull-*shit*.'" Harper is retired from Hormel now, after more than thirty-three years working on the line. He started in 1968 as an executive trainee but asked to be moved to a line job after just a few months because, in those days, the work paid better and was more secure. He and his wife, Linda, still live in the same house on the north side of Fremont where they raised their two boys. They were able to save up for a few upgrades, like a sunroom with an electric fireplace, and they vacation for two weeks in Hawaii every February now, but there is otherwise little trace of the upper-middle-class existence that Hormel workers once enjoyed.

Harper told me that the union at Hormel had tied one hand behind its back when they trusted Knowlton in 1978 and accepted his new contract. The agreement bound the union to the no-strike provision and production standard established in the Austin plant but without benefit of a new plant in Fremont or promises of re-duced workloads there. It was, in Harper's estimation, a misplaced show of good faith in the new corporate leadership—the result of a generation of union presidents who had never faced significant conflict with management.

Worse still, at exactly this time, the Amalgamated Meat Cut-ters union, moving to widen its sphere of influence, merged with the Retail Clerks International Union to form the United Food and Commercial Workers (UFCW). The goal was to match the expanding vertical integration of the food industry by organizing workers on every link of the supply chain. But the UFCW bosses didn't stop at recruiting meatpackers. Focused on building membership and consolidating power within the AFL-CIO, they expanded their ranks to include barbers and beauticians, then retail workers and insurance agents. The butchers and grocers had resented the comparatively high wages of the packinghouse workers right from the start, Harper told me, but barbers and insurance agents were even less interested in protecting the take-home pay of people they considered overpaid factory grunts. So when Knowlton proposed the steep cut in pay, Hormel workers, both in Austin and Fremont, were ready to walk out as soon as their no-strike clause expired, but their union brothers were not. "Amalgamated Meat Cutters lost their teeth," Harper said.

When UFCW Local 22 in Fremont formally rejected the wage cut, Hormel simply informed the union that the company intended to close the plant. The clause requiring fifty-two-week notice of layoffs was still in effect, so Hormel sent out registered letters to each individual production employee. The UFCW national leadership refused to intercede. So the Fremont local gave in and agreed to a two-tier wage scale. Under the compromise, new workers would start at $8.25 per hour as Knowlton had requested; workers with seniority would get $9 per hour with the promise to increase wages to $10 per hour in a year. (Knowlton later claimed that the idea for this arrangement came to him in a dream, waking him "in the middle of the night from an uneasy sleep.")

Austin workers, however, refused to accept the cut. They walked out on August 15, 1985, the very day the no-strike clause expired, and Hormel temporarily shut down the Austin plant, expecting that all parties would be able to reach a quick agreement. Instead, the negotiations dragged on—and tensions rose to new heights on October 26, when Hormel first made a public announcement that it had posted a record quarter despite the strike and then reopened some parts of production with management manning the workstations. On January 20, 1986, with still no resolution in sight, Knowlton decided to fully reopen the plant, welcoming in union workers who wished to return and filling any vacant positions with strikebreakers, many of them young farmers who had been pushed by the farm crisis to look for work in the cities. Within twenty-four hours, tensions and threats of violence had spiraled so out of control that governor Rudy Perpich called in the National Guard.

The P-9 leadership in Austin decided to mount a company-wide strike of Hormel workers without the sanction of the UFCW. They sent out roving pickets with the intent of closing down one plant after another. They arrived first in Ottumwa, Iowa, where Dale Chidester was working, and formed a picket at the plant gates with members of UFCW Local 431. Almost all of the Ottumwa workers honored the line—and Hormel responded the next day by firing 478 union members and locking the factory doors. When P-9ers arrived in Fremont in the early hours of the next day, they were called back by leaders in Austin, who had just learned of the mass firing in Ottumwa. But not everyone got the message. A small P-9 picket was established at the Fremont gates, but Local 22 issued a warning to members that workers who stayed out might simply be fired as they had been in Ottumwa. Most members of Local 22, including Harold Harper, reluctantly decided to cross the picket. Of the sixty-five workers who honored the line, some fifty were fired. In the end, the UFCW stepped in and ended the strike, arguing that it was the only way to save jobs for all workers at Hormel.

Less than a year later, however, Hormel announced the total closure of the Ottumwa plant and the shutdown of nearly half the Austin plant. Hormel would continue to run the refrigerated packaging side there, but the cut-and-kill operation would be taken over by a new company called Quality Pork Processors Inc., which would pay its workers $9 per hour. In August 1988, Hormel, citing "poor profit margins," informed the UFCW Local 22 in Fremont that the company would likewise lay off 324 cut-and-kill workers—more than 40 percent of the plant's total workforce—unless the local union agreed to another reduction in pay, matching their hourly wage for new workers in the warm room to QPP's pay-scale. Wounded and abandoned, the Fremont local acceded to the wage cut without a word of protest.

Those were dark times for the Harper family. Harold remembers wondering if the Fremont plant would be next in line for closure. Linda told me that because of the first wage cut she had started babysitting neighbor kids after school, turning their house into an unofficial day-care center to pick up a few bucks; after the second wage cut she had to go to work full-time, eventually finding a job at the 3M plant, down the road in Valley. Through it all, their younger son, Blake, was suffering from a series of unexplained illnesses, which eventually landed him at the Boys Town National Research Hospital in Omaha. Doctors there prescribed a potent dose of antibiotics that killed off the infection but also left him with severe-profound hearing loss.

Meanwhile, Hormel's corporate profits were soaring. Between 1983 and 1993, sales doubled on increased output. But more tellingly, earnings rose more than 350 percent, and the stock price among investors bullish on those numbers went from $4 per share to $24. Soon, the only way for Hormel to further improve the bottom line would be to find a cheaper workforce.

"I didn't know anything," Raul Vazquez told me, remembering the day in 1991 when he began his long journey from the sierras of Chichihualco to the rolling prairies of the Midwest. "My mom, she make some call to my cousin and we go." Vazquez's father, already living in Chicago and working toward obtaining legal status, had been advised by his attorney to bring his wife and two sons across the border before Raul, then sixteen years old, became a legal adult. The process would be much harder after that. So they took the winding mountain road through the Sierra Madre down to Chilpancingo, where they could catch a northbound bus to Mexico City. From the capital, they took another bus, thirty-six hours to Ciudad Juarez. At last, within sight of the U.S. border crossing, the *coyote* hustled everyone through a hole in the corrugated steel fence and down the embankment into the concrete containment chute that channels the Rio Grande between Juarez and El Paso, Texas. At the shift change for the border guards, Vazquez and the others were pulled across the river, one by one, on an inner tube tied between two lengths of rope. From there they were told to go to a city park, where they were given their false identification and bus tickets north.

Vazquez and his family were part of a first wave of people to make the arduous trip from Chichihualco to the United States with the hope of becoming citizens. When they were children, Raul's parents had worked as braceros, picking their way from the lettuce fields of California to the cherry orchards of Washington State each year at harvest time, but it was only after the multiple economic crises and devaluations of the peso in the 1980s and President Reagan's declaration of general amnesty for millions of undocumented immigrants in 1986 that they began thinking of returning and settling permanently north of the border. But if immigrant families like the Vazquezes were going to be able to put down roots, they could no longer rely on seasonal jobs in the fields; they needed year-round employment. They found those steady incomes in the meat processing plants all over eastern Nebraska and Kansas.

The work is strenuous and dangerous, especially compared to the supporting industry of Chichihualco—making soccer balls. All over the town, people sit on their patios hand-stitching balls and chatting with neighbors, but the piecework, a few pesos per ball, rarely adds up to more than $40 per week. So the risky journey to the United States and the backbreaking and dangerous labor in the meatpacking plants (Vazquez lost the index finger on his right hand working in Chicago) seem small sacrifice given the relatively high pay of $500 per week—$25,000 per year. For those who work even two years sending half their paychecks home, they can return to Chichihualco with the equivalent of fifteen years of savings. Or for those, like Raul, who decide to stay, they can set aside enough to buy a house and even a small business.

By the late 1990s, it wasn't just Hormel attracting illegal immigrant labor to Nebraska; there was also Fremont Beef (next door to the Hormel plant), Cargill-owned plants in Schuyler and Columbus, Tyson plants in Madison and Norfolk, and Wimmer's in West Point. Caravans of minibuses made the pilgrimage from Chichihualco to Chilpancingo every month, driving north from Mexico City through Monterey to Piedras Negras, just across the border from Eagle Pass, Texas. "After a rest and once their supplies are set," *Business Mexico* magazine reported in 2003, "it's only a few hours through the desert mountains of southern Texas to the safe house—a motel where the groups split off either to Schuyler or Fremont in Nebraska or Liberal or Dodge City in Kansas."

In an interview with the *Herald Mexico* in 2005, Chichihualco's mayor Leopoldo Cabrera estimated that nearly $250,000 flowed into the town each month from Nebraska and Kansas. With those funds, Vazquez told me, the highway into town was paved, the narrow main thoroughfare was widened into a tree-lined avenue, and new homes were built among the old tin-roofed adobe huts. And the annual festival for the town's patron saint, San Miguel, now features a Migrant's Day celebration. A group of Tlacololeros, the traditional dancers of the sierras, collects cash at the Labor Day parades in Schuyler and Columbus, and then sends the money home to pay for a rodeo, hire a band,

and give soccer balls to the local kids. "That day everything is free," Vazquez told me.

Ironically, the newfound prosperity in Chichihualco has created a younger generation less driven to make the northward journey—especially knowing that their only reward is long days of relentless work. The improved highway opened the city to easier commerce with Chilpancingo, making it much simpler to bring in farm equipment and get crops to market, but it also ushered in the drug cartels, which have muscled out corn growers in favor of planting fields of pot and poppies. And many locals in Nebraska—and, indeed, in the U.S. Drug Enforcement Administration—worry that the well-worn human smuggling routes into the United States may open the way for drugs and weapons and gangs bent on gaining control of the Midwest (still relatively virgin territory, where meth, low-potency marijuana, and other homegrown drugs dominate the black market trade). By 2012, more than 1,500 people in the highlands of Guerrero had been displaced by fighting between the Sinaloa Cartel and the Zetas gang. And a new cartel, calling itself El Cartel de la Sierra, had emerged.

This latest group of narcoterrorists has adopted the particularly chilling practice of leaving their assassination victims in public places, dismembered into tidy, blood-drained pieces. The cuts are expert, made with sharp blades and practiced hands—intended not for disposal but display. As you look at the neatly cut corpses arrayed at the entrance to the grade school in Chilpancingo or on the sidewalk outside the city's science museum, it's hard not to wonder if the butchers of the sierras learned their skills on the kill floors of eastern Nebraska, whether the humanity squeezed out of workers slicing apart more and more bodies every day hardened their souls to this grisly task. "It's not a slaughterhouse of pigs," Alfredo Velez, owner of Tienda Mexicana Guerrero in Fremont, said of Hormel. "It's a slaughterhouse of people."

Some white residents of Fremont and Schuyler express fears about such violence arriving in their sleepy neighborhoods, but more often anti-immigrant rhetoric focuses on how much money is hemorrhaging from the local economy, how Mexicans are stealing American jobs. But Raul Vazquez told me that Hormel and other packers almost always have vacancies. "They have a big sign: *tell your friends, tell your families*," he said, but, with white workers refusing to apply for jobs at decreased wages and the increased line speed permitted by the HIMP agreement with the USDA, the workforce at the Fremont plant is now more than three-quarters Hispanic. "The owners learned that the Hispanics work harder," Vazquez said. Another Hispanic worker at Hormel said that in his time on the line, he watched the speed increase from 5,000 hogs to 9,000 hogs per shift—made possible by employing a greater and greater percentage of immigrant workers. "They don't ask for breaks. They don't ask for raises," he said. "They just work harder and harder, because they *need* to work."

But then in May 2008, Bob Warner, a member of Fremont's city council, taking his cue from other small towns passing anti-immigration laws, introduced a local ordinance with the goal of preventing illegal immigrants from working or renting inside the city limits. Though Vazquez and his family were all legal citizens now, the renters they depended on to help make their monthly mortgage payments were not. When word of the proposed ordinance spread among the workers at Hormel, Raul's tenants, already two months behind on their rent, cleared out without warning—or payment. He searched frantically for new tenants, but it seemed everyone was fleeing. Within two months, Raul defaulted on his loan. One of Miguela's cousins, the one who owns Tienda Chichihualco in Schuyler, told him about the liquor store coming up for sale, so Raul and his family picked up and left town, too. "My plan was to do something else," Raul told me.

"My plan was to live in Fremont." But now, he was again at the vanguard of a mass exodus.

The ordinance's architect, for one, was pleased. "When they find out that Fremont is not a haven for illegal immigration," Warner said at the time, "they will leave."

Chapter 5

THEY THREW ME AWAY LIKE TRASH

By March 2008, four months after the Minnesota Department of Health's visit to Quality Pork Processors and the immediate removal of the brain machine, the most acute sufferers from the neurological disorder now known as PIN were still convalescing and getting by on short-term disability, waiting for their workers' compensation to kick in. But then each worker, one after another, began receiving single-line letters from QPP's insurer, American Home Assurance Company, a unit of American International Group (AIG), informing them that their claims had been rejected for lack of information—essentially asserting that there was still too little evidence to certify that PIN was a workplace injury. The workers were stunned; QPP itself had guided them through the application process and submitted their forms. The Centers for Disease Control and Prevention (CDC) had issued a preliminary report, finding that, after testing ten confirmed or suspected patients, researchers had developed the hypothesis that "worker exposure to aerosolized pig neural protein might have induced an autoimmune-mediated peripheral neuropathy."

Workers appealed to QPP to contact AIG on their behalf.

What they didn't know was that QPP's company attorneys were already engaged in a protracted argument with AIG over long-term workers' compensation liability. Worker benefits—which in a case like this could cost millions, mostly in medical claims—were covered by QPP's policy, but the deductible clause contained ambiguous language, stating that QPP as policyholder had $600,000 of liability for "Each Accident or each Person for Disease." QPP argued that the outbreak constituted a single "accident." AIG responded that PIN was a disease, and, therefore, QPP was responsible for $600,000 per person. With thirteen claims already filed and the Mayo Clinic and the Department of Health discussing ruling in the cases of a dozen more workers, QPP was facing possible liability of $15 million or more. Worst of all for QPP, a successful claim—in which the injured party can receive wage-loss, medical, and rehabilitation benefits—is not dependent on employment eligibility or immigration status. Even if an employee were found to have been working without proper documentation, QPP would still be held responsible, because the company had screened applicants and hired and employed the worker. So QPP contested the claims. Six months after Kelly Wadding's grand gesture of removing the brain machine and presenting it to the investigative team from the Department of Health, QPP told AIG that there was still no definitive proof that PIN had originated from within its plant.

Susan Kruse retained attorney Ray Peterson of the firm McCoy, Peterson & Jorstad and sought out an independent medical evaluation by a board-certified neurologist in the Twin Cities. The doctor concluded that exposure to aerosolized brain matter was "a substantial contributing factor to the development of the disease." The finding was vindication for Kruse—but also galling. The story of an unexplained neurological disorder among QPP's workers was, by then, becoming a national story. Carole Bower told the *New York Times* that it was nurses in the medical department who had first noticed a pattern emerging and alerted doctors. During the fall of 2007, she said she had seen three workers complaining of "heavy legs." After a fourth came in with the same symptoms, she had realized, "Something is out of sorts." This version of events not only contradicted the accounts of the doctors at the Austin Medical Center and Mayo Clinic but also made Kruse wonder why her case had never caught Bower's attention. Kruse told me she went to the nurse's department every week for six months to collect her short-term disability check. "Not once did any of the nurses tell me that other workers from the head table were having the same symptoms and were getting sick," she said. She told me that she thought the company was stalling for time, hoping that workers would improve or quit before they found each other. In early April, she filed suit against QPP.

Kelly Wadding publicly blamed the denial of coverage on poor sharing of medical information among the Mayo Clinic, MDH, and CDC, and he said that some workers still hadn't been interviewed, so the medical research remained in process and, therefore, inconclusive. "Once it's determined that they've contracted the illness at work, they'll be eligible for workman's comp," he told the *Austin Daily Herald*. This statement was a stark contrast to Wadding's comments for national news stories, in which he always portrayed QPP's medical staff and upper management as fighting on behalf of workers, without waiting for final findings from MDH. "It's a new disease," he said now, "so there's a lot of things they need to determine."

After Kruse filed suit, ten other workers, most of them undocumented immigrants, banded together and retained Paul Dahlberg of Meshbesher & Spence to represent them in preparation for filing their own complaint. "They're really scared," Dahlberg said at the time. Many had already accrued medical expenses of $30,000 to $100,000—several years' income for anyone working at the head table—and their conditions seemed to be declining.

"They may be going back to work," Dahlberg said, "but they have so much fatigue, it's about all they can do."

In May, AIG contacted Kruse's attorney with news: they would no longer contest the claims and had assigned an outside social worker, Roxanne Tarrant, to guide employees through resubmitting workers' compensation claims. As the workers began filling out their forms, QPP offered Dahlberg's clients about $20,000 each as a preemptive settlement. But the deal required workers to forfeit coverage for medical benefits and any future claims against the company. Dr. Lachance was telling them that researchers at the Mayo Clinic were still determining whether nerve damage caused by PIN was temporary or long-term. In several of the most severe cases, workers didn't seem to be showing the signs of recovery that Lachance had initially expected. There was no telling whether they would ever be able to work again or faced permanent disability. The workers collectively rejected the offer.

Days later, on the Monday morning after the long Fourth of July weekend, Miriam Angeles was told to report to Human Resources, where she was informed that there was a problem with her identification. Angeles, who'd been working under the assumed name Felicitas Olivas, knew she was about to be fired. Would she continue to have her health insurance? Would she still qualify for workers' compensation?

"They said, 'That's your problem.'"

As Angeles told me about that day, her voice turned soft, lost in the memory.

"I feel thrown away," she said, finally. "Like a piece of trash. Before, I worked hard and willingly for QPP, but after I got sick and needed restrictions and told them I was in pain, they threw me away like trash and were done with me."

Bob Warner is in his eighties, with weatherworn features and a persistent cough, but he retains the booming voice and wagging index finger that marked him as an attack dog on the Fremont City Council for twenty years. During much of his time representing Ward Four, however, he had felt powerless against the demographic shift his town was experiencing. He watched Mayor Skip Edwards kowtow to Hormel from the time he took office in 1988, while the company steadily increased its Hispanic workforce. Many of these employees, Warner was convinced, were in the United States illegally—an assertion he supported by pointing to the prevalence of Spanish-speaking adults in Fremont. "How could a person be a twenty one year-old adult and have no knowledge of the English language at all?" he asked me, then dismissed his own question with a wave. "That's all bullshit."

On May 13, 2008, Warner, who had already announced his plans to retire from the council that fall, decided he'd had enough. He was fed up with rising crime, with grade schools overrun with non-English speaking students, with unpaid medical bills at the local hospital, with immigrant families crowding into rental houses on the west side of town, and with everything from having to wait in line at the bank while people wired money to Mexico to having to press 1 at the ATM for English. Just the day before, U.S. Immigration and Customs Enforcement agents had arrived at the Agriprocessors plant in Postville, Iowa; in all, they had hauled away nearly four hundred undocumented workers—more than 20 percent of the town's total population. Warner couldn't help imagining how Fremont would be transformed if its undocumented population disappeared in a single, swift action. Before the close of the monthly council meeting, he surprised his fellow members by proposing that city attorney Dean Skokan draw up an ordinance to ban "any resident or any business from harboring, hiring, or transporting illegal immigrants." Skokan agreed to work on a draft but warned the council that similar municipal ordinances were facing stiff—and expensive—constitutional challenges from the American Civil Liberties Union (ACLU). "I'm not telling you this can't be done," he said. "I'm telling you it's going to be very difficult."

Despite this concern, a draft of the ordinance was scheduled for its first public reading on the evening of July 8. But just before four o'clock that day, Warner was tipped off that the entire second shift had called in sick at Hormel; they were carpooling to the Fremont Municipal Building. By the time he reached the council chambers, Warner told me, the room was already nearly filled with Hormel workers—and the police had been dispatched to maintain order. Warner demanded that the balcony be opened to let more people in, but the room was filled to capacity and people were spilling out into the halls by the time the meeting commenced.

Skokan announced that language in the ordinance was still rough but had been modeled on similar measures drafted by the Immigration Reform Law Institute. When he was done reading, council members informed the crowd that they would hear constituent complaints at this meeting (and two more to come) before making a decision. First the council heard from several landlords, who protested that Fremont had 4,247 rental units—and estimated that between a quarter and a third of the occupants were Hispanic. It would be impractical to check everyone's status, they said. And trying, complained one landlord, would lead to "targeting Hispanics"—a violation of the Fair Housing Act.

Norm Pflanz, a staff attorney with the Nebraska Appleseed Center, echoed this concern. But Warner responded angrily. "Illegal is illegal," he said, "and it has nothing to do with discrimination." But according to people present in the meeting, Warner's comment sparked several pro-ordinance supporters in the crowd to begin pointing around the room: "There's an illegal. . . . There's an illegal. . . . There's an illegal. . . ." Warner leaned over to Mayor

Edwards and said, "Skip, you're opening a can of worms." He didn't think that Pflanz—or anyone else who lived outside the city limits—should be allowed to speak. "He shouldn't have taken testimony from anybody, unless they was a resident of Fremont," Warner told me. "It's a *city* issue. It's not county, it's not state, it's not federal." The atmosphere was so tense that night that, when Pflanz and a group of Hispanic testifiers started for the door during a recess, a police officer interceded. According to Pflanz, the officer said, "I think I'm going to escort your group to your cars." Before the meeting was adjourned, Warner and Skokan scheduled a reading of a revised version of the ordinance for July 29.

When Roxanne Tarrant, the social worker assigned to help QPP employees with their workers' compensation claims, first met Pablo Ruiz, he was slumped in a recliner in the living room of his ramshackle rental on the east side of Austin. The kitchen was almost too tight to turn around, and the lower reaches of the plasterboard walls were covered with crayon scrawls. Ruiz sat impassively, taking in the swirl of activity around him with a sluggish indifference induced by high doses of his pain meds. He had been experiencing searing pain in his legs for months, he told Tarrant, as well as pounding migraines that made it impossible for him to sleep. His voice was so reedy that every word seemed eked out in the midst of a spasm, and his eyes often fluttered closed from the throbbing in his temples. He appeared in such acute pain that Tarrant immediately called Dr. Lachance.

Ruiz had first seen Lachance in January 2008, when he was hospitalized at the St. Mary's division of the Mayo Clinic. After Ruiz's fall on the floor of QPP in November, he had appeared to make a speedy recovery. Doctors at the Austin Medical Center prescribed pain medication and put Ruiz on crutches. For a few weeks, he worked at a desk job in the QPP office. Then one morning just into the new year, Ruiz awoke in such pain that he couldn't stand. He screamed to his wife, begging her to get him to the hospital. His head hurt so much he thought his skull might split wide open.

He was given a full workup—a spinal tap, EMG, MRI of his head and spine, blood work. He was released a week later, but follow-up visits revealed signs of decline. His lumbar nerves were inflamed; the steroid treatments recommended for PIN patients had induced type 2 diabetes in Ruiz. He was taking antidepressants. Now, when Tarrant reached Lachance in Rochester, he reported that on reviewing Ruiz's latest MRI, he had found brain inflammation. He prescribed sleep medication and Paxil for anxiety over the phone and asked Tarrant to arrange for Ruiz to resume steroid treatment immediately.

Despite the steroids, Ruiz's condition continued to worsen. Lachance worried that he might be suffering from some form of meningitis, and Tarrant was unable to get him into counseling for his depression because she couldn't locate a Spanish-speaking psychologist closer than the four-hour round-trip it would require to go to the Twin Cities. When a Mayo Clinic psychiatrist brought in for consultation recommended another hospitalization for depression, AIG objected. They asserted that family troubles (his dying mother, his monetary stress) were the source of Ruiz's anxieties—and, as such, his depression was not covered by QPP's workers' comp insurance.

Meanwhile, Ruiz's blood sugars soared to over 300, and he suffered from severe all-over inflammation—an attempt by his body, a Mayo Clinic physician told him, at "desensitizing itself." Ruiz was referred to the chronic pain clinic, but nothing seemed to be working. Lab results indicated that the steroid treatments were having little effect. His sweat tests showed advancing neuropathy in his arms and legs. The numbness in his hands had spread as far as his elbows now, and his arms were too weak to comb his hair or brush his teeth.

In early August, Ruiz was notified by QPP that his six months of health benefits were up. By then, the pain in Ruiz's right leg was so agonizing that doctors ordered a bone scan. "I most worry about my leg," Ruiz said. "It feels like it's going to explode or something." But AIG refused to pay for the test. By fall, Ruiz was only able to get around with the help of a walker, and each round of sweat tests kept coming back abnormal. The bills were mounting when QPP contacted Ruiz's attorney to up their previous buyout offer from $20,000 to $22,000. But, as with the previous proposal, Ruiz would have to agree to quit his job effective immediately, with no chance of return or any future claim against QPP. The payment wouldn't have even covered his outstanding medical bills, Ruiz told me, and he was beginning to fear that he was permanently disabled. On advice of his attorney, Ruiz turned down the deal.

Fremont was threatening to boil over into violence. In the weeks after Bob Warner proposed the anti-immigration ordinance, upstart opposition group One Fremont, One Future documented dozens of incidents of hate-based intimidation—anonymous callers threatening to burn down Hispanic-owned businesses, rocks hurled through front windows from passing cars. When Maggie Zarate turned away a salesman at the door of her home, the man began cursing at her and shouting at her children playing in the yard, "Go back to Mexico!" (Zarate's children are fourth-generation Americans.) Andy Schnatz, local leader of the anti-immigration Nebraskans Advisory Group, sent emails to the mayor and members of the city council. "We're in a battle right now with illegals coming across the border," he wrote. "We shed blood to build this country and we will shed blood again to take it back."

Republican leaders, from Governor Dave Heineman to state senatorial candidate Charlie Janssen, both from Fremont, urged ordinance supporters to seek out expert legal advice, in order to steer debate toward matters of law, rather than matters of race. "That's when they went to Kris Kobach," Warner told me. By that time, Kobach had become a minor celebrity in conservative circles on the strength of his work on the other local ordinance cases as counsel for the Immigration Reform Law Institute—the legal arm of the Federation for American Immigration Reform (FAIR). With Kobach's help in reshaping the language of Warner's proposed ordinance to closely resemble the local ordinances working their way through the courts in Kansas, Pennsylvania, and Texas, city attorney Skokan felt he could come up with a proposal that would be deemed constitutional should the ordinance pass a council vote—and, with any luck, help quell the anger bubbling to the surface citywide.

But one morning soon after, Alfredo Velez, owner of Tienda Mexicana Guerrero, arrived at his shop in downtown Fremont to find a police car waiting in the parking lot and his storefront window shot out, broken glass everywhere inside. Velez told me that the shot appeared to have been fired from across the street, maybe from a moving car. For him, it was more than simple vandalism; it was an insult, an attack on his family and all they had worked for. Like so many in the area, he had grown up near Chichihualco, but he'd been born to a wealthy Mormon family on a sprawling mountain estate, dotted by tall trees and an enormous herd of cattle. The land had been in his family since it was deeded to his grandfather by the king of Spain in the 1860s, and Velez himself, with his silver temples and gentle accent, still retains something of that regal air. When Velez was a young man in the 1970s, however, the Mexican government seized his family land for corn and bean plantations. He came to the United States legally and obtained citizenship in 1985. To support himself, he worked at area packinghouses and set aside money every month. In 1998, he had enough to buy his small grocery space along D Street and supplemented his income, at first, by working on the kill floor at Hormel. He put his four children through college, determined that they would never have to work on the meatpacking line as he had.

After his window was shot out, Velez considered leaving Fremont, maybe joining his daughter in Omaha or his eldest son in Lincoln; he even flirted with the idea of returning to his native Chichihualco. But he didn't want people to think he had been in Fremont illegally or that he had been run off by threats. He resolved to speak out—but then, on the night the ordinance was scheduled for its second public reading, Velez received an anonymous letter. "It appears that your business is the drop off point for illegal immigrants," it began. "This could be a violation of the federal immigration laws. I also heard that you cash checks such as payroll checks from Hormel without asking for identification. That also could be a violation of the federal immigration law. The illegals are costing every legal resident of this city a lot of money and they are destroying Fremont. It is the responsibility of every American to insure that this stops and that those people harboring them are held accountable." Velez decided to stay behind the counter to protect his store and listen to the hearing on the radio.

The second reading of the ordinance drew more than a thousand people—so many that the gathering was moved at the eleventh hour to the high school auditorium. Some fifty police officers and a bomb-sniffing dog patrolled the crowd, and more than seventy residents, both citizens of Fremont and people from surrounding areas, were allowed to take the lectern for more than four and a half hours of testimony. Jerry Hart, a retired IRS agent, voiced outrage that the ordinance hadn't already been passed and implemented. John Wiegert, a fifth-grade math teacher in nearby Yutan, told the council that Fremont needed the ordinance to reduce the strain on schools. "Racism has nothing to do with this ordinance," Wiegert insisted. "This ordinance is about what is legal and what is illegal. If the federal government is not going to watch out for us, then we need to watch out for ourselves."

After public comments concluded, the council voted to suspend the rules and place the ordinance on immediate final reading in order to vote that night. They explained later that they worried about waiting another three weeks for resolution, but when the measure came to a vote, the council split—4 to 4—leaving Mayor Edwards to break the tie.

Edwards had clearly foreseen this possibility. It was nearly midnight as he took out a prepared statement. "This has weighed very heavy on me," he said, then began reading. "Control of illegal immigration is a federal issue," he said. "I'm bound by the law, too." The proposed ordinance, he explained, overstepped the city jurisdiction. He said he had consulted with Nebraska attorney general Jon Bruning and two outside attorneys. They agreed that immigration matters should remain in federal hands and voiced their belief that passing an ordinance would pull Fremont, already struggling economically, into a long and expensive legal fight that it would ultimately lose.

"I vote no," Edwards concluded—and the room roared, but not everyone was cheering.

Chapter 6

THIS LAND IS NOT YOUR LAND

Two weeks after the city council vote in Fremont, nearly 150 people gathered for an anti-immigration rally at the Oak Park Mall in Austin. Ruthie Hendrycks, founder and president of Minnesotans Seeking Immigration Reform (MinnSIR), warned the audience not to believe it when Hormel said that the company was forced to rely on undocumented labor, that Hispanic immigrants were just doing the jobs that American citizens were now unwilling to do. "Who was doing these jobs before?" she demanded. The crowded erupted into applause and hoots of approval.

Hendrycks had launched MinnSIR with her husband, Scott, from their home in Hanska, Minnesota, in early 2006 after seeing a report issued by Governor Tim Pawlenty's office estimating that eighty-five thousand undocumented immigrants were living in the state. Hendrycks was angry that Swift & Company in Worthington and Hormel in Austin had attracted so many Latino workers to southern Minnesota, spilling over into the Tyson plant in Sleepy Eye and the Armour-Eckrich plant in St. James, not far from her home. According to Pawlenty's report, these new immigrants were costing taxpayers $188 million a year for education and health care. Hendrycks, who worked as a dental hygienist, saw these immigrants coming into her office in increasing numbers, paying for dental cleanings for themselves and their children with Medicaid. She didn't like that her tax dollars were supporting their health care while they took jobs away from Minnesotans.

She began writing to the leaders of FAIR, the Minuteman Project, Brotherhood Organization of a New Destiny, the John Birch Society, and other anti-immigration groups, asking them to endorse her organization and speak at a series of rallies to be held in the Twin Cities and then other cities in southern Minnesota. Within a few months, ICE had carried out a massive enforcement action at six different Swift plants across the Midwest, including the one in Worthington. Hundreds of workers were taken away in handcuffs and eventually deported. Hendrycks believed the enforcements were sparked by MinnSIR's spotlight on the region and called for similar actions at Hormel and QPP in Austin—and when Susan Tully, Midwest field director for FAIR, told her about what was happening in Fremont in summer 2008, Hendrycks began to think that the time was right for a rally in Austin, to see if citizens there would get behind a similar ordinance.

Many Austin locals pointed out that the town—devastated by the farm crisis as well as the strike—would not have survived the Reagan era without the immigrant influx, and that the appearance of Mexican restaurants and bakeries was proof that some Hispanic influences had been embraced. But many more felt, like Hendrycks, that these immigrants had stolen union jobs and were leeching off of government services to which they did not contribute. The immigrants themselves countered that payroll taxes were withheld from their paychecks, though they would never be able to claim Social Security. And if they were injured at work, they would be unlikely to file workers' compensation claims, for fear they would face firing and receive no backing from the white-run union.

On this one point, Hendrycks seemed to agree with pro-immigrant advocates. These thousands of undocumented immigrants were a perfect corporate workforce: thankful for their paychecks, willing to endure harsh working conditions, unlikely to unionize or even complain. That's why she called on the Austin Police Department and the Mower County Sheriff's Office to step up the number of arrests made under the provisions of a new executive order, issued by Governor Pawlenty as part of the run-up to his presidential bid, that effectively deputized local officers in enforcing federal immigration laws. But that wasn't enough, she said; something had to be done about the federal government.

When an audience member wanted to know why Hormel had never been raided the way that Swift or Agriprocessors had been, Hendrycks suggested a larger conspiracy. "Three times raids were scheduled, and every time, a directive straight from Washington, D.C., called that raid off," Hendrycks said. She claimed that she had it on direct authority from Mower County sheriff Terese Amazi. Amazi wouldn't confirm that claim, but she later said, "We've sat down with ICE, and they've said, 'We won't do a raid. Period.'" She told another reporter, "We're having to build a new jail for a reason." Amazi's comments hinted at the deeper message that organizers meant to send. Though they insisted that their aim was squarely on companies like Hormel, Hendrycks kept warning that Austin's crime numbers were poised to increase unless something drastic was done—unless the "illegals" were sent packing.

At the end of the evening, after the speakers had finished, a local newspaper reporter covering the event asked one of the attendees if he thought it was really the place of local law enforcement to step in, if ICE wasn't taking the lead. The man, a bus driver from Albert Lea, responded by warning against making the issue "too complicated."

"It's like us against them," he said.

No doubt Dale Chidester was right when he told me that anti-immigrant anger was held-over animosity from an earlier era, but it runs deeper than the strike in the 1980s. Missing from the usual creation myth of P-9, both in union literature and the sanitized corporate history presented at the Spam Museum, is a crucial story, told decades later, of Hormel's abortive efforts to undercut the all-white workforce with African American workers in the early years of the Great Depression.

At that time, Austin was a segregated town—but divided by class lines, not race, with poor packinghouse workers living on the eastern side of the Cedar River near the plant and the city's wealthy families living on the far bank with its idyllic Main Street and thriving shops. The arrival of the Great Depression, just as Jay C. Hormel was taking over the family business, widened the schism. Though Jay would come to be romanticized as "the owner who cared," workers at the time regarded the Princeton-educated son of privilege as a mere inheritor who knew nothing about meatpacking—and they were keen to test his resolve. The unrest grew when slumping sales of canned goods caused the company to post a loss in 1931, its first in three decades, and Jay instituted an across-the-board wage cut without informing workers in advance.

The lost income pushed many Hormel families out of their homes. They erected shacks on the right-of-way easements along either side of the railroad tracks leading to the plant or squatted in an abandoned shed in the nearby brickyard. "We had people that lived in tar paper shacks," Hormel worker Marie Casey remembered later. "We had 'skunk hollow,' where people lived in tents." Casper Winkels said even before the Depression that Hormel workers made "just enough to pay your room and board, buy a few clothes, and then maybe you'd have a couple of bucks left to go out on a Saturday night and have a little fun." Now all they could hope for was enough to buy food and some fuel to heat their hovels. It was about this time that Casper and his brother

John Winkels began talking with Frank Ellis about organizing the workforce into a formal union. In the midst of this nascent organizing, "Hormel hired 40 niggers," Winkels remembered, "and they put 'em all in the plant at one time."

The Winkels brothers had seen this strategy before, he explained. When the Great Railroad Strike of 1922 hit Austin, Union Pacific brought in an entire boxcar of black workers to man the roundhouse. Several of the railway brotherhoods had earlier denied membership to African American workers to appease southern locals; now these excluded workers were only too happy to come north and fill positions, to show leadership that the union needed to protect all workers to sustain a strike. But the Winkels brothers, even in those days, didn't see it that way.

John Winkels was at a dance in downtown Austin when a cousin arrived to tell him that a mob was forming. Winkels remembered his cousin saying, "We're gonna chase the niggers out of town." He handed Winkels a sawed-off shovel handle, and they headed for the railroad yards. There had been violence all over the country that summer, with mobs attacking and killing strikebreakers, so Union Pacific had housed the African American workers in the roundhouse. "We went in there and run the niggers out," Winkels recalled. "Hit them over the head, you know, and tell them to get going! Albert's Creek runs through there, and some of them run that way, and we was after them, chased them, and one of them fell in the creek. He got up on his feet and he says, 'Lordy mercy, if I ever gets on my feet again, I'll never come in this town again!'" Within a year, a crowd of twenty thousand watched as the Ku Klux Klan initiated four hundred new members at a meeting in an open field outside Austin.

And Winkels told this story to labor historian Roger Horowitz more than seventy-five years later, as context and precursor, a way to explain what he had done almost a decade later when "Hormel hired them forty" in 1931. Winkels and his brother led a group down to the woods on the edge of town, an area locals called the jungle. The story was less animated this time, less detailed, but he didn't shy away from what they'd done or why. "After supper we got clubs and went down there and we run them out," he remembered. "After that they didn't come in no more."

With a unified, all-white workforce in place, Winkels was able not only to unionize all Hormel workers but also to carry off a strike in 1933 that radically reshaped the labor-management balance in Austin. But the fifty years of labor peace that both sides lionized—and later lamented passing—was built on a shared understanding that the union would come to the bargaining table if Hormel did not bring in scab workers, usually minorities, from outside the community. This became the central, unspoken rule of the Austin local: nonwhite workers would destroy the union.

So what must Pete Winkels, the son of Casper Winkels, have thought when he was fired by Hormel for his participation in the 1980s strike? Pete had grown up on stories of union fights. He had spent nearly two decades in the plant before getting a job as the business agent for the union. When the international union betrayed the local and fired Austin's leadership, Winkels applied to be reinstated by Hormel but was told that his position no longer existed. While his lawsuit wound its way through court with no support from union leadership, Pete watched as Hormel was subdivided into Quality Pork Processors and his fellow union workers remained unrecalled as the cut-and-kill operation was steadily staffed by fresh workers bused in from Mexico.

Not long after the city council vote in Fremont, John Wiegert got a phone call from Wanda Kotas, who was then the manager of the local veterans' club. Both had spoken passionately in favor of the ordinance in the high school auditorium, and both were fuming that the council had suspended the rules to vote early and that Mayor Edwards had cast the deciding vote from a prepared statement—evidence, as they saw it, that the decision had been made ahead of time, that the whole process of gathering the town had been a sham.

"How do you feel?" Kotas asked.

"I'm pretty upset," Wiegert said.

"Well, it might not be done yet," Kotas told him. She said she had been contacted by John Copenhaver, an anti-immigration activist in Omaha who had called the Comprehensive Immigration Reform Act of 2006, which was defeated by Republicans in the House of Representatives, a "blueprint for the destruction of America." Copenhaver had told Kotas that she should draft a petition to put the ordinance to a public vote. They would need to get three sponsors and then collect three thousand signatures. She wanted to know if Wiegert would sign on as a second petitioner; he quickly agreed and suggested contacting Jerry Hart, the retired IRS auditor who had also spoken at the meeting, to be the third person.

Not long after, Wiegert spotted Hart in the Wal-Mart parking lot, collecting signatures for a pro-ordinance candidate to run against Skip Edwards for mayor. Wiegert honked and waved Hart over to his truck. "Hey, you don't know me," he started, but he introduced himself and explained how the petition would work.

"Would you be willing to help out?" he asked.

"You bet," Hart said.

They had petitions printed up and started collecting signatures. They stood outside the Veterans Club, across the street from the high school football stadium, passing clipboards through car windows as people waited in line to park for the games. They went table to table at the Eagles Club. They divided the city into a grid and went door-to-door. They got a list of registered voters from Charlie Janssen, who had voted for the ordinance as a member of the city council and had just been elected to the state legislature, and started making phone calls; when they found someone willing to sign, they dispatched a runner to drive a petition right to the front door. They got Bob Warner to call his constituents during the day and went out to meet with them at night. When Wiegert's Christmas break came around at school, he began working full-time. He spent every morning making phone calls and accumulating commitments from citizens willing to add their names to the petition and then ventured out into the snow and cold every afternoon with a list of addresses, driving to each house to collect those signatures.

As the deadline for submitting the petition approached, Hart and Wiegert started to believe they could gather not only the three thousand signatures required but several hundred additional names, in case any were thrown out. Hart published an editorial in the *Fremont Tribune*, as both a statement of purpose and rallying cry for the measure they were about to put on the ballot. "The more that I look around Fremont, read the paper, talk to people," he wrote, "the more that I am sickened by what is happening to this town. It disgusts and angers me that this city is being destroyed by the greed of Hormel, Fremont Beef and like minded places." Two weeks later, Hart, Kotas, and Wiegert submitted their petition—with a total of 3,300 signatures.

At the next city council meeting, however, members voted unanimously to file petition for a declaratory judgment action in the Dodge County District Court, seeking a ruling on whether the proposed ordinance was constitutional. City attorney Skokan argued that the proposed ordinance would be preempted by federal law, would not provide sufficient safeguards to protect constitutional property rights, and would violate the Fair Housing Act. John Copenhaver contacted Kris Kobach to see if he would represent the three petitioners. Kobach drove up to Fremont from Kansas, along with representatives from FAIR in Washington, and met with Wiegert and Hart at the Big Red Keno Club, not far from Wiegert's house. Over burgers and fries, Kobach offered to represent them pro bono.

Remembering that moment later, Kobach said he had made the offer because he was touched by what he saw in Fremont. "It was a refreshing vignette," he began then stopped himself. "No, let me use the English word—a refreshing *little picture* of citizens who were taking this issue on, who were trying to get expert help, and who were just delighted that I was willing to help them." He said he would waive his fee on the sole condition that the petitioners totally commit to the case, with the full knowledge that it could be a protracted fight.

"We're willing to help you out," Kobach said, "but you just have to promise that you don't get cold feet halfway through—because this could take several years."

Wiegert told him not to worry. "Once I get started on something," he said, "I go through with it."

At the end of November 2008, a group of about twenty picketers gathered on Hormel Drive outside QPP. They held signs that read: HORMEL AND QPP GUILTY FOR OUR DISEASE and SCIENCE DOESN'T HAVE CURE FOR OUR DISEASE. Centro Campesino, the Hispanic cultural center assisting immigrants suffering from PIN, issued a statement alleging that QPP and Hormel had been ignoring the concerns of sick workers, violated their work restrictions, and, in some cases, simply fired employees who could no longer work. Centro Campesino called on QPP to make amends, demanding the rehiring of fired workers and taking "appropriate steps to assure access to workers' compensation benefits for all the affected employees."

Roberto Olmedo-Hernandez—a father of three in his late thirties who had worked until March at the viscera station, opening and draining pigs' stomachs—sat hunkered against the wind, a dark scowl on his face. He told reporters that he had been reassigned to light duty in the laundry room at QPP but still struggled with "intense fatigue, headaches and foot pain." He said that doctors at both the Mayo Clinic and Austin Medical Center had run multiple tests on him, but none knew how to help him—and his symptoms were worsening. Once, he had gotten into an argument with Dr. Lachance, accusing him of working for Hormel. "People are scared," he explained to reporters. "I'm not scared for myself now, but my kids, my wife. My kids are asking me if I'm going to die."

When the local newspaper in Austin reached Kelly Wadding for comment, he was clearly shocked by the negative press. The public attention, up until that point, had been almost universally positive. Now Wadding acknowledged that he had been contacted by Centro Campesino and said he had done his best to address their concerns. "They made a lot of accusations," he said, "but they didn't give me any names or any specifics." He insisted that he knew of no instances in which supervisors had not honored employees' work restrictions and no instances of anyone with the disorder being denied workers' compensation. Wadding did acknowledge that some workers had been fired when they couldn't provide documentation of legal work status. But he steadfastly maintained that he knew of "no one that was fired" because they had filed claims against the company.

And yet, during the week that followed the small protest, several additional workers who had filed workers' compensation claims were summoned to the office of Dale Wicks, director of human resources, to answer questions about their immigration status. Among them was Pablo Ruiz. As with Miriam Angeles—and, by then, several other workers—Ruiz was informed that QPP had received an inquiry from ICE about his immigration status. The company, Wicks said, had reason to believe that Ruiz had filed a false job application and was working in the country illegally.

Ruiz was stunned. He had grown up in Mexico within sight of the Rio Grande, but when he was ten years old, he crossed the river with his parents and went to work in the fields of South Texas — on a legal temporary agricultural worker visa. "I was so young that they got to go to the lawyer and get a couple of witnesses, and the farmer signed the papers," Ruiz told me. In 1996, when he turned eighteen, he applied for full citizenship, and it was granted.

Now he looked back on his job interview at QPP, many years before, and suspected that key questions were subtle ways of trying to assess his immigration status. "When was I last in Mexico?" he gave as an example. "Are my parents there? It's kind of tricky." He told me that, he believes, QPP had assumed for nine years that he was working without proper documentation—and, once they realized the extent of his injuries, had tried to dupe him into fleeing for fear of deportation. Ruiz stiffened and told Wicks what he later told me: "I'm a citizen since 1996 so with me there is no problem with that."

Wicks apologized for the error and told Ruiz he could go—but Pablo Ruiz's problems were just beginning.

Part Three

Chapter 7

FROM SEED TO SLAUGHTER

On September 15, 2008, Lynn Becker got the phone call every hog farmer fears.

For months on end, pork producers across the Midwest had been struggling against record-low prices per head, but Becker had taken steps to protect his family's farm against contractions of the market. He had signed a producer agreement with Hormel Foods, maybe the one company with a recession-proof demand for pork, and he had planted enough of his own corn to sustain his herd for the next year, insulating his operation from skyrocketing feed prices. With another Minnesota winter already in the air, Becker was out walking his fields one last time before starting the harvest. "When I got in and checked the answering machine," he told me later, "there was a message from Matt Prescott with PETA." Becker was soft-spoken but bristled with nervous energy. His jitters, together with his work-honed physique and fair hair, made him seem much younger than forty. But he insisted that the four years since receiving the call from the People for the Ethical Treatment of Animals had aged him by more than a decade.

"They had 'damning evidence,'" he said haltingly. "Undercover. Of animal abuse. On a farm that we own."

Becker described his hog operation outside Fairmont, Minnesota, a little more than an hour due west of Austin on Interstate 90, as a "good old-fashioned, American family farm"—and it might appear that way at first. Everything about the old homestead suggests its age, from the weathered, brick-red Dutch Gambrel barn emblazoned with the name, LB PORK, to the simple farmhouse that Becker's grandfather built in the 1940s—the house where all big decisions are still made on Sundays around the dinner table. But in truth, Becker was already a major supplier, providing more than fifty thousand pigs to Hormel each year, and he was making a bid to double that number by bringing the whole supply chain, from seed to slaughter, under his control. He owned 1,500 acres of prime farmland, where he raised corn and soybeans, which he put up in a colossal grain bin and ground at his own feed mill and then trucked to more than a dozen sites in Minnesota and Iowa to feed to thousands of pregnant sows in his breeding barns and tens of thousands of weaned piglets at separate finishing facilities. The company was sprawling and complex, employing dozens of full-time and part-time workers, and it was only getting bigger. Still, Becker insists that he always personally monitored every phase of his business. And as the voice message claiming animal abuse started to sink in, his shock and disbelief quickly turned to indignation.

"Wait a second," he remembered thinking. "Not on any farm *I* own."

Then it dawned on him. The farm in question wasn't LB Pork or even his breeding facility, Camalot, about ten miles away outside the town of Welcome. The farm that PETA had investigated was a large barn complex, housing some six thousand sows and tens of thousands of newborn piglets, that Becker had acquired less than a month before in Iowa, an operation he had purchased from Natural Pork Production II and renamed MowMar Farms but had only ever seen a few times. Becker phoned his day-to-day management company, Suidae Health & Production, based in Algona, Iowa, and asked them to reach out to Prescott and see if they could get their hands on this "damning evidence"; maybe the video they claimed to have in their possession had all been shot before the facility was under his ownership.

Meanwhile, Becker worked his connections. He was the president of the Minnesota Pork Board, and his wife, Julie, had been the Minnesota Pork Promoter of the Year in 2007. In fact, she was, at that very moment, on Capitol Hill with the Minnesota Pork Producers Association, the lobbying arm of the Pork Board, meeting with members of Congress. Becker called his wife so she could alert her fellow lobbyists. Then he placed another call to Cindy Cunningham, the assistant vice president for communications at the National Pork Board in Des Moines, Iowa.

Soon Becker heard back that PETA wanted to meet with him one-on-one and then stage a joint press conference. Everyone advised against it. Instead, with the assistance of Himle Horner, a public relations firm in the Twin Cities, he decided to issue a written statement, and Cunningham mobilized several agribusiness organizations to help answer press inquiries. But nothing could have prepared them for the onslaught of negative attention. The next day, when the Associated Press released the video online along with a wire report describing its contents, the story became worldwide news almost instantly. The video's camerawork was shaky and low-definition, captured with recorders hidden in the hat brims of undercover workers, but it had been cut together into a concise and harrowing five minutes.

In one shot, a supervisor was shown beating a sow relentlessly on the back. In another, workers turned electric prods on a crippled sow and kicked pregnant sows repeatedly in the belly. A close-up showed a distressed sow knocked out, her face royal blue from the

Prima Tech marking dye sprayed into her nostrils by a worker who said he was trying "to get her high." In one of the most disturbing sequences, a worker demonstrated the method for euthanizing underweight piglets: taking them by the hind legs and smashing their skulls against the concrete floor. Fellow workers whooped and laughed as he tossed the bloodied and twitching bodies into a giant bin. The AP story revealed that PETA had already met with Tom Heater, the sheriff of Greene County, Iowa, and he had agreed to open a criminal investigation.

That night, Becker played the PETA video again and again on his iPad. He told me he felt numb as he watched his inbox fill with more than a thousand angry emails. He was starting to see what an ordeal the release of this video was going to be. But worse, he feared that Hormel would terminate its production contract with him—the contract he had used to secure a loan of more than $1 million to mortgage the breed barns in Iowa, with his family's homestead in Minnesota as collateral. If Hormel decided that Becker had become a liability, he and his family could lose everything.

Before World War II, American meat production, especially in the Midwest, was necessarily seasonal. Cattle, hogs, and chickens were part of small, diversified farms that sustained livestock year-round, but farmers tended to fatten and bring animals to market only after harvest, when feed was plentiful and cheap. So northern meatpackers offered workers long hours during late summer and fall, then laid them off during the winter and early spring. But, after the industrialization of the war, major meat producers like Hormel were eager to keep increasing output (and sales) by turning packing into a year-round activity. To make this possible, the companies encouraged farmers to turn away from diversified, seasonal farming and to begin specializing and modifying their operations to produce market animals throughout the year.

During the 1950s, the midwestern stockmen who embraced this shift usually raised either cattle, which were hardy enough to withstand winter cold, or chickens, which could be easily cooped when temperatures plummeted. But hog farming on the icy, windswept plains was difficult in those days. Even in milder winters, farmers often suffered deaths among their herds, and periods of sustained bitter temperatures naturally suppressed sows' fertility, which meant they could be bred only once a year. But, beginning in the 1960s, some enterprising hog farmers began building confinement barns large enough to house hundreds or even thousands of pigs throughout the winter. Such enclosures not only overcame mortality due to bad weather but, with even basic space-heating systems, also allowed farmers to successfully breed sows twice a year.

By the close of the decade, family farmers worried that hog confinement was so effective that the innovation would encourage highly capitalized meatpackers to begin building their own barns and buying up cheap cropland, establishing monopolies that would effectively squeeze out small operations. Between 1972 and 1982, various forms of the Family Farm Protection Act passed in North Dakota, South Dakota, Nebraska, Kansas, Oklahoma, Minnesota, Wisconsin, Iowa, and Missouri. A template law introduced with identical language in each state, the goal was to defend small farm operators against large packers. But almost from the moment those measures were passed, packers were looking for a way around them.

From a business perspective, their determination to control the supply chain made perfect sense. In a marketplace already at the mercy of weather, disease, feed and fuel prices, and the changing American appetite, Hormel, like most large meatpackers, was always searching for opportunities to curb and regularize input costs. If they could buy up enough cornfields to manipulate feed prices or invest in enough hog operations to depress the market price for pork, then all of the major packers stood to benefit from pushing out small farmers. So when the Midwest passed laws against vertical integration, a handful of the nation's largest hog producers, with a shared focus not seen since the industry united against Upton Sinclair and Teddy Roosevelt's efforts to break up the Meat Trust, financed a building boom in the unregulated American South, where they could erect larger and larger barns capable of holding thousands of animals without fear of interference from state officials.

The epicenter of the boom was in North Carolina. During the 1990s, the hog population of the Tar Heel State tripled to more than 8 million, and Smithfield Foods opened the world's largest meat processing plant there. But the unbridled growth sparked intense debate about the environmental safety of the massive cesspools of manure, so-called lagoons, produced by tens of thousands of hogs in small confines. Concern turned to outrage in 1999 after a containment dyke at Ocean View Farms ruptured and spilled 25 million gallons of waste into the New River, poisoning the water and killing thousands of fish. Then a few months later, floodwaters from Hurricane Irene overflowed lagoons all across the state. As the *New York Times* reported, "Feces and urine soaked the terrain and flowed into rivers." The ensuing backlash pushed many southern politicians to start embracing tighter regulation, while midwestern governors and lawmakers, especially those in heavily Republican states, argued that industrialized meat production was a way of reviving farms that had never fully recovered from the farm crisis of the Reagan era. But first they needed to roll back bans against vertical integration.

In 2002, Smithfield, joined by livestock subsidiaries Murphy-

Brown and Prestage-Stoecker Farms, filed suit against Iowa in federal court, arguing that the state's packer ban violated their rights under the Commerce Clause of the U.S. Constitution by discriminating against out-of-state companies. In fact, the ban applied to corporate processors both in and out of Iowa, but—because the language of the Family Farm Protection Act provided an exception for small-town farmer co-ops—the federal district court nullified the law. The appellate court agreed to hear an appeal, but in September 2005, before the scheduled court date, Iowa attorney general Tom Miller made a devil's bargain: consenting to an injunction prohibiting the enforcement of the packer ban with specific respect to Smithfield. Predictably, other out-of-state meatpackers immediately filed suits of their own.

By April 2006, both Hormel and Cargill had negotiated exemptions with the state of Iowa—and began buying up existing confinement barns and offering financing for the construction of new, large-scale facilities. Because the ban was still technically on the books, only hog producers under contract to Smithfield, Cargill, or Hormel had permission to own farmland and raise hogs. Faced with the looming threat of competing against these feed-to-market monopolies, many farmers sold off their hogs and hog operations. Many more agreed to risk everything by shouldering thirty-year mortgages on multimillion-dollar barn complexes, with only short-term contracts, and often their family land, as collateral to secure the loans. Packers were then free to dictate industrialized herd management techniques, requiring farmers to raise genetically engineered hogs, to artificially inseminate their sows, to hold them throughout pregnancy in gestation crates, to inject newborn piglets with high doses of preemptive antibiotics, and to raise weaned pigs on feed additives that promoted rapid growth and leaner animals.

As the sole limit on Hormel's exemption from Iowa's anti-vertical-integration law, the attorney general stipulated that the term of their agreement with the state would be ten years, at which point these few by-name exemptions would all be reviewed to assess whether they had created market monopolies. But rather than encouraging Hormel, Cargill, and Smithfield—and later Tyson, Christensen Family Farms, and a few other producers that obtained subsequent exemptions—to proceed with caution, the term agreement spurred these companies to build as many large-scale farms in Iowa as they could and as rapidly as they could, in order to grab as much market share as possible.

Hormel was especially eager to get a jump on increasing hog production. Their southern competitors had seen production grow by leaps and bounds during the 1990s, while Hormel's Midwest-based operations had been limited by the number of hogs they could raise. With an agreement in place in Iowa, Hormel could finally take advantage of the sweetheart deal they had secured with the USDA in 2002 allowing them to run the lines at their processing plants at speeds higher than any other packinghouse in the country. This was their chance to gain ground on Smithfield. Even before the agreement with the state of Iowa was official, Hormel began providing loans to hog farmers, pushing them to build multimillion-dollar large-scale confinements in the northern counties, just south of the Quality Pork Processors plant in Austin, and in western Iowa, within trucking distance of the Hormel plant in Fremont, Nebraska. On the very day the exemption was publicly made known, Hormel issued a press release announcing that they would be increasing production at the Fremont plant from 9,000 hogs per day to more than 10,500.

In 1946, Hormel hosted the first National Barrow Show in Austin. Hog farmers from thirteen states brought truckloads of their best castrated boars to the plant to be slaughtered, weighed, and judged. Each cut was scored not just according to raw weight but by its lean-to-fat ratio. The top-scoring hog was 49.7 percent lean meat and 21.3 percent fat; the bottom-scoring hog was 44 percent lean and 23.6 percent fat. The difference was slim—and nearly undetectable on the hoof—but Hormel had discovered, at that early stage, that they could standardize production and dramatically improve margins if they were paying for hanging carcass weight and grade, instead of live weight. So they began offering premiums, as much as $2.50 per pound, for hogs that yielded above-average ratios of meat. As the annual show grew, Hormel instituted a rule that breeding animals would also be brought to the fairgrounds—and auctioned on the final day. Most of the farmers buying the boars and gilts were Hormel suppliers, thus improving the lean quality of the company's stock. Soon, Hormel launched the Fort Dodge Market Hog Show in cooperation with the Agricultural Extension Service of Iowa State University to improve the company's breeding stock in Iowa as well.

In 1957, Hormel persuaded the Minnesota legislature to go one step further—authorizing the establishment of the state's first swine testing station in Austin. State-funded research scientists tested hogs of every breed for their overall size, lean-to-fat ratio, and yield of particular cuts. Then in a barn leased to Hormel by the state for $1 per year, the Minnesota Swine Breeders Association bred the most desirable members of each breed—and, eventually, crossbred them—in an effort to create a leaner market hog. But all that research had one serious limitation: even as custom-bred animals improved overall stock, Hormel couldn't dictate feed or care to individual farmers, especially after the institution of the packer bans in the 1970s. What arrived at the grading station still varied tremendously, which made yield unpredictable.

After the rollback of the bans, however, pork producers, with Hormel at the forefront, began dreaming of having enough farm-level control to prescribe particular growing techniques, allowing their meat scientists to custom-design the perfect hog. If each and every pig could be optimized and standardized according to the particular needs of the processing plant where they would be slaughtered, then butchering at the plants could be sped up through further automation and market share could be grown by providing the steadiest supply to retailers. In the early 2000s, for example, when Hormel approached major retailers about stocking their prepackaged fresh cuts, Wal-Mart demanded identical, exact-weight pork chops, loins, and roasts. But if Hormel was going to provide 10-pound packages of pork chops, pre-portioned into identical cuts, and trimmed with no more than an eighth inch of fat as Wal-Mart required, then each hog would have to be raised to have the same amount of back muscle with the same amount of fat. And, ideally, the same would be true for hams, bacon, loins, roasts, and every other part of the animal.

Hormel was no longer willing to receive hogs of varied breeds and ages at their weigh stations, where they would then have to go through sorting according to size and leanness. Instead, the company's systems engineers wanted trucks to arrive at Hormel's loading docks each morning carrying thousands of hogs as nearly identical to one another as possible. And so the modern hog confinement became the test laboratory for a grand-scale experiment in reverse engineering.

Hormel developed a chart that measures carcass weight against body fat with an optimal "red box" at the center, offering their contract growers a sizable bonus for hitting the target and paying for the bonus by extracting a penalty from those growers whose animals fell too far outside the desired parameters. On average, hogs that hit the red box (yielding hot-weight carcasses of between 174 and 222 pounds, with less than 1.1 inches of backfat) earn about 105 percent of base price, compared with 88 percent of market price for hogs outside the box. For contract growers, that can mean a price swing of as much as $25 per hog. Hitting the red box can increase the value of a single shipment by more than

$4,000, which, in a typical year of roughly sixty truckloads from a single large-scale facility, can add up to the difference between a healthy profit and a crippling loss. So growers are constantly chasing promises of improved methods (antibiotics, growth enhancers, metabolism-altering beta-adrenergic agonists, acidifiers, enzymes, and other feed additives), but in pursuit of those improved profit margins, farmers are also steadily increasing their overhead.

Rigid standardization, however, has been nothing but beneficial for Hormel. Its sophisticated network of interrelated growers, each producing just the right number and age of hogs, keeps a steady stream of uniform carcasses moving from the kill room to the chain to be butchered each day. The system ensures there is never a scarcity of hogs that would drive up their input costs, and there is never a surplus that would force them to pay too much overtime at processing plants.

From a pure business standpoint, the project of industrializing hog production has been an unparalleled success—and a logistical wonder. Every working day, about 175 trailers in various parts of Iowa, eastern Nebraska, and southern Minnesota are loaded with 170 hogs each; they converge onto one of a dozen loading docks in Fremont and Austin, arriving within a one-hour window of each other, in order to deliver roughly 30,000 hogs for slaughter. That's every day for 260 working days, every year—7.7 million hogs, herded through a tiny set of chutes, slaughtered, butchered, and sent out for additional value-added processing, at just those two plants. For the system to work, a four-month growing cycle must culminate with an exact-weight animal at just the right time. That precision must be carried out at hundreds of feeder sites, and the whole cycle, from insemination to slaughter, must be exactly replicated three times a year.

The industry despises the term "factory farm," but the fact is that modern hog farming is designed on a factory model, carried out with the exactitude of a factory, and built around serving the

needs of other factories—the packinghouses, the packagers, shipping warehouses—farther along the supply chain. Each step can
be replicated and repeated countless times in identical or near-
identical facilities almost anywhere that residents of nearby communities will allow it.

In the first years following the unofficial repeal of the vertical
integration ban in Iowa, the factory model also convinced business developers, many of whom had extensive experience in lo-
gistics but no knowledge of agriculture, that raising hogs was no
different than managing any other factory. To them, building hog
confinements looked like easy money. After all, major meatpackers were effectively cosigning on loans worth millions of dollars by
guaranteeing a constant market for years to come. It seemed like a
sure thing—that is, until the whole system, under the strain of its
own runaway success, threatened to fall apart.

A couple of miles north of Bayard, Iowa, at the crossroads of two
wide gravel tracks, there are three enormous sow barns: the site of
Lynn Becker's MowMar Farms. It's now operated under the name
Fair Creek, though you'd never know it; there are no company
signs, no indication at all of what's going on inside. The barns
gleam white in the sun and seem, by all appearances, to be well
ventilated, well supplied with water from giant external holding
tanks, and generally well turned-out, right down to their square
corners and tightly tacked aluminum siding. Gary Weihs (pronounced WISE), the site's original developer, saw to it that the
facility was clean, inconspicuous, and odor-free. It took him two
years of disputes and disagreements to get a permit recommendation from the board of supervisors for Greene County, so he
wanted to be sure there were no complaints once the facility was
built.

After spending years working with large corporations like Pepsi, Procter & Gamble, and Monsanto in operational management, Weihs had decided to return to his native Iowa. He planned to combine the experience he had gained growing up on his father's hog farm outside of Harlan with the statistical analysis of three decades of corn pricing and hog yields he had performed to complete his MBA at Harvard Business School. "We flat price everything," Weihs told the *National Hog Farmer*, "so that we make a little bit per head and base our profits on quantity." Under the name Natural Pork Production II (NPPII), he lined up investors and, when he had the start-up money in place, began building facilities, about one per year. The three barn complex in Bayard was the fifth unit—a 6,000-sow farrow-to-wean operation, where returns would be generated for investors by selling roughly 130,000 weaned pigs each year to finishing operations at $36 apiece. All told, NPPII facilities were supplying about fifteen different hog farmers with close to 800,000 weaned pigs, for gross annual earnings of nearly $29 million—but all while carrying precarious overhead, including roughly $5 million in construction costs per site and millions more invested in the breeding sows housed inside.

To make the ambitious plan possible, Weihs enlisted Daryl Olsen, president and CEO of the Audubon-Manning Veterinary Clinic (AMVC) in Audubon, Iowa, to oversee building and operations. AMVC's name makes it sound like a small mom-and-pop animal hospital, but it is, in reality, one of the ten largest pork producers in the United States, with more sows in the mid-2000s than Tyson or Hormel and already in well-established relationships with, by Weihs's estimate, more than a dozen finishing operations. If Weihs could scrape together the start-up capital for a facility, Olsen could staff it quickly and provide guaranteed buyers.

But by 2003, when the facility was first proposed in Bayard, many Iowans had grown suspicious of factory farming. Though

Weihs was the first hog developer to come into Greene County, many builders—particularly Smithfield's Prestage Farms from North Carolina—had been erecting mega-barns in other parts of northern Iowa. Bayard residents had observed the problems there and wanted to see NPPII's plans to mitigate environmental impact from waste and to hear how the animals would be cared for. Weihs pledged that NPPII could "raise 800,000 hogs a year and pollute less than my dad used to" and that the hogs would be "treated like royalty." In describing the facility to the *Midwest Ag Journal*, Weihs made it sound like a paradise for hogs: "We put them in separate crates, so they have their own water and feed and they can't fight. That way, even the weaker ones are productive." When some countered that Weihs seemed to be describing factory farming, he went on the offensive. "We *are* a factory," he said, "and there's nothing wrong with that. Would you want your car to not be made in a factory? There's quality control in a factory. There's good treatment of people and animals in a factory." He argued that the meat from factory farms, thanks to hormones and antibiotics, was leaner and, because of high-volume, could be produced at a lower cost. "So the consumer gets cheap pork loins, and lots of them, and they're high quality," he said. "I think it's the American way."

But in 2006, everything changed. The rollback of Iowa's vertical-integration ban created an instantaneous boom in the building of hog confinements, which signaled an influx of start-up capital but also attracted dramatically more competitors. In 2000, there had been thirty-eight applications statewide to build confinements large enough to require permitting through the Iowa Department of Natural Resources. In 2005, the year Smithfield was given an exemption to the law, that number vaulted to 203 applications. The following year, with Cargill and Hormel now granted the same exemption, the number jumped again to 318.

In under two years, Iowa went from having an outright ban on corporate involvement in hog farming to having more than half of its 17 million hogs in confinements owned by or under exclusive contract to three large meatpackers.

In the midst of this period of sudden competition from corporations, the per-bushel price of corn shot up from $2 to more than $3. New supports encouraging the production of ethanol had instantly increased the demand for corn. Meanwhile, in late 2006, the USDA revised its harvest estimate downward by 200 million bushels because of weather. These factors, combined with the smallest on-hand corn reserve since the drought years in the Clinton era, sparked a run in commodities speculation, driving the price to heights it hadn't seen in more than a decade—and defying the downward trajectory of prices seen since the early 1970s. Depending on whether you were a corn grower or a livestock producer counting on that feed, the *New York Times* wrote, "you have daydreams—or nightmares—of that $5 mark.

"When corn started going from two dollars to four dollars, it was pretty clear that it wasn't going to be profitable," Weihs told me. He sold out his personal interest in NPPII and moved on to developing other industries. Meanwhile, feed prices continued to soar on climbing energy costs, reaching as much as $8 per bushel of corn, and suddenly the model Weihs had sold to investors as a can't-miss business opportunity proved utterly unable to withstand the market shift. Investors started pulling out—and, soon, NPPII was in a position of needing to sell its facilities quickly, just to keep its backers from ruin. "Eight-dollar corn has a way of doing that," Weihs told me, but he defended his original business plan. "The economic models weren't built for even four-dollar corn, much less eight-dollar corn. And unfortunately, we got it wrong. As a developer, I was looking back and corn was two and three dollars for thirty years. I just didn't see it coming. That was my mistake."

By May 2008, rumors were flying among the workers at the sow barns that NPPII was on the brink of bankruptcy. According to at least one person who toured the facility during this time, the "quality of the husbandry" had begun to decline, and, according to another source, things had finally gotten so bad that a group of workers went to the farm manager, Jordan Anderson, with their concerns. Anderson initially claimed not to know what they were talking about, then laughed them off, saying there was nothing to worry about "as long as PETA don't find out." When one worker, identified by others only as Dave, finally threatened to report his concerns directly to Daryl Olsen at AMVC, he was terminated. Soon after, PETA received a message from the fired worker, describing the conditions at NPPII in stark detail. Overmatched and undertrained, workers were often kicking sows and beating them with herding boards or gate rods just to move them from one part of the facility to another. But, more than that, in the void left by a lack of management, some workers seemed to be finding a sadistic joy in taking out their frustrations on the hogs.

"This is cruel treatment of the animals," Dave wrote to PETA, "and I thought you should know."

Chapter 8

DON'T BE AFRAID TO HURT THEM

When Robert Ruderman showed up at Natural Pork Production II's sow barns to apply for a job in June 2008, he didn't know anything about the history of the facility or even who they were supplying. He was an undercover investigator, working for PETA, and knew only that a whistle-blower had alleged that animal abuses were occurring at the threadbare operation. Ruderman's cover story was thin—a vague account of meeting a girl online, coming to Iowa to be with her, but then things not working out. He was hired immediately, no questions asked.

Ruderman spent the morning of June 10, his first day, watching training videos, but by the afternoon he was assigned to shadow Shelly Mauch, a senior employee who worked in the farrowing facility: a single barn accommodating 15 rooms with 68 stalls per room—and each stall housing a sow that was either close to birthing or had recently given birth. Mauch explained that about 15 litters were born each day, with an average of 11 piglets per litter. Roughly 20 percent of those were classified under one of four headings: abortions, mummies, runts, or deformed. An abortion is a piglet that has developed fully but is born dead. A mummy has died earlier in the pregnancy and is born still wrapped in its embryonic sac. These dead deliveries along with birthing waste—placentas, umbilical cords—were deposited in the dead room at the end of each day and collected for composting. Runts and piglets born with deformities—displaced hips, spraddled legs, tumors—were more problematic. They had to be thumped, the euphemism for killing a piglet by smashing its skull against the concrete floor.

Of the remaining three-quarters of each litter, all had their tails docked—the males were also castrated with the same metal clippers—and sprayed with an iodine solution to prevent infection. According to Ruderman's daily logs, the piglets' screeching during those procedures was so loud that workers wore earplugs to protect their hearing. "Never do I hear the piglets cry and screech like that at any other time during their stay on the farm," he wrote, not even when they are weaned from their mothers after twenty days and loaded up in trucks to go to finishing operations.

In the weeks that followed, Ruderman managed to shoot undercover video of piglets as they were castrated, including some with unrecognized scrotal hernias, dubbed "ruptures," whose intestines would fully protrude when snipped. He got close-ups of bloody piglets after being thumped—skull-crushed, paddling their legs and twitching, gasping for air, as others were piled on top of them in giant bins. He secretly made detailed transcripts of AMVC's own records: the thousands of piglets tail-docked, the two hundred thumped each week. But none of what he captured was illegal—or even frowned upon. The industry insists that tails and testicles are clipped to prevent them from being bitten off by littermates and becoming infected. And thumping is not only legal but also an industry-sanctioned method of "humane euthanasia." In fact, what legal protection does exist is a law requiring that piglets euthanized by blunt-force trauma must receive only one blow. And, again and again, Ruderman noted: "I did not see any piglets thumped more than once."

But then, on June 27, Ruderman was helping to take sows out of their farrowing stalls for herding back to the breed barn. One of the sows was moving out of her stall and into the sheltered hallway between the two buildings when Marvin Mauch, the manager of the breed barn and Shelly Mauch's father, reared back and struck the sow hard across the back with his herding cane. Ruderman was shocked; according to his notes, Mauch had raised the cane "like a tennis serve" and then brought it down "like an ax." The sow squealed and rushed ahead into the hallway.

But Marvin's real anger, it appears, was directed at an intern who had seen him smoking in the breed barn—a violation of Iowa law—and reported him to Jordan Anderson. In the lunchroom, Marvin confronted the intern. According to Ruderman, Marvin shouted that he hated snitches and made physical threats. The intern shouted, "I can't handle this!" and stormed out, never returning. The next day workers learned that Marvin had been suspended, pending an investigation both by AMVC and the Department of Health. Not long after, Marvin was fired "for harassment and intimidation of an employee," and the intern was persuaded to return to work at another farm. "This is a small victory for the animals," Ruderman wrote in his log, "as Marvin was likely the cruelest, most abusive member of the staff."

But by then, Ruderman had noticed that many sows arriving in the farrowing barn from the breed barn bore the signs of abuse—red welts across their backs from the herding canes and unexplained bloody gouges in their rumps. Even with Marvin gone, the breed barn was little improved with Richard Ralston now in temporary command. He wasn't cruel like Marvin, but one of his fellow workers told me, bluntly, "Richard was a moron." He was nervous around the five-hundred-pound sows and often indecisive in ways that endangered coworkers and harmed the hogs.

On one day, for example, Ruderman watched Ralston attempt to put down two seriously ill sows by using a captive-bolt gun (CBG). According to Ruderman's log, "He retrieved the CBG and loaded a small metal shell into the device. The first CBG shot, administered into the middle of her forehead, did not kill the sow. The sow was still very much alive, on the ground, moving her head and torso and kicking her limbs. She appeared to be writhing in pain as a result of the first shot. She grunted and wailed. The second shot further debilitated her and she died about a minute later." The second killing went much the same.

PETA made the unusual decision to dispatch a second investigator, in hopes of getting him hired on in the breed barn where Ralston could be monitored more easily. But PETA would need to work fast. By then, Jordan Anderson had called a meeting to confirm the rumors: Natural Pork Production II was trying to sell out. Prospective buyers would be coming to inspect the place, so everyone was instructed to keep the blood from thumping and docking cleaned up. And they should be aware that new ownership might mean new management; everyone's job was potentially on the line. In late July, Ruderman recorded that a buyer had been found. In his notes, the name is entered first as "Momeyer," then "Momar," and finally the correct name: MowMar Farms.

The history of the Becker family farm in Minnesota could double as a microcosm of what has occurred in the hog industry as a whole in the last half century. Lynn's grandfather, Walter, was just six years old when he moved with his parents to the farm west of Northrop in 1920—and he never left, building a second home for his own family a stone's throw from the original farmhouse. When Walter took over in the 1950s, the operation was still an old-fashioned diversified farm, raising cattle, hogs, and chickens, along with a variety of crops. But in 1966, he decided to build a hog confinement, maybe the first in Martin County, with slotted floors and a pit below to catch manure.

By today's standards, Walter's farm was still quite small when he passed it on to his son, Larry, in the 1980s: just two hundred sows, which were only confined during nursing. But Larry named the operation LB Pork and began expanding capacity enough to make room for his sons Lynn and Lonny as partners. Larry built a gestation barn, bringing the sows permanently indoors, and added a two-ton on-farm gristmill, so that the family could grind its own feed. In 1995, Lynn returned from the University of Minnesota with his new wife, Julie, both with degrees in agriculture business management; they took over daily operations for the family, bringing the latest in ag science with them.

Lynn quickly revamped their whole system. The family had been using three "continuous flow" nursery barns—a simple method of maximizing barn space by moving pigs from one pen to the next as they grew. But diseases that once were held in check when pigs were exposed to Minnesota winters now flourished in temperature-controlled confinement barns. When a spate of Methicillin-resistant *Staphylococcus aureus* (MRSA) tore through the barns in the winter of 1996–97, Becker decided to switch to a two-step process: gestation to weaning in one set of barns, finishing in another.

He also set about aggressively expanding. Within five years, LB Pork was a full-scale, farrow-to-finish operation with 1,500 sows housed at two sites and more than 32,000 weaned piglets at 37 finishing barns spanning 12 sites. LB Pork was also part owner in Camalot, a 2,200 sow unit, and annually bought 15,000 heads of "isoweans"—piglets that are medicated and weaned early to prevent them from being exposed to adult illnesses. Between their own facilities and facilities they managed as contract growers, LB

Pork had roughly 24,000 pigs on inventory at any one time. They even launched Granja Becker, a 500-sow farrow-to-finish operation in Minas Gerais, Brazil. As dramatic as the expansion of LB Pork seems, it is reflective of a larger trend in the pork industry—one where hog producers either had to choose to keep their operations small and make only small profits or get big and do their best to compete amid (and sometimes against) the forces of industrialized agriculture.

The trouble was—and is—that in order to get big, farmers had to acquire more of everything: more land, more row crops, more animals, more equipment, more loans, more overhead. All of which steadily put more of the business and the profit but also more of the risk and the fixed costs onto fewer producers. When Lynn Becker joined the family business in 1995, there were more than 10,000 hog farms in Minnesota; by 2007 that number had fallen to 4,700. But over the same period, Minnesota's overall hog production went from just under 5 million head per year to nearly 8 million. In other words, half as many farms were producing nearly twice as many pigs. And no place was going bigger than Martin County—with LB Pork, both geographically and economically, at its very center. Already the state's top hog-producing county, Martin went from turning out 240,000 hogs per year in 1990 to 790,000 in 2008—with a full 10 percent of those hogs coming from LB Pork.

When, in the mid-2000s, the big meatpackers filed their lawsuits and obtained their exemptions from vertical integration, the timing couldn't have been better for the Beckers. They were continuing to expand their farming—from 900 acres of corn and soybeans to 1,500 acres—and had recently erected a new 150,000-bushel grain bin. When the sagging global economy drove up feed prices and drove down demand for meat, creating the worst hog market in history, the Beckers were insulated. They had raised enough corn, stored directly on the farm, to get them through.

At the same time, LB Pork's main customer, Hormel Foods, was experiencing a spike in demand for cheap meat, especially Spam. So Lynn Becker found himself in the enviable position of having a store of cheap feed and a buyer lined up to purchase as many hogs as he could bring to market.

And Becker recognized the opportunity. He shifted from looking for sites to build expanded facilities to searching for beleaguered companies in Iowa that he might be able to take over. "Calculated growth and modifications to our operation are how we've steadily maintained growth," he told the *Progressive Farmer*. "We need to position ourselves so that when good opportunities arise, we can jump on them." About that time, Becker met Gary Thome through their mutual veterinarian, Daryl Olsen, the president of the American Association of Swine Veterinarians and the CEO of the Audubon-Manning Veterinary Clinic. Thome, like Becker, had what Hormel itself describes as "a long-term agreement" with the company. "Because of this agreement," according to Hormel's own literature, Thome had access to "the capital required" to build a finishing facility.

Now Thome and Becker were both looking for another chance to expand, and Olsen had not only an opportunity but an urgent need. Natural Pork Production II—whose hog barns near Bayard, Iowa, were managed by AMVC—was on the verge of bankruptcy and, with twelve facilities to offload in a hurry, the company was offering bargain-basement prices. Becker visited two Natural Pork sow barns in May, where he told me he found a "sinking-ship feeling." But he chalked it up to neglect by an unraveling company. "It's kind of like when you know you're going to sell your car," he said. "Are you going to put new tires on it fifty miles before you sell it? Naw, you run them down to the wires."

So Becker and Thome reached an agreement with NPPII on a complex of barns housing six thousand sows near Bayard, Iowa, renamed the operation MowMar Farms, and officially took possession on August 18. The facility was exactly what Becker's company needed, but he acknowledged that the barns were not initially up to snuff. "The animal care had been slacking a little bit," he told me. "I think the manager would see somebody at the coffee shop that morning and might ask them to help do some chores." Becker said his management company, Suidae Health, had reinterviewed all of the employees—and many had quit rather than face retraining or termination. "That's always made me feel good," he said. "They could see there was a new sheriff in town."

On July 23, 2008, about the same time that Lynn Becker was finalizing the purchase of the hog barns in Bayard, Michael Steinberg, the second PETA operative, arrived in Iowa and was hired for one of the new openings in the breed barn. On his first day, he watched training videos, then at lunch met with two representatives from Suidae Health & Production, who explained that the new ownership would be taking over the farm on August 18. Steinberg then began his on-the-job training with Richard Ralston, who had been made the temporary head of the breed barn until a permanent replacement could be found for Marvin Mauch. Ralston was in a foul mood that day; he had sustained a long cut that morning when he was bitten by a boar brought into the breed barn to detect which sows were in heat. He admitted to Steinberg that, knocked down and bleeding, he had wanted "to beat the hell" out of the boar.

Barely a week later, Steinberg was able to get Ralston on video, admitting to a series of abuses—including anally penetrating the sows with gate rods and herding canes. "When I get pissed or get hurt or the fucking bitch won't move," he says in a portion of the video, "I grab one of those rods and I jam it in her asshole."

"You take the gate rods and shove it in their asshole?" Steinberg can be heard asking.

"Yeah, fuck 'em," Ralston says.

When pressed, Ralston told Steinberg that he knew he could get in trouble. "Half the shit I do nobody else is supposed to do," he said. But the very next day, when Steinberg was having trouble moving a frightened and balking gilt from isolation back to the brood barn, Ralston and another worker, Shawn Lyons, jumped in and started kicking the agitated hog. Finally, Ralston turned to Steinberg and said, "Stick your finger in her butt." When Steinberg refused, he says Ralston replied, "Stick it in her pussy then. . . . Just whip your dick out and get some pleasure." Later, in the break room, Ralston bragged about "giving it" to a sow with his cane. Steinberg, at first, understood him to mean that he had been beating her, but Ralston shushed him and told him to lower his voice. "I was shoving it in her pussy," he said. Steinberg asked if this helped move the sows along, but Ralston shook his head. "Just fucking around," he said. Weeks later, when the deputy sheriff was investigating the case, Ralston admitted to boasting he had penetrated sows with his cane but said he was just trying to act "macho" in front of his coworkers, particular his assistant manager, Alan Rettig.

Rettig was the one, Ralston said, who was always shouting to show the sows your dick. At sixty, Rettig was significantly older than twenty-seven-year-old Ralston and the other men, most of whom were in their late teens to early thirties. But he had more on his coworkers than just years; Rettig had cultivated a hard-ass mystique. He told everyone he had been a member of the Iowa Sons of Silence, a motorcycle gang that had been broken up in 2001 for trafficking drugs and firearms, and he was rumored to have served prison time. He certainly relished his image as a vicious, unpredictable presence in the barn, and he not only perpetrated violence but also frequently egged on his coworkers.

One day, after weaning a group of piglets, Steinberg, Rettig, and Lyons started returning sows to the breed barn. Rettig grew impatient at how long it was taking Lyons to move a particular sow. He took the gate rod out of Lyons's hands and cracked it down on the sow's back twice, each blow echoing through the barn. "Don't be afraid to hurt 'em!" he shouted. Another time, Rettig exhorted Ralston, "Hit 'em hard! Show 'em your dick! Show 'em your penis!"

One afternoon, barely two weeks into his employment, Steinberg went around with Rettig to adjust the feed for the sows. Rettig wanted Steinberg to jab each one with a wooden handle until they stood up, so he could judge their weight. When Steinberg didn't hit them hard enough, Rettig repeated his usual refrain—but with a new wrinkle. "Hurt 'em," he said. "Nobody works for PETA out here!"

On the hidden camera video, there is a tense moment, as Rettig asks Steinberg, "You know who PETA is?"

Steinberg mutters a reply, apparently fearing that he has been discovered. But Rettig is too busy searching his memory to notice Steinberg's hesitation.

"That's Protection for the . . ." Rettig begins. He seems to be scanning his thoughts, still oblivious to Steinberg's reaction. "Protection for the Environmental Treatment of the Animals. I hate them. These motherfuckers deserve to be hurt!" By now Rettig seems lost in reverie; he raises the handle and shouts, "Hurt I say! Hurt, hurt, hurt, hurt! If you've got to hurt 'em, hurt 'em!"

Steinberg says something about a mild tap on the head being enough to get the sows to their feet, but Rettig isn't listening.

"Take out your frustrations on 'em!" he says. In a portion of the video not released to the public, Rettig concludes, "Just make believe that one of these motherfuckers scared off a seventeen-, eighteen-year-old voluptuous little fucking girl that's hornier than a bitch! And it scared her off. Then you beat the fuck out of her."

Soon after, the word went out to employees that the new owner, Lynn Becker, would be coming to the barn on August 18. There were going to be some changes, and Becker wanted to address the staff directly. The workers were nervous going into the meeting, but Becker's low-key demeanor seemed to set them immediately at ease. He introduced himself and Pat Thome, one of the sons of his business partner. Then Becker explained that the biggest change under MowMar would be thumping more runts. With corn at $8 per bushel, it was just too expensive to stick with undersized piglets that weren't putting on weight quickly. "Everything else will remain the same," he said.

On the secret audio recording of the meeting made by Robert Ruderman, the first of the PETA investigators, an unidentified woman sounds quite concerned about how to know which piglets would now be deemed undesirable. She had seen Becker and Thome personally thump some two hundred piglets that morning.

"Did you guys get rid of the ones that you didn't want me to ship tomorrow?" she asks. She was trying to understand, she said, what path they intended to pursue with regard to runts.

"There's a trail of blood out there for you to follow," Becker says.

From the back of the room, Al Rettig lets out a relieved holler: "And the boys are back in town!"

Looking back, it's hard to understand how management and workers at any hog barn under Hormel control in 2008 could have been so blind to the possibility of infiltration by undercover animal rights activists. Even if workers like Al Rettig couldn't conjure what the PETA acronym stood for, the upper management of Hormel was very aware of People for the Ethical Treatment of Animals, as well as the Humane Society of the United States (HSUS). In fact, the company was actively involved in efforts to discredit the undercover investigations of these organizations—and hoped to garner support for the controversial step of criminal-

izing covert taping of animal abuse at factory farms. The reasons
were simple: recent undercover operations had resulted in major
recalls, costing the meat industry billions of dollars, and had even
netted some criminal prosecutions.

In the fall of 2007, investigators from HSUS secretly videotaped workers at a Hallmark/Westland Meat Packing Company
plant in Chino, California, kicking downer cattle and shocking
them with electric prods, in an effort to get them back to their feet
and into a slaughtering station. In February 2008, the video led
to two employees being charged with felony counts of animal cruelty and the pen manager being charged with three misdemeanor
counts of illegal movement of a nonambulatory animal. Under
pressure from the USDA, Hallmark/Westland recalled more than
143 million pounds of beef, the largest meat recall in U.S. history.
In little more than a year, the company was bankrupt and permanently out of business.

At the exact same time the HSUS operation was under way in
California, a PETA investigator managed to get hired at a 3,500-
sow breed barn owned by Murphy Family Ventures, a major supplier for Smithfield. Over the next two months, he covertly video
recorded five different workers at the facility near Garland, North
Carolina, dragging hogs by their ears, beating them with metal
gate rods, and gouging their eyes—all in an effort to get stubborn
sows to move from gestation crates to farrowing crates, where they
would give birth and suckle their piglets. He even captured one
worker bragging, after suffering an attack by one of the barn's
boars, that he had "cut the shit out of his goddamn nose with a
fucking gate rod." In June 2008, that man and another caught
on the video were charged with multiple misdemeanor counts of
animal cruelty.

Even before these most recent videos, Hormel had been aware
of—and worried about—the prospect of being targeted by PETA
and HSUS, raising the prospect that the whole factory-farming

system could come under scrutiny. If anyone were to look too closely, there was the possibility that these crimes could be judged the result of a broken system, not the actions of a few cruel workers. If the government imposed industry-wide strictures, the massive expenses involved in retrofitting could dwarf the cost of even a major recall. So Hormel decided to take an active role in attempting to curb and even criminalize such undercover investigation. In 2006, CEO Jeffrey Ettinger had provided major backing for the production of a low-budget documentary film called *Your Mommy Kills Animals*, which made the case for prosecuting animal-rights activist groups, particularly PETA and HSUS, as homegrown terrorist organizations under a controversial piece of legislation then before Congress, known as the Animal Enterprise Terrorism Act (AETA).

Back in September 2003, the American Legislative Exchange Council (ALEC) had issued an early version of the law as a piece of model legislation then called the Animal and Ecological Terrorism Act. Like so many bills drafted by the free-market think tank, AETA was handed over, ready-made, to legislators with the idea that it could be introduced with minimal modification. Under the measure, it would become a felony to "enter an animal or research facility to take pictures by photograph, video camera, or other means," and, in a flush of Patriot Act–era overreaching, those convicted of making such recordings would also be placed on a permanent "terrorist registry."

After several years on the shelf, the bill was overhauled—modifying the ban on shooting video to "damaging or interfering with the operations of an animal enterprise," eliminating the section on terrorism, and only imposing prison terms if protest actions resulted in a person's injury or death. This defanged version, renamed the Animal Enterprise Terrorism Act, was repackaged to congressional leaders as a needed revision of existing laws protecting medical research from unlawful interference. Though it wouldn't become apparent until much later, it was the beginning of lobbyists and lawmakers conflating radical Animal Liberation Front–type incidents with the undercover work done by PETA and journalists.

In an effort to persuade lawmakers, the Center for Consumer Freedom, a nonprofit front for food industry über-lobbyist Richard Berman (immortalized by *60 Minutes* as "Dr. Evil" for his efforts on behalf of the tobacco and gun industries), hatched the idea of producing *Your Mommy Kills Animals*. Nonprofits don't have to reveal their donor lists, so ordinarily we would have no idea who exactly was financing Berman's efforts. However, Berman later sued the filmmakers because, contrary to his wishes, they had made a movie that was too evenhanded. Court filings in the suit revealed that Hormel was the film's principal backer. Berman, when confronted with a canceled check for $50,000, signed by Jeffrey Ettinger, conceded in testimony that the company was a "supporter."

In the end, the film was unnecessary. The bill sailed through the Senate by unanimous consent, and in the House only encountered resistance from Representative Dennis Kucinich of Ohio. Kucinich warned it would "have a chilling effect on the exercise of the constitutional rights of protest"—then left the chamber, allowing the bill to be ushered through. And soon, just as Kucinich had warned, the FBI announced, "The No. 1 domestic terrorism threat is the eco-terrorism, animal-rights movement," and legal cases began stretching the application of AETA in a way that nipped at the heels of First Amendment freedoms. Most notably, a small New Jersey–based activist group, which had been the central focus of *Your Mommy Kills Animals*, was found guilty of conspiracy for publishing the home addresses of researchers at Huntingdon Life Sciences, an animal test lab. The jury handed down convictions for seven members of the group.

Far from backing down in the face of such aggressive legal tactics, national organizations like PETA began stepping up their efforts across the country, focusing on more and more agricultural operations, especially those owned by large meatpackers. Hormel, as a matter of routine, required employees in every part of its operation to receive training on proper treatment of hogs. But the lack of knowledge about what was happening in barns before they were acquired by Hormel and its affiliates, as well as the lack of oversight once those barns were officially under contract to the company, is evidence of just how rapidly the hog industry was growing in Iowa at that time. Not even Lynn Becker really knew what was going on inside the barns near Bayard, and Hormel didn't want to know—so long as MowMar Farms, and hundreds of other facilities like it, kept raising more and more hogs and shipping them out on trucks in time to arrive in Austin and Fremont each morning, fully loaded and ready for slaughter.

On September 5, Jeff Kayser, the production manager at Suidae Health, called a lunchtime staff meeting and distributed the MowMar Employee Handbook. After running briefly through standard guidelines, he asked everyone to turn first to the page marked "Animal Rights Statement" and then to one marked "Mistreatment of Animals Statement." Kayser read both statements aloud. The second warned that any employee caught abusing an animal would be fired on the spot, and any worker "observing mistreatment of animals by another employee is also subject to termination unless he/she reports the mistreatment to MowMar, LLP during that current working day." Kayser told everyone to sign the statements, right then and there, and hand them in to him as they left the meeting.

Afterward, Rettig was fuming. He didn't care if he saw someone gut a pig right in front of him, he said. "I'd rather suck an elephant's dick than rat on anyone for anything." Greg Hackler, another worker in the breed barn, chimed in: "Gotta do what you gotta do to push those fucking pigs." Rettig said the new owners should make the pigs sign a pledge not to kick him in the shin, slam him into a gate, stomp on his feet, or try to break his arm. As the other workers seemed to ponder the implications of this change, Rettig was having none of it. "Motherfucker hurts me," he said, "that fucker gets a caning."

Two days later, Robert Ruderman decided to put this new policy to the test. With his recorder rolling, he went to Randy Vaughan, the new farm manager hired by Suidae and MowMar to take over from Jordan Anderson. In his log notes, Ruderman wrote, "I reported to Randy the following abuses that I had witnessed on the farm: the hitting of sows, seeing cuts on sows after being loaded into the farrowing barn, the improper thumping of piglets (piglets who are not dying immediately or even shortly after being thumped), and the spraying of spray paint into the faces of those sows who have attacked/killed their own babies."

Vaughan seemed unsurprised and unconcerned. "I'm not gonna get too shook up about it," he said, "unless somebody's really abusing 'em, is all—somebody's beating the piss out of 'em, and not feeding 'em, no water, that kind of stuff." Ruderman countered that the cuts and welts on the backs of the sows was evidence that they were being beaten. "Don't get too excited about it," Vaughan instructed. Some of those injuries might have come from the sows scraping up against the metal gates. As for the injuries squarely on their backs and hindquarters? "Ya know, I mean, you got to do something if they won't move. You got to move 'em." Ruderman left that Friday evening angered that Vaughan had dismissed his reports of animal abuse, but he hadn't expected any consequences for making the complaints. So he was shocked the following Monday when he was called into Vaughan's office and told that the farm was cutting back. Vaughan told Ruderman that he was being let go.

Things were turning chaotic for Michael Steinberg in the breed barn as well. Al Rettig was rumored to have been injured over the weekend—crushed against a gate by a sow—and was out for days. Greg Hackler was nowhere to be seen, and Richard Ralston, without explanation, was no longer in charge of the breeding facility. With the hierarchy unraveling and the prospect of a mass turnover that might scatter the workers, PETA decided to conclude the operation and go public. They summoned Ruderman and Steinberg back to the east coast and prepared to make the phone call to Lynn Becker.

Chapter 9

AG GAG

By the time Lynn Becker actually received the voice message, Daphna Nachminovitch, vice president of cruelty investigation at PETA, was already on a plane bound for Des Moines. She met with deputies from Sheriff Tom Heater's office, turning over CDs of video footage and a black binder of paperwork labeled "Abuse and Neglect of Livestock at Sow Farm." Heater assigned Deputy Sheriff Russell Hoffman to investigate and met briefly with Jeff Kayser from Suidae Health. By then, the edited five-minute video was everywhere on the Internet, and Kayser requested that Hoffman accompany him to MowMar, where he planned to terminate Alan Rettig and Richard Ralston immediately.

That afternoon, directly after the meeting, Kayser went to MowMar and fired Ralston, who then agreed to answer some of Hoffman's questions outside in the deputy's official pickup. Shown the video, Ralston dropped his head in shame. He told the deputy that he felt "like shit," seeing himself beat the sows. "But in the environment," he said, "you don't realize that it's right or wrong. You're here to get as much done as you can. You're the only one that knows what's going on. People just stand around and watch."

Deputy Hoffman asked Ralston to write out a statement there in the cab of his truck. When Ralston protested that he wasn't a good writer, Hoffman agreed to have him go through everything again while he wrote it down for him.

In the coming weeks, Hoffman began tracking down the other workers to question them about abuses itemized in the PETA list. Shawn Lyons tipped off the sheriff that Al Rettig was packing up and planning to skip town before he could be charged. Hoffman went to Rettig's home in Scranton and asked him to come out to his pickup parked in the alley. Rettig, predictably, was unapologetic. He told Hoffman that he had only been at this facility since March 2007, but he had worked as the manager of two breed barns previous to this one—a total of eighteen years handling sows—and he was willing to do "whatever it takes to keep hogs moving and not get hurt and not get the hogs hurt." Everything he did, he said, was to protect himself, and all that stuff about seventeen-year-old girls and showing them your dick was just "bullshitting." He told Hoffman that "people don't have a clue as to what really goes on in there and what you have to do to survive—to keep your body, to keep your health, and to keep your job."

From there, everything began falling into place. Hoffman got Shelly Mauch to admit to huffing angry sows with marking dye to calm them, but she said she had been instructed in this technique by farm manager Jordan Anderson. Greg Hackler admitted to kicking sows, to jabbing them hard enough with clothespins to make them bleed, and to hitting sows multiple times with the captive-bolt gun—one sow six times. Jordan Anderson admitted to instructing workers on huffing sows and the use of clothespins.

Finally, almost as an afterthought, Hoffman interviewed Shawn Lyons. Lyons acknowledged to the sheriff's deputy then—as he did to me later—that he had prodded sows with clothespins, hit them with wooden herding boards, and pulled them by their ears, but only in an effort, he told me, to get pregnant sows that had spent the last 114 days immobilized in gestation crates up and moving to the farrowing crates.

As Lyons remembered his conversation with Hoffman, he rocked nervously in his recliner chair in the living room of the tiny, tumbledown house he shares with his wife and two kids, the same house he grew up in, just two blocks off of Main Street in Bayard. His watery blue eyes seemed on the verge of tears as he tried to explain himself, and he spoke in a skittish mutter that would sometimes disappear all the way into silence as he rubbed his thin beard. Lyons said he never intended to hurt the hogs, that he was just "scared to death" of the angry sows "who had spent their lives in a little pen"—and this was how he had been trained to deal with them. "You do feel sorry for them, because they don't have much room to move around," he said, but if they get spooked coming out of their crates, "you're in for a fight."

On October 22, Deputy Sheriff Hoffman preferred charges of livestock abuse against six workers at the sow barns: five counts each against Alan Rettig and Richard Ralston, two counts against Greg Hackler, and one count each against Shelly Mauch, Shawn Lyons, and Jordan Anderson (who was also charged with two counts of aiding and abetting livestock abuse).

Hoffman then began calling them, one by one, with instructions to come in and surrender at the Greene County Courthouse.

While the Greene County Sheriff's Office was still conducting its investigation, Lynn Becker, as the public face of MowMar, led an effort at damage control, with assistance from Julie Henderson Craven, the spokesperson for Hormel; Cindy Cunningham, the assistant vice president for communications at the National Pork Board; and John Himle, founding partner at Himle Horner, the PR firm in the Twin Cities hired by Becker at the recommendation

of Hormel. Authored by Himle and released through Cunningham's office, a statement issued on September 17 read: "Representatives of PETA and MowMar's farm managers had a frank
and open discussion in a meeting this morning about what PETA
discovered and the actions being taken to correct this unfortu-
nate situation." Among the actions Becker pledged to undertake:
firing all employees found to have abused animals, instituting a
zero-tolerance policy against abuse, and investigating the possibility of installing a video monitoring system. "I've known the hog
producers who own that company for years," Cunningham said
in an interview at the time, "and they will do everything possible
to run that facility the right way. I know they are in there today,
cleaning it up, and they will turn it into one of the best-run facilities anywhere."

Craven, for her part, reiterated that MowMar "shares our commitment to animal welfare and humane handling" but also told the
Associated Press that, as she understood it, "the abuses took place
before the change in ownership." PETA vice president Daphna
Nachminovitch disputed this claim and pointed out that the new
farm manager, Randy Vaughan, who had been hired by MowMar,
was guilty of abuses as well. To back up the claim, PETA released
a second video, showing Vaughan using a "hot shot" electric prod
on an injured sow. Michael Steinberg, who recorded the video, described it that day in his notes: "She tried to stand up as he walked
over, but both of her back legs were in very bad condition. In my
opinion, she had a possible broken pelvis, hip, or legs, although
nobody suggested this to me. Both of her legs were underneath the
left side of her body. Randy continuously stomped on and kicked
her bad legs and shocked her the whole time he was doing this."
The second video brought renewed attention—focused this time
more squarely on Hormel. "One month later, the pigs at this farm
are still at the mercy of the same manager," Nachminovitch wrote
in a public statement issued on October 21. "We have yet to see

any action from Hormel that would spare these mother pigs and their babies one iota of suffering."

Craven went on the offensive. "We are appalled that PETA representatives not only witnessed incidents of improper animal handling without reporting the abuse, and after several months, have not released all of the video footage," she said in a statement of her own. "If they are truly concerned about animal welfare, they should release information when they obtain it." But Craven's statement ignored the fact that PETA had turned all video over to the Greene County sheriff for investigation only after Robert Ruderman was fired by Randy Vaughan in apparent retaliation for bringing these abuses to his attention. After the story broke publicly, PETA had offered five times to deliver those same materials to Hormel's offices but never received a reply.

Craven also repeated her belief that most of the abuses occurred before MowMar's ownership and added that the farm had only become a Hormel supplier after that change. Hormel's own corporate literature, however, issued just months before the whole scandal erupted, identified the previous management company, AMVC, as one of "our partners." The report said that the company's CEO, Daryl Olsen, met representatives from Hormel "during an industry meeting almost nine years ago [in 1998]. Soon after, AMVC began its business agreement with Hormel Foods and began supplying Hormel Foods with hogs." The report goes on to quote Olsen as saying, "We meet regularly to discuss ways we can help [Hormel] produce a better product and work together to meet that goal." Even more strikingly, the only other "partner" highlighted in the report was Gary Thome—Lynn Becker's co-owner of MowMar, who had first met Becker through Olsen.

In the midst of the second uproar—and perhaps in an effort to quell it—Sheriff Heater announced the indictments against the six former and current employees. He had pressed charges against nearly all of the offenders identified by PETA, with the exception of Randy Vaughan, who, based on the sheriff department's interviews of suspects, seems to have avoided prosecution simply by steadfastly denying all charges. So it was a special irony that on October 22, when Deputy Sheriff Hoffman was unable to reach Shawn Lyons and Shelly Mauch, he wound up calling MowMar—and reaching Vaughan. Hoffman asked Vaughan to inform Lyons and Mauch that they had twenty-four hours to turn themselves in at the courthouse. Vaughan agreed to relay the message, but he seems first to have called Hormel for guidance. At the end of the day, as workers sat around the break room, talking, Vaughan came in and told Mauch and Lyons that they had been formally charged—and that they were being let go. According to Lyons, Vaughan told him, "We don't want to do it, but we got to—because Hormel will quit taking the pigs."

Lyons called his wife, Sherri, and told her to get ready to go out. He had been fired and charged with a felony; he would explain everything as they drove to the county seat in Jefferson, Iowa. Once there, Sherri was shown to Holding Room 3 while Shawn filled out paperwork and had his mug shot taken. While she waited, Sherri's cell phone buzzed again and again; Shawn's name was already on the evening news. Hoffman released him with instructions to go find a lawyer. He might be able to beat the charge, considering that Lyons's supervisor had emphasized what a good worker he was.

"Well, they fired me," Lyons replied.

"You got fired?" Hoffman asked. "I didn't want that to happen to you."

"I was pretty pissed," Lyons told me later, with a rueful chuckle. "What'd you think was going to happen?"

In early September 2008, the Minnesota Agri-Growth Council played host to AgNite—one of the largest private parties during that year's Republican National Convention, held in St. Paul. The official mission of the Minnesota Agri-Growth Council is "to represent the most vital interests of Minnesota's diverse food and agricultural community," but in reality its executive committee and board of directors are composed almost entirely of higher-ups from the state's largest agribusinesses — such as Hormel, Cargill, General Mills, Land O'Lakes, the Schwan Food Company, and Syngenta seeds—as well as the heads of individual agricultural lobbying groups, including the Minnesota Corn Growers Association and the Minnesota Milk Producers Association. Hormel's vice president for legislative affairs, Joe C. Swedberg, in his capacity as the newly elected chair of the Minnesota Agri-Growth Council, organized the event, and it exceeded all expectations.

A crowd of more than five thousand attendees, including delegates and elected officials from the Republican convention, gathered in the Depot in Minneapolis for drinks and ag showcases and live musical performances, including a late night set by aging rockers Styx. Among the attendees, John Rusling Block, the secretary of agriculture under Ronald Reagan and cochair of presidential candidate John McCain's farm and ranch committee, called the night a celebration of technological progress in agriculture—from pesticides to genetic engineering. "We raise a good, clean crop," he said, "and we do it so efficiently."

To promote the event, Swedberg had hired John Himle's PR firm. Himle had been the executive director of the Minnesota Agri-Growth Council when he was first elected as an Independent-Republican to the Minnesota House of Representatives in 1981; he had founded Himle Horner soon after and always kept the council as one of his steady clients. AgNite was still in the post-convention PR phases when Himle Horner began advising Lynn Becker. Indeed, in an interview Himle gave with the Agri-Growth Council's newsletter, he listed among his greatest "success stories": "this year providing media and strategic counsel for the successful

AgNite event" and assisting several clients with "crisis issues," including "PETA/livestock issues."

Two weeks after AgNite and less than twenty-four hours after the PETA video went online, Joe Swedberg traveled back to St. Paul for a meeting of a legislative working group on immigration reform at the State Office Building. At that meeting, the committee, chaired by Minnesota House minority whip Rod Hamilton (on Swedberg's nomination), committed to addressing immigration issues in the state by developing "economic arguments supportive of rational immigration" and to informing their strategies by coordinating with similar working groups from Illinois and Iowa. The effort, in short, was to come up with policies that would shift public opinion on the immigration debate by bringing together members of the Latino advocacy community with business interests like Hormel, represented by Swedberg and Hamilton himself, who had preceded Lynn Becker as president of the Minnesota Pork Board and was then the communications director for Christensen Family Farms, the third-largest pork producer in the United States. Discussions around that meeting may also have been the seeds of the legislative effort against undercover investigations into animal operations in Minnesota and Iowa.

Two years later, Hamilton and Doug Magnus, recently appointed chairs of the agricultural committees in the Minnesota House and Senate respectively, were invited by Swedberg to deliver the policy lecture at the Minnesota Agri-Growth Council monthly luncheon together. The talk, according to the council's newsletter, drew one of the largest and most varied arrays of attendees in the group's history. Ten weeks later, during the 2011 legislative session, Hamilton and Magnus introduced identical bills that would make it a crime to "produce a record which reproduces an image or sound" inside an animal facility—or even "possess or distribute" such a recording.

"It's absurd," said Amanda Hitt at the Government Accountability Project. She told me that activist videos were akin to airplane black-box recorders—evidence for investigators to deconstruct and find wrongdoing. Ag gag laws, as they're known, don't just interfere with workers blowing the whistle on animal abuse. "You are also stopping environmental whistle-blowing; you are also stopping workers' rights whistle-blowing." In short, "you have given power to the industry to completely self-regulate." That should "scare the pants off" of consumers concerned about where their food comes from. "It's the consumer's right to know, but also the employee's right to tell. You gotta have both." She said she couldn't believe that an industry that had been so regularly recorded breaking the law "would then have the audacity to come to any state legislative body and say, 'Hey, we're sick of getting caught doing crimes. Could you do us a favor and criminalize catching us?'"

But Daryn McBeth, then the president of the Agri-Growth Council, told the *Minneapolis Star-Tribune* that the law would be "an important deterrent tool in our toolbox" against videos shot by "fraudulently hired employees." He pointed to a case that rocked Minnesota a few months earlier, when workers at the Willmar Poultry Company—the country's largest turkey hatchery, producing 45 million birds a year—were filmed by Humane Society undercover activists throwing sick, injured, or surplus birds into grinding machines while still alive.

It was a spotlight on another horrifying but legal practice. No surprise, then, that lobbyists from the poultry industry soon helped the effort to move similar bills onto the legislative agenda in Florida and Iowa, as well as Minnesota. Wilton Simpson, an egg farmer and now a member of the Florida Senate, pushed the legislation in the Sunshine State. In Iowa, where egg mogul Jack DeCoster was under a federal investigation that eventually found that filthy conditions at his facilities had led to a salmonella outbreak and nationwide egg recall, the Iowa Poultry Association freely admits the role it played in shaping the bill. Introduced by then–state representative Annette Sweeney, former executive director of the Iowa Angus Association, the bill—supposedly composed around Sweeney's kitchen table—was nearly identical in language to the bill introduced by Hamilton and Magnus in Minnesota.

When I reached Hamilton by phone at his office at Christensen Family Farms to inquire about the origin of the bill, he searched his computer for his notes. "Was that House File 1369?" he asked. "Let me pull that up again—because I know that was brought to me from an ag group, and I introduced it." I asked if the group in question was the Minnesota Agri-Growth Council; Hamilton ignored the question. "So it was brought forth," he said, "and I said that, yeah, I will put my name on it, so that we could have some discussion around that." Later that same day, he sent me an email to revise his statements: the issues of farm trespass, hiring under false pretenses, and the shooting of undercover videos was "brought to me by a number of people and not simply a single group or organization."

Sally Jo Sorensen, president of the McLeod County Farmers' Union, wasn't buying it. "At a time when a significant share of the consumer food market is clamoring to know about their food, the Agri-Growth Council seeks to impose a government-enforced ban on information," she wrote. "Maybe that's what that big party the Council threw for the RNC in 2008 that the journos loved so much was all about."

In the meantime, back in Bayard, Shawn Lyons had hired a lawyer in hopes of mounting a defense against the charges against him, but he was dead to rights. His abuse of sows at MowMar Farms had been captured on video, and he'd confessed to the deputy sheriff.

"They got you, dude," Lyons said his attorney told him. "Do you want to plead guilty?"

Lyons shook his head remembering. "Might as well."

His lawyer met with the county attorney and worked out a plea agreement—six months probation and a $625 fine plus court fees. On January 15, 2009, Lyons went to the magistrate to plead guilty to one count of livestock neglect and sign an admission of guilt: "On or about August 27, 2008, I did the following: intentionally cause pain and suffering, or otherwise fail to provide livestock care consistent with customary animal husbandry practice." The date cited for the abuse was ten days after MowMar Farms had taken ownership of the facility. Despite all the denials from Julie Craven, the eventual conviction for Lyons and others was for actions documented after the facility was under contract to Hormel—but the press didn't seem to notice. And, with no more ceremony than that, Shawn Lyons became the first person ever convicted of livestock abuse on a midwestern farm—and, according to PETA, only the third person convicted of that crime in the history of the American meat industry.

What Lyons remembered more clearly were the months it took him to pay off that fine now that he had no job and the immediate cold shoulder he received from everyone in Bayard. Every time he went to Sparky's, the local watering hole, all of the farmers shunned him and gave him dirty looks. "They completely snubbed him," Lyons's wife, Sherri, told me. "It was brutal for six months after that." Then, at the end of June 2009, Richard Ralston, Alan Rettig, and Greg Hackler pleaded guilty to multiple counts of livestock abuse and received two-year suspended sentences along with fines. Jordan Anderson pleaded guilty to aiding and abetting livestock abuse and was fined as well. (Shelly Mauch's charges were listed at the time as still "in process"—and appear to have since been dropped.)

In all, it was six convictions—a major PR win for PETA, which often appeals to local authorities to make arrests but rarely gets the kind of cooperation they got from the Greene County Sheriff's Office. But it was also a hollow victory. "Who in their right mind would want to work in a dusty, ammonia-ridden pig shed for nine bucks an hour but somebody who, literally, had no other options?" asked Dan Paden, the senior researcher at PETA who helped run the investigation. "And at the end of a long, frustrating day, when you are trying to move a pig who hasn't been out of its crate in [months], that's when these beatings occur—and people do stupid, cruel, illegal things." PETA was urging prosecutors to go beyond plea agreements for farmworkers; they wanted charges against farm owners and their corporate backers, to hold them responsible for crimes committed by undertrained, overburdened employees. But the sheriff's office closed the investigation and never seems to have taken a look at charging Gary Weihs or Lynn Becker or any of the other off-site managers, much less anyone at Hormel.

The crackdown, however, has had some broader effects. Today, workers at MowMar Farms, now renamed Fair Creek, watch weekly training videos on a large flat-screen TV in the break room, where they are reminded of the fundamentals of "day one" piglet care. Piglets are now kept warm with heat lamps, and sows are moved much less frequently. "We try to leave pigs home with Mom," Becker's health manager told the *National Hog Farmer*. "Never move more pigs than you have to." The new system has dramatically reduced piglet mortality rates—and, according to one worker, runts are now euthanized via the carbon monoxide system preferred by PETA, rather than the blunt-force thumping of old. "I didn't completely buy into it when we first started focusing on day-one pig care," said the new farm manager, "but it really works."

These changes have not only improved conditions for the hogs at the facility in Iowa, but also helped increase the profit margin for its owners. In the end, improved care has been touted as a win for everyone. But would it have occurred without the harsh light of public scrutiny? I asked Becker if the industry might not be better served by increased transparency, rather than tightened security. Why not open up Fair Creek to journalists to prove that it no longer resembles the days when it was MowMar Farms? He gave a list of reasons—sow health, proprietary practices—why it wouldn't be possible. Months of follow-up requests went unanswered.

Shawn Lyons, who spent two years unemployed after being fired from MowMar Farms, finally got a job with a security company. He installs video cameras in hospitals, nursing homes, and schools for twenty-four-hour monitoring. Before I packed up my things and left his tiny house, Lyons asked me whatever became of Becker's promise to investigate the possibility of installing security cameras in his hog barns. "That's what I do now," he said.

His wife, Sherri, chimed in. "They could have some kind of a committee set up that can come in and check anytime that they want, someone that's not associated with the company. I think that would be the better way to do it. So that people are well aware of the fact that there's cameras here, and there's this group of people that can come in anytime and look. So, you know, be on your best behavior."

Part Four

Chapter 10

I THOUGHT IT WAS FISHY

On March 19, 2009, Roxanne Tarrant received a phone call from AIG Claim Services, informing her that she should complete an R-8 Notice of Rehabilitation Plan Closure form for Pablo Ruiz. Tarrant knew that Ruiz was still suffering from the same blinding migraines and searing pain in his hands and lower legs that she had first recorded in his file more than a year before. In fact, his condition had worsened with diabetes from his steroid treatments, and Dr. Lachance at the Mayo Clinic had expressed concern that Ruiz might be suffering from some form of meningitis. When Tarrant asked AIG why coverage for someone as obviously unwell as Ruiz was being terminated, she was referred to his attorney. Thomas Patterson, the lawyer now handling the claims of the Hispanic workers from QPP, told her that he had been mailed a VHS cassette containing short clips of secret surveillance video, crudely cut together into a montage of Ruiz performing everyday tasks—tasks that AIG said would be impossible if he were being honest with Dr. Lachance about his pain levels. They were terminating coverage on the assertion that Ruiz was lying about the extent of his injuries.

To this day, it remains unclear what motivation Ruiz would have. The implication was that he intended to sue QPP in hopes of receiving an out-of-court settlement, but after more than seven years, Ruiz has never sought compensation for anything more than his medical bills, and he has repeatedly told me that his examinations and treatments are often excruciating: spinal taps, sweat tests, bone scans, MRIs—the kinds of procedures no one would choose to endure. More than that, a number of Ruiz's symptoms were measurable by those tests. Before the termination call, his most recent sweat test indicated lingering effects of poly-radiculoneuropathy, and his blood work still showed spikes in his sugar levels brought on by his type 2 diabetes. Drs. Lachance and Dyck believed that Ruiz's recovery was being slowed by clinical depression and chronic pain; they had jointly recommended refer-ral for Ruiz to the Mayo Clinic's Pain Management Program as "a charity case," which the hospital had already approved. According to Ruiz's insurance file, the doctors felt it was "imperative that Mr. Ruiz receives immediate treatment for his depression and chronic pain," noting that they both believed that "these are as a result of his 11/20/07 date of injury."

Still, the video showed a sequence of short scenes that AIG claimed were hard evidence of Ruiz's physical fitness. In the first segment, shot on December 8, 2008, just days after Dale Wicks brought him in to question his immigration status, Ruiz is shown returning from an appointment in the Gonda Building of the Mayo Clinic. His wife gets out of their car to pump gas, and Ruiz walks gingerly with their six-year-old son into the station to pay. "I was walking slowly, because that day the winter was pretty bad," Ruiz told me. During the appointment, Lachance had given him 40 milligrams of OxyContin, more than enough to temporarily dull Ruiz's pain. "After I take my medicine I can be out for a little bit of time, walking slow. But I still had the headaches. The headaches never go away," he said. "And I never said that I can't walk. I walk short distances. Longer distances make me tired and short of breath and a lot of pain."

The second video was shot at the Old Country Buffet in Rochester on December 12. This time Ruiz was shown leaving a consultation for his diabetes. "I had to check out my blood, do my insulin, and eat something," Ruiz explained. In the video, someone has to carry Ruiz's tray from the buffet line back to the table, but he manages to walk that distance on his own. In the third segment, shot on December 18 at the Value Store, Ruiz is shown in the parking lot after buying Christmas presents. He lifts several boxes from their cart and hands them to his wife to load into the car.

Ruiz told me that when his attorney saw the video, he started "kind of freaking."

"This is bad for us," Ruiz remembered him saying. "What do you think Dr. Lachance thought when he saw those videos? What do you think he's going to say? He's going to say, 'Oh, he can walk. He can work.'"

And, in fact, when I asked Lachance specifically about Ruiz's case, he seemed clearly to have been swayed by the video. Bound by confidentiality, he couldn't answer my questions as directly as I had asked them, but—slowly, carefully—he explained his interpretation. "For most patients that have gone on to have complaints, their complaints consist of a purely subjective phenomenon which is pain—something you really can't measure," he told me. "One example is an individual who was apparently severely affected by pain, dramatically so, who, it turns out, was investigated and videotaped secretly by workers' comp investigators and was found, outside the context of the office, to behave completely normally."

I asked Lachance what possible reason there would be to lie, for months and now years.

"I think there's a whole psychology that relates to work injuries—people's response to being injured in the workplace, the possibilities of compensation and secondary gain."

Lachance smiled to be sure I understood his meaning.

"Put yourself in the place of these people who do these godawful jobs," he said. "Who wouldn't want to see if there was some alternative for their livelihood?"

In the early morning hours of June 12, 2009, police arrived at Eleventh Avenue SW. The neighborhood is poor even by Austin standards—tiny clapboard houses clustered along unlit streets that dead-end into a muddy oxbow of Turtle Creek—and officers had been dispatched after Patricia Rodriguez-Sanchez called 911 to report that her husband had tried to strangle her. When she came to the door, her face was scratched, and her neck bore the bright red imprint of a man's hand. "You're lucky to be alive," one cop told her. He arrested the young woman's husband and told her to get an order for protection as soon as the courthouse opened. The police loaded her husband into their cruiser and took him to jail.

At the detention center, officers discovered that Sanchez's husband had a Matrícula Consular card, a form of identification issued by the Mexican government to nationals living outside the country, with the name Delfino Sanchez-Hernandez but he was also carrying paperwork from Quality Pork Processors with the name Richard Morones-Hernandez. He explained that he was Richard Hernandez and claimed that the Matrícula Consular card was his brother's. Not sure who they had in custody, police obtained a warrant to search the couple's home for anything that could prove that the man they had arrested was living in the country without legal documents and had received government identification in violation of state law.

The next morning, Patricia Sanchez filled out the paperwork for a protection order at the court clerk's window before going to work at QPP. While she was beginning her shift, police arrived at her home to execute the warrant. In the bedroom of the house, officers searched two purses. In one, they found QPP pay stubs for Lisa Salazar, a letter from the IRS to Lisa Salazar, receipts for money orders sent to Mexico by Lisa Salazar, and a Minnesota Health Care Program card for Salazar's five-year-old son. In the other, they found a letter from the IRS to Patricia Sanchez, letters from Mower County Human Services to Patricia Sanchez. Then one officer noticed a QPP Employee of the Month plaque from 2006 hanging on the living room wall. Mounted on the plaque was a photograph of the woman who had identified herself to officers as Patricia Sanchez, posing in her hard hat and white smock, but the name plate was engraved "Lisa M. Salazar."

As the officers were leaving, Sanchez returned home from her shift at QPP. Through an interpreter, police asked her to identify herself, pointing out that the picture on the plaque appeared to be her. Sanchez admitted that she worked at QPP under the name Salazar. After later checking state records, police learned that a fraudulent Minnesota driver's license had been issued to Lisa Salazar. And QPP confirmed that the license was among the pieces of identification presented at the time of her hiring. Sanchez was brought to the police station, read her Miranda warning, and then presented with the evidence. She waived her rights and again admitted to working at QPP under the name of Lisa Salazar. Police informed her that she was under arrest on two counts of aggravated forgery.

The arrest was in accordance with the law, but it didn't sit right with Detective Sergeant David McKichan. As a member of the Southeast Minnesota Narcotics and Gang Task Force, he knew from fellow police officers in Worthington that Hispanic immigrants there still refused to cooperate with police investigations

out of fear of deportation, more than two years after the Swift
raids. There was already a climate of fear among immigrants after
Austin police investigators recently had strung together an unusually interconnected set of stolen identities, resulting in twenty-
two cases of aggravated forgery. Stories in the local press were
beginning to make note of the fact that almost every case involved
either QPP or Select Foods, and anti-immigration activists had
not only renewed their push for the city government to implement
a measure similar to the ordinance proposed in Fremont, but more
extreme elements had begun to surface.

Only days before Sanchez's arrest, Samuel Johnson, a member
of the neo-Nazi National Socialist Movement, had staged the
first in a series of anti-immigration rallies at the Mower County
Veterans Memorial in front of the county courthouse. For two
hours, Johnson and fellow NSM member Robert Hester took
turns barking into a megaphone, decrying immigrants for stealing American jobs and bringing gang violence to the streets of
Austin, while supporters held banners reading DEPORT ILLEGALS
and yelled at counterprotesters and passersby. Johnson shouted at
Hispanics gathered in the park, "You think America's going to let
you get away with this? Not a chance." Another protester called
out, "Hitler is not dead; he's alive in our hearts." Austin police
had served as peace officers at those events and worried that immigrants wouldn't come forward to report crimes against them or
yield information vital to major crime cases already under investigation if they in turn would be investigated for aggravated forgery.

McKichan told Jeremy Clinefelter, the assistant Mower County
attorney, that he didn't think the office should prosecute cases like
Sanchez's. Clinefelter agreed with the sentiment. "It didn't feel
right morally," he later told the *Minneapolis Star-Tribune*. "We're
prosecutors. But more than that, we're here to be fair and just."
But, until Clinefelter could get higher-ups to agree to an official
policy, the only action would have to originate from within QPP.

In an unusual move, both CEO Kelly Wadding and human resources director Dale Wicks agreed to speak to the *Austin Daily Herald* about the process they used to clear potential employees— but only to defend their hiring practices. QPP, they explained, asked all applicants to fill out a standard I-9 form, which required a name, address, date of birth, Social Security number, statement of citizenship, and documents to support identity and eligibility to work. Human Resources would then run that information through the U.S. Department of Homeland Security's online E-Verify program, as well as a Social Security database purchased by QPP to check that the date and place that the card was issued matched the date and place of birth on the I-9. They said that the process occasionally raised red flags—sometimes turning up an invalid birth certificate or passport, sometimes uncovering a Social Security number with a date of issuance before the applicant's stated birth date or a number registered as belonging to someone deceased. But more often, everything would come back okay. In such instances, Wadding said, "We're obligated to hire them."

But he denied any suggestion that QPP was intentionally hiring undocumented workers. "There is no advantage for us to hire someone illegal to work here," Wadding said. "None."

Even after his diagnosis with PIN, Emiliano Ballesta couldn't bring himself to request a transfer from the head table to another part of the production line. His job, removing sinewy cheek meat from the tight nooks of the skull (a job known as "chiseling"), required more precise handwork than almost any other position in the plant. In the era of Upton Sinclair's *The Jungle*, workers at the head table used an actual chisel to pry open and dislocate hogs' jaws, then hacked away muscles from the cheeks and temples. But today most factories use a mechanized jaw-puller for the brute task, and the meat is harvested by a single highly skilled worker making precise cuts with a straight blade, honed to razor sharpness and handled with a chain-mail glove. The dexterity and mastery it takes to perform this task while keeping pace with the speed of the line made Ballesta's job one of the most prestigious and (at $13.15 per hour following a raise) highest-paying positions at QPP. Younger workers with straight-blade jobs at other stations often sought out Ballesta, hoping to apprentice in his technique—to study the angle and speed at which he drew his knife along the hone, to count the number of strokes he used to achieve his edge and the number of cuts he made before he dressed it back again.

In the kitchen of his rented apartment in a house on the east side of the Cedar River, Ballesta showed me a technique. He turned the blade of a butcher knife over, checking both sides.

"You have to be sure there are no dents in the blade," he said, as one of his sons translated. "Then you sharpen it against the steel rod."

He slid the blade out and back along the sharpening steel in a fluid motion that made the knife hum and sing. During the early days of the new plant, veteran workers complained repeatedly about the introduction of mechanical knife sharpeners, which were replacing the personal stones and steels used to hone and feather their knives. They insisted that the mechanical sharpeners never gave knives a proper edge, leading to more strain while cutting and eventually to carpal tunnel syndrome. Some continued to use their own sharpeners. Ballesta said there wasn't time for the mechanical sharpeners. Cutting through the dense hide of the hog's head and slicing away the meat meant he had to redress his blade, a few precise strokes against the hone dangling from his belt loop and then back to cutting, almost every minute of his shift.

"The skin of a hog is very thick and the blade would wear out quickly," Ballesta said. "I had to keep sharpening it all day."

Everything about him was commanding, from his trimmed mustache to his iron-gray temples. Once, I spotted him among the crowd of congregants arriving for Mass at Queen of Angels Catholic Church, his bright red western shirt pressed and perfectly creased, the sleeves buttoned to conceal the circular scar of a Whizard knife slash on his left forearm. He had always hated the mechanical knives after that incident long ago and resolved ever after only to use a blade under his exact control. But even on the day of that injury, he had gotten patched up at the Austin Medical Center and returned to QPP to finish his shift. It must have been nearly impossible for him now to accept that something invisible—something he referred to always as "the infection"—had robbed him of sensation and fine motor function, turning what had been surgical skill into a fumbling hazard.

After his diagnosis, Ballesta was given work restrictions and assigned to other jobs: weighing and packing parts, running the circular saw that clips off snouts. He even tried going back to a less skilled job trimming head meat with the Whizard. But by March 2009, Ballesta's work with the humming blade—performing the same motion 400 to 500 times per hour—had worsened the tingling in his right hand and left his middle finger completely numb. "I strongly suspect this is carpal tunnel syndrome," Dr. Lachance wrote to Carole Bower. Ballesta was given lighter duty washing ears, then taken off the line altogether to work in the box room alongside Matthew Garcia. He couldn't take it. In May, Ballesta asked to be put back at his chiseling station, but he had trouble keeping up, and his need for breaks jeopardized his ability to hang on to the job. Under his contract, he had to meet standard in order to keep the job—and the high-paying position was coveted by other workers.

Bower sent an email to Lachance. "Rather difficult," she began. "He really likes the chiseling job and does not want off of it." She explained that Ballesta had asked to return to chiseling full-time.

But Lachance believed he would still need fifteen-minute breaks every two hours, something that Bower doubted could continue to be accommodated. Still, she wrote that Ballesta "is a very good and ethical man so wants to work hard and please his employer. Can we see how it goes for awhile?"

In July, Bower told social worker Roxanne Tarrant that QPP had been reviewing the job lineup sheets for the workers with PIN, and it was becoming increasingly difficult to manage their required accommodations. She asked Tarrant if Ballesta could possibly chisel cheek meat without taking breaks. For the first time, Ballesta balked. He said that he still had terrible burning in his feet if he stood too long; he had tried to work full shifts without a break, but he just couldn't do it. On October 1, Ballesta finally gave in and requested to be put on cutting and cleaning intestines—despite a 20-cent-per-hour pay cut. He was dismayed but joked to coworkers that, after years at the head table, he would finally graduate to another station. That Saturday, October 3, would be his fifteenth anniversary at QPP. He called it his *quinceañera*, his coming of age.

But that Saturday, when he arrived at work, Ballesta was summoned to Human Resources. It was his last day at QPP.

Kelly Wadding didn't want to talk to me. I called and left voice messages dozens of times. I sent long emails assuring him that I wanted to hear his side of the story. After months of silence, I got a phone call one day from his assistant. Wadding was on the road; she didn't say where. She explained only that he was in a hotel room, traveling for business, and had a few minutes. She gave me his cell phone number and told me to keep it short.

At first, when I got Wadding on the line, he was tense but cordial as we talked through the history of QPP, the unfolding of the PIN cases, and the unexpected spotlight it had shone on immigration issues. But when I said something vague, simply that I had been struck by how many of the people affected by PIN had turned out to be undocumented workers, Wadding plunged into a defensive monologue. "We go above and beyond what the government requires as far as documentation. So we feel very comfortable with the documents of the people we hire. Now, there is an issue with people having forged documents. That is a problem—a big problem. I speak for myself and my company: we're in support of immigration reform, we would like to see something done on that. Now, having said that, we're very diligent in our process, making sure people have the proper documents. When these people—"

He caught his breath, and then, without prompting, turned adamant.

"I know where you're headed and I'll tell you right now: anybody that's contracted PIN or any other illness or injury at work, we never, ever, ever go back and check their documentation." I could hear his fist bang on something hard. *Never, ever, ever.* I imagined a buckling nightstand, the Gideon's Bible rocking inside its drawer. *Bang, bang, bang.*

I told him that I wasn't implying anything, but many former workers insisted that Dale Wicks had targeted sick workers for immigration review. I explained the larger facts as I understood them. His company had experienced an outbreak among its workers. Before bringing in the Department of Health, he transferred all of his shares to a holding company. Later, he shifted large parts of his workforce to a new company, one without an existing union contract. And when ICE had come down on him for violating laws against employing undocumented immigrants, he had begun removing workers from his rolls. The only question was whether there was any truth to the claim that Wicks began with—and focused on—employees who had filed workers' compensation claims.

"That is not done," Wadding said emphatically. His voice was

insistent. "The only time we go back and review the documentation and confront the employee about their legal status is if we're
contacted by the Social Security department or the unemployment
department, those state agencies or federal agencies that contact
us, and notifying us that they have suspicions of somebody's identity. At that point then we do go back, and we will check records,
and we will confront the person. And that happens regardless of
if they've had an injury, regardless of what their status is here at
work. We do that. And that is commonplace, more commonplace
than I'd like to say, but that happens on a regular basis to people.
And, yes, some of these people had PIN. We were contacted by
Social Security that they had questioned their documents and we
confronted them and found out they were illegal and we had to
take action. We cannot employ them lawfully, so once we have
that information . . . but at no time did we go back and check their
records after they contracted this disease."

He breathed again, exasperated this time. "You know, you guys
just don't understand stuff," he said.

In April 2010, Matthew Garcia was called in to talk to Dale
Wicks in Human Resources. Wicks told him that a man had been
arrested in Texas; his name was Matthew J. Garcia—and he had
the same date of birth and Social Security number as this Matthew J. Garcia. Wicks asked if his papers were his own. By now,
workers—who had formed a support group that met weekly at
Centro Campesino—had learned not to confess the way Miriam
Angeles did, the way Emiliano Ballesta did. Of the fourteen workers who had workers' comp claims, six had been fired for working
under forged or stolen identities.

"I told them, yeah, they're my papers," Garcia said. "I have my
ID, I have everything."

During his illness, Garcia had enrolled in classes at Riverland

Community College, and his English was now good enough for him to get by without an interpreter; he was not as frightened as other workers had been. Wicks warned that law enforcement was investigating, that they had already found records of Garcia's information being used in five other states. Garcia didn't budge; he insisted he didn't know anything about that, that those people must have somehow stolen his information.

Garcia wasn't fired—but, in June 2010, his condition suddenly worsened. Lachance ordered a fresh round of tests and found no evidence of relapse. Instead, in a letter to QPP, Lachance attributed the symptoms to "a chronic fibromyalgia like condition," which he said he had also observed in "several individuals" with PIN. The tests did reveal residual nerve damage that Lachance said was hindering his ability to walk and "affecting some degree of permanent impairment of bowel and bladder function." Lachance now regarded Garcia's illness as a chronic condition. "I think his symptoms will be long term," Lachance wrote to Bower, urging QPP to find a place for Garcia to perform light work—perhaps, now that his English skills were improving, even a desk job in the office. "Hopefully some day his pain syndrome will gradually remit and his tolerance for physical activity improve but for the foreseeable future, especially concerning work-related activities, I think it is reasonable to assign some permanency here."

Roxanne Tarrant told me that she understood the difficulty that QPP faced in finding light-labor positions for the injured workers. "It's a slaughterhouse," she said. "There really are no light jobs." Still, she was dubious of the claim that Immigration and Customs Enforcement just happened to be investigating so many affected workers whose doctors had recommended lighter duty. (Indeed, it's not clear ICE did.) "When the first firing happened, I thought it was interesting," Tarrant said. "When the second, then the third happened, I thought it was fishy."

In the end, fourteen of the twenty-three workers who tested

positive for PIN were approved for workers' compensation. Of that group, six were fired for working without proper documentation between the time when claims were filed in June 2008 and April 2010: Miriam Angeles, Emiliano Ballesta, Santa Zapata, José Díaz, Lupe Treviño, and Humberto Paz. Zapata, Ballesta, and the young man I have called Matthew Garcia have all now been classified as permanently injured. And Pablo Ruiz, despite earlier skepticism from Lachance, successfully challenged his insurance suspension and was eventually allowed to resume care at the Mayo Clinic, where he continues to show permanent nerve damage on his periodic sweat tests.

Meanwhile, even as Kelly Wadding was assuring me that QPP had made no special effort to remove workers with PIN from employment, company attorneys were in the final stages of negotiating a settlement with up to a dozen employees. After attorneys' fees, each received $12,500, a half year's pay—all except Ruiz, who refused the settlement and still has not received any payment from QPP. Garcia, because of the extent of his injuries, got a one-time payment of $38,600—and, as a condition of the settlement, voluntarily terminated his employment at QPP. "I felt pushed into it," Garcia told me. "My attorney said, 'If you don't do it, you'll end up with nothing.'" He used some of the money to pay for more courses at the community college, but when I spoke to him last, the settlement money was going fast. He asked me not to use his real name, fearing it might hurt an application he had pending at McDonald's.

Chapter 11

YOU ARE NOT WELCOME

Shortly after the start of the morning shift on a cold and blustery day in early March 2010, ICE agents from the Omaha Field
Office entered the Fremont Beef processing plant, directly across
South Platte Avenue from the Hormel plant. Fremont Beef's
President Les Leech was informed that his company was one of a
thousand businesses nationwide that had been selected at random
and audited against the Federal Trade Commission's identity theft
database. Agents presented him with a list of names, and those
employees were summoned to a conference room. Managers did
not tell the workers why they were called in, only to cooperate
and answer all questions. In the hallway outside, ICE agents—all
dressed in civilian clothing, their firearms concealed—divvied up
case files. Then they entered the room and began calling names.

David Gran, a special agent with nearly two decades at ICE
and the former Immigration and Naturalization Service, took a
seat behind the conference table and called the name of Olga Ar-
guelles. A woman rose and came to sit beside him. Gran showed
her his agent identification and asked the woman for her true and
complete name. "Rosaura Carrillo-Velasquez," she replied. She

told him that she had been born in Guatemala, that she was thirty-two years old, and had been living in a trailer park in Schuyler. She admitted that she did not have immigration papers and had entered the country illegally. Gran informed her that she would be taken into custody on an administrative arrest and transported by van to the detention center in Omaha. He asked if she had any conditions that required the retrieval of medications, or any small children at home who would require caretaking. She did not. Agent Gran then escorted her across the hall to a holding room. Eventually, agents arrested eighteen workers from among Fremont Beef's dayside crew, roughly half the shift.

To Jerry Hart, the sweep was proof of what he and his fellow petitioners had been saying all along. "To those people who want proof that Fremont has a problem with illegal aliens, here it is. To those that still think that the problem is not that big, think again," he wrote in an editorial for the local newspaper. "Had the ordinance prohibiting the hiring, renting to or harboring of illegal aliens been in force, these identity thefts might not have happened. It is appalling that citizens have to fight the City of Fremont, have to take the time and effort to circulate petitions to force this city to enforce federal laws. I am enraged that these crimes were committed in Fremont. I am more enraged that this city could have prevented these crimes simply by preventing illegal aliens from being in Fremont in the first place." Les Leech protested that Fremont Beef, and the Hormel plant directly next door, were already using E-Verify but had been denied access to the FTC database—so they had less information available about their own workforce than ICE did. "This ordinance will not change the complexion of this county one bit," Leech told the *New York Times*, "because E-Verify doesn't work."

But panic spread quickly. "We heard that this happened at Fremont Beef," Raul Vazquez told me, and the rumor flew: "This is going to come to Hormel." An email circulated, in Spanish, saying that ICE was planning a raid at Hormel, that immigrants should stay away from Wal-Mart because ICE agents might be positioned there as well. A story went around that there were middle-of-the-night arrests in Schuyler. The sheriff's office was called out to the Hormel plant to investigate a bomb scare—and, upon finding a device in an employee locker, the federal Bureau of Alcohol, Tobacco, Firearms and Explosives and Nebraska state troopers sent in a robot to retrieve the suspicious mechanism and detonate it in the west parking lot. Fear and mistrust began feeding on themselves among the residents of Fremont.

In the meantime, Kris Kobach, the aggressive young attorney from the Immigration Reform Law Institute, pressed for taking the ordinance and its mission to the state level. He advised former Fremont city councilman Charlie Janssen, by then a state senator, on the authorship of LB 1001—a bill to repeal Nebraska's Dream Act, allowing in-state tuition for undocumented aliens who graduated from high school in the state. Kobach personally filed suit against the University of Nebraska–Lincoln, the Nebraska State College System, and the Nebraska community colleges on behalf of six legal residents—his in-laws in Fairbury—claiming that their taxes were being used to support tuition breaks for illegal aliens in violation of federal law. Last but not least, Governor Dave Heineman, himself a former councilman in Fremont, entered into an agreement with ICE for a new program called Secure Communities. The new initiative took fingerprints, obtained through arrests by local and state law enforcement, and shared that biometric data with the Department of Homeland Security to check against immigration databases.

While these new battles commenced on the legislative and executive sides, legal challenges to one part or another of Fremont's proposed ballot measure—whether or not the ordinance would violate the reserve clause, whether or not the wording of the ordinance was consistent with state law—made their way through the

Dodge County District Court and the Nebraska Supreme Court. For Kobach, this was just one front in a larger war on immigration policy. His boss at the IRLI, director Michael Hethmon, had called these local ordinances and state bills "field tests"—a kind of spinning-plate strategy, whereby the organization hoped to keep enough legal cases going at once, trying slightly different strategies, that they would occasionally find sympathetic judges and establish precedents to advance all of their other cases at once. The goal was to eventually bring each piece to the U.S. Supreme Court and cobble together a new broad-ranging immigration policy, bit by bit. In late April 2010, Kobach scored a major victory, when Arizona governor Jan Brewer signed the Kobach-authored SB1070, which made it a misdemeanor for any alien, legal or not, to be present in Arizona without federally required documents on their person and not only empowered but obligated police officers to determine a person's immigration status during any "lawful stop, detention or arrest." The measure was criticized by pundits as the "show me your papers" law, but Kobach argued that the law merely brought state statutes into harmony with existing federal mandates.

When I spoke with Kobach in his office in Kansas, where he is now the secretary of state, he leaned way back in his chair behind an imposing mahogany desk. He conceded such legal maneuvers were part of a larger strategy—a coordinated effort at "attrition through enforcement." But he took umbrage at critics who asserted that this amounts to harassment, achieving an extralegal end by making life miserable for an already sorely mistreated immigrant population. "That's not it at all. It's just changing the calculation," Kobach insisted. He pointed to Fremont's ordinance as an example. "If before Fremont adopted the ordinance you had an eighty percent chance of finding a job and successfully getting that job illegally, now maybe it's a thirty percent chance. So it changes the calculation of a rational decision maker. Maybe a person says, 'I'm not going to go to Fremont. I might not even go to the United States.' So it's all about changing the calculation: you ratchet up the costs, and you ratchet down the benefits, so that people make the rational decision to follow the law."

By the spring of 2010, enough immigrants—legal or not—were choosing to leave Fremont and Hormel behind that the company decided it was time to intercede, albeit covertly. But before Hormel could effectively band together with the unlikely alliance of the ACLU, Nebraska Appleseed, and the Fremont Chamber of Commerce, a ruling came down from the Nebraska Supreme Court: the ordinance language was deemed constitutional. And a date was set—June 21, 2010—for a public ballot measure. After more than two years of legal wrangling, Fremont's future would come down to a single popular vote in just a few weeks.

The short deadline allowed little time to organize a campaign on either side. Kristin Ostrom, a Fremont resident who held a law degree with certification as a master mediator and previously served as the executive director of the Nebraska Justice Center, decided to form an ad hoc coalition to fight the ordinance. She reached out to Gabby Ayala, a member of the mayor's task force on immigration, and convinced her to join in founding the group they eventually named One Fremont, One Future. But by the time they held their first meeting, Ostrom told me, they had only about a month to organize.

Adding to the confusion, no one seemed to know exactly where city limits were drawn or how far municipal jurisdiction would extend to contiguous areas. Somehow, in all the arguments about the ordinance, no one had considered the bounds of its reach if it were passed. The Hormel plant, for example, had been built outside the city's southern boundary, but its latest expansion pushed one wing across the line. Would they be subject to the ordinance?

The Regency II Mobile Home Park, a largely Hispanic community of neatly rowed trailers (which counts among its residents many Hormel and Fremont Beef employees), fell right along the city limit as well and appeared, in places, to have grown outside the official boundaries. Would the ordinance be enforced on one block and not another? And who in this neighborhood was eligible to vote?

Volunteers from One Fremont, One Future went door-to-door at Regency II, registering people. But rumors continued to fly—there would be police at the poll checking identification (and, in fact, a Charlie Janssen–sponsored voter ID law was under debate in the legislature), there would be immigration officials outside the voting stations—and spontaneous intimidation began to target this area of town as well. There were numerous reports of people shouting "Go back to Mexico!" from passing vehicles, of windows being shot out. At a pair of houses under construction just south of the railroad tracks, someone vandalized the Habitat for Humanity sign in the yard, so that it read, "Habitat for Mexicans." In the midst of it all, the Schuyler Public Schools announced plans to revise their standards for residency, barring noncitizens from attending, until the ACLU issued a warning letter—and, likewise, vowed to fight the Fremont ordinance in court if it cleared the vote.

One Fremont, One Future made no yard signs or bumper stickers or buttons; they managed only to get out a few mailings. But then Ron Tillery, executive director of the Fremont Area Chamber of Commerce, reached out to Les Leech at Fremont Beef and Don Temperley, the plant manager at Hormel. Tillery had received word that the national press was preparing to descend on Fremont; it was a grand opportunity to build opposition to the ordinance by shining a spotlight on the battle, but it also presented a peril. Any misstep could be costly. In a group meeting on June 11, it was decided that Leech would go to Hormel's corporate headquarters in Austin, Minnesota, for meetings, presumably to establish common talking points. In the meantime, Hormel would dispatch Bill McLain, then Hormel's manager of external communications, to Fremont to give media training to anyone who would be speaking to the press. In an email copied to a business-backed committee opposing the ordinance and a local real estate agent who is also one of the city's largest property managers, Tillery assured everyone at the Chamber of Commerce that McLain was an "expert at dealing with situations like this" who would be arriving soon "to review a number of things." Tillery also mentioned that Temperley had agreed to seek $10,000 from Hormel to bolster their anti-ordinance television ad campaign

The following Monday morning, McLain arrived in Fremont. Together with plant manager Temperley, he met with Kristin Ostrom in Tillery's office at the Chamber of Commerce. McLain offered "to teach me," Ostrom said, "how to deal with the press and how to stay on my talking points—but I couldn't say anything to anybody about it."

"Did you take them up on it?" I asked.

"I took them up on the information," Ostrom said. "I didn't promise a thing."

She still stiffened at the thought of accepting assistance from Hormel. In the progress of the whole sordid mess, the beleaguered liberals of Fremont had found themselves forcibly aligned with the meatpacking giants that had made a killing exploiting immigrant labor. And the city council that had been convinced by those liberal constituents to vote down the first version of the ordinance was now represented by Kris Kobach, the attorney who authored the ordinance they had opposed. The sheer madness of the situation was infuriating to Ostrom. But then, she softened a bit. The representatives from Hormel, especially Bill McLain, "were very easy to work with, very kind," she said. They offered constructive and insightful advice in helping her steer far away from the ironies of the situation and took a strong hand in coaching her through several radio interviews, which everyone agreed would be critical in swaying potential voters.

One morning, as Tillery and Ostrom prepared for a joint interview on KHUB radio in Fremont, Bill McLain sent a long email, hoping to help Ostrom turn the interview toward certain talking points. "I've drafted a list of questions that I think could be topics of discussion during the show tomorrow," he wrote. "I will start drafting proposed responses to these questions and send them to you. If you prefer to run through these questions in person, please do not hesitate to let me know." Later that night, he sent long, detailed answers—nearly 2,200 words in all—to each of the questions he had posed. If asked about Hormel, they could say that the "company supports the Chamber of Commerce's position that immigration reform should be addressed by the federal government and not on a state or city basis," but they were told to "note that the company voluntarily started using the E-verify system in April 1999 when it was called the Basic Pilot program" and emphasize that both Hormel and Fremont Beef "are outside the city limits." Tillery and Ostrom stuck closely to the script, and McLain called after the show to applaud their performance.

Despite all the hands-on involvement, Hormel never took a public stance on the ordinance. When I reached him by phone to ask why, McLain, who is now the dayside manager at Hormel's Fremont operation, refused to answer any questions. Every time I started to speak, he cut me off, shouting over my queries that I would have to speak to Hormel's media relations department. When I asked if we could speak off the record, he hung up. The company, in a prepared statement, did eventually concede that McLain had traveled from Austin to Fremont "to provide communications support for media inquiries that we had started to receive." They further explained that while "Hormel Foods supported the Chamber's position in opposition to the ordinance," they had considered it "most appropriate to communicate through the Chamber to enable a constructive dialogue and to speak on behalf of all of its members about this issue." On the weekend before the election, Ostrom and other opponents of the measure went door-to-door in a final push—two hundred volunteers, knocking at some nine thousand homes. Their hopes were high that they had rallied sufficient support to defeat the measure, but, as the national press arrived in Fremont for the day of the actual vote, few residents were willing to publicly share how they intended to mark the ballot. Even at Regency II, there was only a simple white sign at the entrance—VOTE NO—and nothing more.

On the night of June 21, the supporters of One Fremont, One Future gathered in the old Fremont Veterans Club off Military Avenue—the very spot where the first signatures for the petition had been collected—and waited for the results. It wasn't close. The county clerk's office reported that Fremont voters had approved the measure by a wide margin—57 percent to 43 percent. "There were a lot of tears in this room tonight," Ostrom told the *New York Times*. "Unfortunately, people have voted for an ordinance that's going to cost millions of dollars, and that says to the Hispanic community that the Anglo community is saying they are not welcome here."

One month after the vote was certified in Fremont, ACLU Nebraska announced that they were filing suit to challenge the constitutionality of the ordinance and seeking a permanent injunction against its enactment and enforcement. Blake Harper, the son of longtime Hormel worker Harold Harper, was living in Pennsylvania now, but he had been following the ordinance battle in Fremont at first with a feeling of embarrassment and dismay but then with a sense of mounting horror. "I wasn't surprised that Fremont would bring up such a law," he told me, "but I never dreamed it would pass."

Blake had moved with his wife in 2009 to State College, Pennsylvania, where he was working for Subway Restaurants, selecting sites for new franchise locations and handling the leasing of those properties. But he still owned five rental properties in Fremont, holdovers from the Grant Group, a real estate and property management firm he had founded in the city in 2006. The new ordinance, if enforced, meant that Harper would have to inquire about the immigration status of each of his tenants before he could rent to them legally. He was outraged by the very idea of this, so when he saw word of ACLU Nebraska's planned lawsuit on behalf of several renters in Fremont, he immediately called their offices in Lincoln. He said he thought the case would be even stronger if there was a landlord among the plaintiffs. "I basically told them, 'Send me whatever I need to sign to get me on this suit.'" (Steven Dahl, another landlord in Fremont, also contacted the ACLU and joined the complaint as well.)

Alan E. Peterson, ACLU Nebraska's attorney, contacted Harper, and they quickly crafted a declaration to be added to the brief. Most of the declaration focuses on establishing Harper's legal standing and arguments about the infringement of his rights as a landlord. But he insisted that the document end on a more personal note. "I am very concerned about the negative effect the immigration ordinance is having on Fremont," Harper wrote, "and personally regard the ordinance as a new form of 'Jim Crow' legislation aimed primarily at persons of Hispanic background, race, or national origin. It appears to me to have a real purpose, underlying the intricate legalities, of keeping the minority population very low, both in numbers and in their feelings with regard to their neighbors in this city. I do not believe that one can label a human being as 'illegal'; regardless of immigration status. People are not 'legal' or 'illegal' and labeling them as such is repulsive, unethical, and abhorrent."

When I spoke to Harper, he was reluctant to delve too deeply into the psychology of his swift reaction to the immigration vote, but he conceded that—ever since the mysterious illness he had suffered in third grade, the one that had left him with severe-profound hearing loss and a lingering speech impediment—he had felt a reflexive kinship toward the powerless. After his stint at the Boys Town National Research Hospital in Omaha, Harper had emerged as an awkward and thin-skinned ten-year-old with a pair of clumsy hearing aids. In order for him to be able to hear in the classroom, his parents invested in a microphone that his teacher could wear around her neck, so her voice could be transmitted directly to young Blake's hearing aids. But when he started the fourth grade in the fall, Harper told me his teacher, Marilyn Wiegert, didn't wear the microphone.

I stopped him. "Marilyn Wiegert!"

Harper heaved a deep sigh. "Look," he said, "everybody's had to deal with bullshit in their lives, but I don't think mine was worse than anyone else's. And I'm suspect of the narrative fallacy—to say that I did *this* because of *that*. But, yes, John Wiegert's mother was my fourth-grade teacher at Clarmar Elementary, and I *hated* her."

Harper, however, was quick to remind me that Fremont was a small town. Sure, he had lingering animosity toward the Wiegerts. And it was true that his mother had worked with Cindy Hart, Jerry Hart's sister, at 3M and eventually asked to be transferred to another division because of conflicts they were having. But he didn't want me to come away with the idea that his opposition to the ordinance was somehow born out of personal feuds and provincial rivalries. He didn't even join the suit because of his feelings, one way or the other, about immigration. "I got involved, because, as a landlord, I thought it was a violation of fair housing law," he told me. "And that's completely separate from anything immigration related." Exactly as he had stated in his declaration, he considered the law discriminatory, bigotry cloaked as legality, the real intent of which was to allow those with power to strike fear in the hearts of people who had none. To that extent, he conceded, it was no surprise to him to see the Harts and the Wiegerts lined up in favor of the ordinance, but the real struggle is for the future of Fremont. People needed to stop directing their anger toward exploited immigrants and start aiming it where it really belonged: toward Hormel. The city would never be free to determine its own future so long as it remained tied to its postwar past, looming silent and sphinxlike across the railroad tracks.

"People say that if Hormel left, the town would die," Harper said. "Okay, maybe—so let's build something else. Because Hormel isn't going to change. Hormel is a machine, it's a robot, and it's going to just go and go and go and go as long as you feed hogs into it. But while the manufacturing sector is doing its thing, the city could be deciding to become a progressive enclave, an arts enclave, a local food enclave. Otherwise, kids, like myself, grow up there, go to college, and get the hell out. And all you're left with is Hormel—and a town divided between the Hispanic people who are moving there to work at Hormel and the old guys, like my dad and his buddies, who used to work at Hormel but got screwed over and are bitter. What kind of future is that?"

Chapter 12

BROTHER, ARE YOU OKAY?

When Immigration and Customs Enforcement finally cracked down on Quality Pork Processors, it wasn't the kind of dramatic action that immigration opponents like Ruthie Hendrycks at MinnSIR or Samuel Johnson of the National Socialist Movement had been hoping for. It wasn't like the coordinated raids in 2006, when ICE agents descended simultaneously on six different Swift & Company meatpacking plants across the Midwest, including the one in Worthington. Not like the raid on the Agriprocessors plant across the border in Postville, Iowa, in 2008, in which agents patrolled the air with two black helicopters and loaded undocumented workers onto a caravan of white buses emblazoned with the words HOMELAND SECURITY. Those raids had given the agency a black eye. Minnesota senator Al Franken publicly raised objections over the tactic of swooping in unannounced. "The raids resulted in the arrest of over 1,500 unauthorized immigrants," he said. "They also left hundreds of children—most of them citizens and legal residents—without their parents and with no way of finding them."

Under the newly inaugurated Obama administration, ICE was shifting away from such large-scale work-site raids and the rounding up of undocumented workers for deportation. New policy focused instead on conducting payroll audits, nicknamed "desktop raids," in which the agency compared an employer's I-9 files to the Social Security database and notified the company each time they turned up a conflicting record, known as a "no-match." Under the law, employers were then allowed thirty days to either correct the paperwork in cases of clerical error or terminate the employee. If a company chose not to address the problem or missed the deadline, it faced a fine. The objective of this new policy was to shift the risk of illegal hiring practices away from immigrants seeking employment and onto the companies that had been relying on them for cheap labor. But activists on both sides of the issue complained that minimal fines and protecting the identities of violators effectively allowed companies to continue breaking the law without the worry of either public backlash or serious financial consequences from a plant shutdown.

But the quiet, under-the-radar ICE actions carried out in Minnesota in 2009 touched off a series of events that unexpectedly shifted the balance of power at one of Hormel's subsidiaries. According to sources within the UFCW locals, the agency conducted an I-9 audit at QPP and its sister company Albert Lea Select Foods and returned roughly six hundred no-matches. ICE won't say what finally spurred the audits or even confirm that they occurred, but union leaders told me that ICE launched the investigation after a rash of criminal cases in which the accused were found to be QPP employees working under false identities. According to official reports, Austin police made thirty-two arrests for aggravated forgery involving QPP workers and several more involving Select Foods employees between March and September 2009. Patrick Neilon, the president of Local 6 in Albert Lea, told me that one of those arrested was a woman employed in Human

Resources at Select Foods. According to rumor, she had struck a deal to avoid deportation, agreeing to reveal all she knew about the immigration status of the workforce at Select Foods and QPP.

With inside information now available to them, ICE was able to squeeze Kelly Wadding, the CEO of both companies. They instructed Wadding to reduce his undocumented workforce at each plant by three hundred employees. Neilon said the management team at Select Foods, in particular, had no choice but to embrace the recommendation of the audit. The numbers were simply too overwhelming to dispute and too conspicuous to plead ignorance. "To be realistic," Neilon said, "they *had* to have known that the majority of their workers weren't properly documented." And ignoring that volume of no-match letters would risk a large-scale enforcement action. A one-day raid, with exits sealed and workers hauled away in handcuffs, would have crippled the company. "They would have had to shut down production," Neilon explained. "If they would have lost three hundred and some employees at once, they couldn't run." The bad publicity on top of the shutdown might have been enough to sink Select Foods.

Wadding accepted the deal. However, to avoid production problems or potential line injuries resulting from hiring so many inexperienced workers all at once, investigators allowed Wadding some leeway: he would have six months to slowly turn over his two workforces, and there would be no publicity surrounding the audit. But if, at the end of the allotted time, records indicated that QPP and Select Foods were still relying on undocumented labor, then the CEO could expect steep fines and high-profile raids at both plants. Wadding agreed to the timeline.

But, at the same time, someone within Wadding's management team was negotiating a different kind of deal—one with the Karen Organization of Minnesota (KOM), a St. Paul–based nonprofit tasked with finding homes and jobs for ethnic Karen refugees from Burma and Thailand. If KOM would supply proof that the immigrants they served had legal green cards obtained under political asylum laws allowing them to work in the United States, then QPP and Select Foods would provide them with cut-and-kill jobs in Austin and packing jobs in Albert Lea. The plan, in short, was the wholesale replacement of undocumented Hispanic workers with Karen political refugees.

Albert Lea was founded on meatpacking. Even before the community's formal incorporation as a city, East Front Street had a butcher shop—which, appropriately, was opened and operated by a pair of recent immigrants. Brothers Axel and Charles Brundin were new arrivals from Sweden and still teenagers when they started the Brundin Meat Market in the 1870s. By the turn of the century, the population of Albert Lea had more than doubled, and the Brundin brothers' need for a steady supply of fresh meat had grown with it, enough so that they built their own packinghouse. They slaughtered and prepared hogs at that facility on a corner of Main Street until 1912, when they built an enormous pork processing plant on the banks of the Shell Rock River on the eastern edge of town. The Albert Lea Packing Company was grand and modern enough to rival George A. Hormel's plant on the Cedar River in nearby Austin, but the Brundins soon fell on hard times and shuttered the plant just two years after opening it.

But the facility didn't sit idle for long. It was briefly reopened by a division of Schwarzschild & Sulzberger before being bought up by the heirs to J. P. Morgan and John D. Rockefeller, Sr. These new owners selected Thomas E. Wilson to head their packing venture and called the company Wilson & Company in his honor. From the start, Wilson was the very opposite of the Hormel family in Austin. Where George Hormel and later his son, Jay, had begun their lives as butchers and sought to keep the peace between workers and management, Wilson was a Chicago aristocrat and a throwback to Gilded Age industrialists—an iron-fisted, top-down manager and unapologetic union buster. In 1935, Wilson went so far as to set up a company-run union to compete with United Packinghouse Workers of America Local 6, until the newly formed National Labor Relations Board shut down his union as a violation of the Wagner Act.

Wilson's successor was no better. James A. Cooney, a former federal district judge from Iowa, had served as the company attorney and vice president for labor relations since 1926, and he seemed to delight in trying to intimidate the labor force at Wilson & Company. Cheri Register, whose father worked at the plant, later remembered that in the minds of union members, Cooney was "a Wild West robber baron who maintained a terroristic control over our town." When the union demanded better working conditions, he threatened to move the plant to the South, where there was less union sentiment. And without Wilson & Company, he told the Chamber of Commerce, the city would see grass grow down the middle of Broadway. With that threat forever looming, Cooney made more and more demands of the city and his workers.

Finally, in 1959, members of Local 6, disgruntled over company-mandated overtime, staged a sit-down strike, which soon turned into a full-scale, 109-day walkout. When the company finally resorted to recruiting scab workers to reopen the plant, the pickets erupted into street violence with strikers hurling rocks at replacement workers and smashing out the windshields of their cars. Governor Orville Freeman closed down the plant and called out the Minnesota National Guard to establish martial law. Eventually, a judge declared Freeman's move unconstitutional, but by then the leadership of Local 6 had negotiated improved terms for their members. The strikers had won.

It was a defining moment for a community that had always regarded itself as a second city to Austin. At last they had a labor

victory to match the hard-nosed tactics of Frank Ellis and the
Winkels brothers in 1933, and the modern brickwork of Wilson
& Company became a symbol of labor strength in Albert Lea. In
fact, the plant became so foundational to life in the community
that nothing seemed to shake its central place. Even when Wilson
Foods filed for bankruptcy in 1983, nullifying the union contract
and reducing workers' pay from $10.69 an hour to $6.50, the
community took pride in having averted a shutdown. Even when
Wilson sold the plant to Farmstead, and Farmstead sold to the
Seaboard Corporation, and Seaboard sold to Farmland Industries,
the plant stood as a monument to how Albert Lea had weathered
hard times and held on to its meatpacking heritage. And by 2001,
business at the aging plant had picked up enough that Farmland
had ordered the facility renovated and expanded.

But then, the unthinkable occurred. On July 8, a team of con-
tractors switched off the main sprinkler system, in order to cut
through existing pipes in the plant ceiling and connect them to
new pipe for the plant addition. At the end of the shift, unknown
to the workers, sparks from the cutting torch had fallen into a
pile of cardboard boxes and started a small fire. The workers left
without turning the sprinklers back on, and the flames grew unde-
terred and undetected inside the vacant plant. Soon, someone outside spotted smoke billowing from the roof, but by then it was too
late. The fire burned all through the night and well into the next
day, engulfing and eventually consuming the iconic plant. Firefighters were still on the scene putting out hotspots in the rubble
as five hundred workers lined up outside the Albert Lea Union
Center on July 10 to formally apply for unemployment.

Less than a year later, Farmland filed for Chapter 11 bankruptcy and sold its remaining hog operations to Smithfield Foods.
The ruins of the old Wilson & Company plant, once the symbol
of the city's economic might, were demolished, leaving an enormous empty lot in the center of town. Albert Lea struggled for

years after that. Jean Eaton, the mayor at the time, admitted that it was a hard stretch for the city—with still more setbacks to follow. Local officials made overtures to the Ford Motor Company and Premium Pork and Winnebago Industries, but every time the deal fell through. "We felt like the big losers," Eaton said, "and it was a very depressing time for many of us in Albert Lea." But then Governor Tim Pawlenty launched the Job Opportunity Building Zone (JOBZ) initiative, a program through the Minnesota Department of Revenue that offered businesses twelve years of tax-free operation in return for moving into struggling communities like Albert Lea.

The tax break attracted the attention of Hormel and Kelly Wadding at QPP. Wadding soon announced that Hormel would be building a fifty-thousand-square-foot pork deboning and packaging facility on eleven acres in the Northaire Industrial Park, at an estimated cost of more than $5 million. As with QPP in Austin, Hormel would own the property and the plant, would pay for construction, and would provide all of the raw materials and buy all of the processed meat exclusively, but the business would technically belong to Wadding and would operate under the name Albert Lea Select Foods. Wadding touted the project as a show of support for the community where he had gone to high school and gotten his first job on the floor of what was then the Farmstead packing plant. "We looked at a lot of sites," Wadding told Minnesota Public Radio, "and decided on Albert Lea."

For the hundreds of out-of-work meatpackers still in town, the arrival of Hormel seemed like a godsend. They assumed that the company had chosen Albert Lea as the site for Select Foods in order to take advantage of the town's experienced meatpackers, but just the opposite was true. "We had an available workforce here locally," said Patrick Neilon at Local 6. "But they hired very, very few of them—very few. And there was a reason for that."

Kelly Wadding rises before the sun and arrives at QPP each morning by six o'clock. Every day, he reviews reports of the previous day's productivity and problems, before touring the plant with the vice president of operations and the plant manager. Then he drives to Albert Lea, where he repeats those rounds with the plant manager at Select Foods. Finally, each afternoon, he heads back to Austin to conduct meetings and troubleshoot any bigger problems. It's rare that he leaves before four o'clock. Patrick Neilon at Local 6 told me that he respects Wadding's work ethic. "He started out working on the floor," Neilon said, "just like the rest of us."

After Wadding and Neilon graduated from Albert Lea Senior High School, Neilon stayed and worked in the Farmstead plant; Wadding started out at Farmstead, too, but bounced around, getting management training. He worked at Wilson Foods in Oklahoma City, Iowa Pork Industries in South St. Paul, and John Morrell & Company in Sioux Falls, South Dakota. In July 1993, Richard Knight, who had formed QPP a few years earlier, hired Wadding as general manager. When Knight retired Wadding bought him out. For a decade after that, Wadding continued to run QPP more or less as he'd found it, but when the USDA finally approved implementation of the HIMP reduced inspection model in 2002, granting QPP the opportunity to dramatically increase its chain speed, the company decided it was time for an expansion and reconfiguration.

Hogs would continue to be slaughtered and butchered at QPP, but to keep pace with the increased speed of the line, certain cuts—loins, picnic roasts, and ribs—would be trucked down Interstate 90 to Albert Lea, where they would be deboned and packaged for Hormel co-brands like Famous Dave's and Lloyd's Barbeque. Hormel chose to outsource these jobs partly because they were labor-intensive but also because sending these cuts to Albert Lea took the processing out of the reach of Local 9 in Austin and allowed QPP to claim that Select Foods (despite its identical management team to QPP) was a separate company—and, therefore, not subject to the union contract shared by Hormel and QPP workers.

Because workers at Select Foods opened with a lower wage than union workers just twenty miles away, the plant attracted an even higher percentage of undocumented workers than QPP. And the large number of undocumented workers, in turn, made it difficult to unionize the workforce and demand better pay. Neilon tried to organize the shop in 2006 and again in 2008, but both times the votes fell just short. He said that executives at Select Foods had scared the workforce out of choosing to join the union: "With a wink and nod—we're not going to come right out and say it—but we're going to make you think that if you organize you're apt to get deported."

After the second failed organizing effort, Wadding seems to have guessed that the plant was never going to go union. To take advantage of this cheap labor and the tax-free operations offered by the state, Hormel shifted a greater portion of its processing to Select Foods and, just three years after opening, paid for a $1.5 million expansion, including new lunchrooms, locker rooms, and office space. The workforce too had grown—from 75 employees in 2006 to nearly 500 by 2008. But then in 2009, there was that rash of aggravated forgery cases, and stories in the local press were beginning to make note of the fact that almost every case involved either QPP or Select Foods.

Austin detective Travis Heickley didn't believe that Wadding was as innocent and helpless as he claimed. The detective told the local newspaper that QPP had caught the attention of higher-ups at ICE. "They see the problem. They're interested," he said. The city couldn't have a rash of arrests like this "without getting the attention of someone, somewhere." Soon ICE agents contacted Kelly Wadding instructing him to reduce the number of undocumented workers on his payroll or face the prospect of a full-blown raid.

The Karen (pronounced Ka-REN) are an ethnic minority from the mountainous eastern border region between Burma and Thailand. First converted to Christianity by the American Baptist Foreign Mission Society in the early nineteenth century, the Karen rose to prominence when Burma was annexed as a province of British India in 1886, after the Anglo-Burmese wars. During World War II, when the Japanese occupied Burma, violence broke out between ethnic Burmese and the Karen people, leading the Karen to aid British efforts at retaking the country. After the war, however, when the British ceded control of Burma, they failed to make good on wartime promises to help the Karen obtain their own sovereign state. The newly formed Burmese-led government officially took power in January 1948 and instituted a policy of removing Karen from positions of power, in favor of Burmese nationalists. Many Karen fled into Thailand and joined a cross-border insurgency that, officially, has never ended.

By 2005, however, the ranks of the Karen National Liberation Army were estimated to be fewer than 4,000, while the refugee population of massive camps, such as Mae La in Thailand, had swelled to more than 50,000. When the UN Committee on the Prevention of Genocide launched an investigation into allegations of massacres, widespread rape, the conscription of child soldiers, and attacks on civilian encampments, the U.S. government officially permitted the emigration of registered refugees from the nine camps along the border with Thailand, sparking a wave of re-settlement. The Minnesota Council of Churches Refugee Services in the Twin Cities, which had already taken an active role in resettling Hmong displaced by the Vietnam War and Somalis fleeing their country's long civil war, now led the effort at recruiting the

Karen to St. Paul. That same year, already established members of the Karen community in St. Paul began training with Vietnamese Social Services in order to learn how to navigate American governmental bureaucracy and obtain health care, public housing, and employment for the incoming surge of Karen immigrants.

The Karen Organization of Minnesota was officially formed in 2009, just months before Kelly Wadding was in sudden need of a new workforce at QPP and Select Foods. The companies made an attractive offer to KOM: if the organization would simply provide proof of green cards, QPP and Select Foods would provide jobs. In the end, Select Foods filled nearly 250 of its new 300 vacancies in Albert Lea with Karen workers. Patrick Neilon told me that Wadding thought he had found the perfect replacement workforce. "He knew they were going to be documented correctly," Neilon said, "but because they didn't speak the language and didn't understand the culture, they would still be less likely to organize."

Neilon broke into a wide smile.

"You know, I grew up with Kelly. He's actually a good guy, and I think he's a smart guy. But in this case, he guessed wrong."

Among the new workers on third shift, packing ribs from eleven at night until seven in the morning, was a young man named Tha Wah. He had grown up just across the Burmese border in a part of the Mae La refugee camp run by Baptist missionaries. Eventually, with the help of church donations, he attended university in Thailand and received a degree in philosophy. When the UN High Commissioner for Refugees declared the situation in Burma an official humanitarian crisis, Tha Wah went through the formal emigration process and was sent to live in Maine. But the tiny Karen population in Maine left him feeling isolated and lonely; then he heard through friends that a large group of Karen had settled in Minnesota.

When I first met Tha Wah, at a meeting arranged by Patrick Neilon in the offices of Local 6, snow was swirling outside. Diminutive and fine-boned, Tha Wah was a striking contrast to the immigrants from Eastern Europe favored by the packinghouses a century ago. But he trudged in from the snow in nothing more than a union sweatshirt and smiled warmly as he yanked off his stocking cap, sending up a wild shock of staticky hair. His English was better than I had been led to expect—though Tha Wah seems always to speak, at least in English, in a hesitant cadence and so near to a whisper that I had to lean close to hear him. "In 2009, December eleven, I came with the Karen organization, and then we applied job," he told me. "The government announced that the company need to accept only those who have legal papers. Then most other employees are Spanish, but because they're illegal, they had to quit. They hire Karen, more and more."

Tha Wah was put to work on the rib line, trimming rib plates after the pork chops had been removed. "Some coworkers told me, 'Oh, rib line is easy,'" he remembered with a smile. It wasn't true. The line ran so fast and the workstations were packed so close together that the ribs sometimes piled up and line workers knocked into each other as they tossed trimmed rib plates into large bins behind them. "I don't want to mention, but they treat us not good," Tha Wah said. "They push us." He said his hands were too small to handle the straight knife he was given and the automatic sharpeners never yielded a well-honed edge. So he started using his own knife and learned to use a conventional sharpening hone. When he had mastered the knife, he taught his fellow Karen on the line "how to sharpen the knife with the machine," he said, "how to use our own technique." The work started to go better, and Tha Wah pressed the plant management to ask Karen workers at other stations what they needed to do their jobs, rather than simply shouting at them to work faster.

Soon, Tha Wah's coworkers came to regard him as a leader,

and word filtered back to Patrick Neilon that the new workforce might follow him, if the union could convince him to organize a third union campaign. When they met, Neilon found that Tha Wah was eager to secure better pay for Karen workers, in hopes of bringing family members to the United States, and he spoke enough English to translate for union organizers. Best of all, Tha Wah explained that the Karen people are communal by nature. "The people, they're like a brotherhood. Karen culture is when we are friends, we look out for each other, we trust, and we keep like a relative. We call friends 'brother,' 'sister.'" He promised to explain to his coworkers that they needed to join with "the brother Spanish."

Over the course of 2010, as more and more Karen joined the Select Foods workforce, Tha Wah visited their homes with union officials, organized events in St. Paul, and worked with a translator named Keh Moo, brought in by the UFCW leadership in Washington, D.C., to produce union brochures and fliers in Karen.

On January 31, 2011, Local 6 filed a notice with the National Labor Relations Board (NLRB) of its intention to hold a vote to unionize Select Foods.

All day long on March 11, before and after all three shifts, workers filed into the orientation room at the plant to vote. Finally, at 6 a.m. on March 12, after all workers had been allowed the chance to vote and the morning shift began, a representative from UFCW Local 9 in Austin began tallying the results. As each ballot was read, he marked it down. The lead seesawed between yeses and nos, and it became clear that the vote was going to be very close. At one point, Keh Moo looked down and noticed that the union rep's fingers were trembling. "His hand was shaking when he was writing the numbers," she remembered. "I said, 'Brother, are you okay?'" In the end, the 215 pro-union votes narrowly edged out

the 206 votes for no union, but everyone was still quiet. Keh Moo
was confused. "Did we win?" she demanded. The union rep told
her, "Yes," but almost too quietly to be heard. He knew that any
celebration would be short-lived.

Less than a week later, Select Foods attorneys filed suit, alleging
that the union had duped the non-English-speaking workforce
into returning pro-union ballots by buying them off with gifts
of clothing. The suit alleged that 40 percent of the workforce was
now Karen, but "one-third to one-half of Karen-speaking employees do not have functional reading or writing skills in Karen.
Almost none of the Karen employees can understand spoken or
written English." They had voted in favor of the union, they said,
because the workers had been bribed with free UFCW sweatshirts
and stocking caps—like the ones Tha Wah had been wearing
when I first met him.

When I spoke to Patrick Neilon about the allegations, more than
a year had passed, but he was still palpably upset. "It made it sound
like the Karen people didn't have a brain, couldn't think," he said.
Besides, if the company was so concerned about the workers' lack
of English-language skills and their general illiteracy, why had they
fought union efforts to offer ESL classes at the plant, and why did
Select Foods hold their own closed-door meetings with employees
and distribute English-language literature against the union?

What angered Neilon most of all was the additional allegation
that the twenty-eight workers who had chosen not to vote had
been intimidated by the union. "Before Tha Wah came and before
Keh Moo was here, I knew where Burma was on the globe, but
I had no idea about the country," he told me. He leaned forward
in his office chair, propping his elbows on his desk. His voice had
turned soft, introspective. "You start doing a little research into
their history and what happened after World War II, how they
were killed and imprisoned and had to flee to Thailand. The strug-
gles they went through, none of us can imagine." The idea that

anyone could go through all of that, could brave a trip across the Pacific to a new country and take hard, dangerous jobs in a meat-packing plant, but then allow themselves to be intimidated into voting a certain way was more than preposterous to Neilon; it was insulting. "Man," he said, "how they portrayed their employees, their own people, was pretty bad."

The charges would touch off months of legal motions, but in reality it was merely a last-ditch delay tactic. The NLRB eventually denied all of the company's claims. In August 2011, Select Foods became the first offshoot of Hormel to successfully organize in more than twenty-five years—and, by the end of the year, the workers had negotiated a new contract with increased wages. The deal provided for wage increases of $2.15 over the course of the contract, which expires in 2018. In addition to the pay raises, Select Foods workers now have the option of joining a company-sponsored health plan, and workers specifically negotiated contract language, which provided for the plant to join the UFCW Local 6, in order to have national backing.

The battle had been long and sometimes bitter, but Neilon still gave Wadding a lot of credit for how he handled defeat. "Once their final appeal was disallowed and we got the final certification, the company came around," he said. "I've known Kelly since we were kids. We go way, way, way, way, way back. Kelly is basically a good guy. I tell you what, when he gives you his word on something, you can take it to the bank. It took a while to get the contract done, but whenever they committed to something, they stuck with it. After we got the contract signed, sealed, and delivered, and got everybody on board, they've been really good to deal with. Kelly always says, 'With the union and the company, it's a marriage. It may have been a shotgun marriage, but it's still a marriage.'"

After I left the union offices in Albert Lea, I drove back to Austin. I called several former QPP workers, but their numbers were all disconnected. I went to their homes and was greeted by unfamiliar faces at the door. Evening was coming on, so I went to Queen of Angels Church, where the Friday night Spanish mass was already in swing. Often, in the past, when I was having trouble contacting Emiliano Ballesta or Matthew Garcia, I could find them there, as they shuffled out of the sanctuary. But that night, I didn't recognize anyone leaving the service, and the pews were noticeably emptier than the last time I had visited. Just when I was about to give up, Walter Schwartz, the translator who had run the driving service for sick workers, spotted me near the door. He pulled me aside, letting the congregation continue to pass.

"What brings you back here?" he asked. Schwartz is tall and lean and exudes a welcoming air. Driving as much as he does, he has been stopped countless times by the Austin police, and he told me once that their eyes always light up when they see his Germanic name. They don't know that there were as many German immigrants in his native Colombia as there were in the American Midwest. Rather than turning bitter over having to repeatedly explain himself, he seemed to delight in enlightening the police.

I told Schwartz I was trying to find any of the workers with PIN. I knew where to find Pablo Ruiz, but I had come up empty with everyone else. I listed off the names, one by one, and each time he shook his head: gone, he said—most of them returned home to Mexico to be with family. Of everyone I mentioned, only Emiliano Ballesta's son, who had also translated for me, was still in Minnesota, but he was in prison. When someone who owed him money refused to pay up, he had gone to his home and taken his television; he had been convicted of burglary.

Schwartz told me that so many Hispanic immigrants had left Austin that he could no longer make a living driving people around town. Now he drove people from Minnesota back to Mexico.

When I asked if these were all people who had been displaced by the ICE desktop raid, he said he didn't know. But he was quick to point out that nearly two hundred unauthorized immigrants in Austin had been charged with aggravated forgery in 2009 and 2010, and many people had decided that they didn't want to risk having their families hopelessly separated.

Even among those who decided to stay in the United States, many had still chosen to move on to other parts of the country. With the increased scrutiny on QPP, jobs were harder to come by, and life in Austin had just grown too hard. One group had gone to Arcadia, Wisconsin, to work in the Ashley Furniture plant. Another group had gone, ironically, to Postville, Iowa, where the Agriprocessors raid had occurred barely four years earlier. And a final group had gone to St. Joseph, Missouri. A consortium of hog producers from Minnesota and Iowa had recently opened a plant there under the name Triumph Foods. Back before Select Foods went up in Albert Lea, Triumph had considered building their plant there, but management decided to construct their mega-facility—one of the largest in the United States—in Missouri instead. They were concerned about Albert Lea's support for workers and their history of successfully organizing into unions.

Part Five

Chapter 13

A CLEAN BILL OF HEALTH

Before I could even set foot outside my truck and onto the gravel surrounding the New Fashion Pork hog confinement facility, Emily Erickson, the company's animal well-being and quality assurance manager, was at my door, handing me a pair of stretchy white plastic footies to put over my shoes. It was a blustery day in September 2013—the sky threatening snow, the slate-gray blanket of overhanging clouds betraying the first hint of winter, when cold, dry air stabilizes viruses and biosecurity becomes a topmost concern. With recent outbreaks of porcine epidemic diarrhea virus (PEDv) and Methicillin-resistant *Staphylococcus aureus* (MRSA) devastating herds across the Midwest, Erickson didn't want to take any chances. I had to put on footies, and then additional layers of bioprotective clothing, if I wanted to be allowed anywhere near New Fashion's pigs.

And the company couldn't spare a single animal. Hormel, the buyer for all of New Fashion's gilt hogs inside that particular confinement outside Jackson, Minnesota, would soon post record profits, up 18 percent for 2013, on the strength of export sales of Spam to Asian markets and the expansion of their corporate operations in China. But Jim Snee, Hormel's head of international sales, announced that the company was making an even greater push, to firmly establish Spam in Chinese grocery stores before products from competitor Smithfield Foods, purchased by Shuanghui International (now WH Group) that June, could elbow them out. As a major supplier to Hormel's Spam plants in Minnesota and Nebraska, New Fashion Pork was racing just to keep pace with demand. The last thing they could afford, Erickson told me, was an outbreak.

To me, the hog industry's vigilance against external pathogens seemed strangely at odds with their out-of-hand dismissals of concerns about their facilities' effects on human health. Large producers like New Fashion insist that the enormous, concrete-reinforced waste pits under each confinement—many with a capacity of 300,000 gallons—effectively prevent contaminants from leaching into the surrounding soil. They repeatedly assure the public that the waste is carefully managed by the Iowa Department of Natural Resources (DNR) under a series of laws aimed at accounting for all manure at all times. But everyone at New Fashion was also aware of the mounting research suggesting that an unprecedented boom in Iowa's hog industry has created a glut of manure—and, with it, heightened concerns about the antibiotics, bacteria, and nitrates that the waste, when spread as fertilizer, was releasing into the air, water, and soil.

These growing doubts about the safety of concentrated animal feeding operations were stoking public outcry in northern Iowa and southern Minnesota, where most of New Fashion's confinements have been built, and causing hog producers, especially within the Hormel supply chain, to clamp down into total media silence. So I was surprised when Brad Freking, the CEO of New Fashion Pork, agreed to allow me to tour one of his facilities with his animal well-being manager as my guide—and, to be honest, I wasn't sure the visit would actually happen until Erickson led me into the changing room. I zipped into some navy coveralls and slid a pair of clear plastic boots over a second set of footies. Erickson turned the handle to the barn entrance, opening the heavy steel door a crack. The sound of squealing hogs spilled into the room. "If you've never been inside," she warned, her voice rising to be heard, "it's a lot of pig, it's a lot of metal, it's a lot of noise." I assured her I was ready, and we headed inside.

Erickson was right: it was a lot of pig. Under the yellow light of a series of bulbs suspended from the wind-rattled roof, a thousand hogs, divided according to size and approximate age, jostled and jockeyed in large holding pens. Their wet snouts pressed through the metal gates, snuffling and grunting curiously, but the hogs scrambled away as Erickson led me down the side aisle. Some, in fits of momentary panic, let out high shrieks, which echoed off the steel ceiling, setting off cascades of squeals and scattering their pen-mates.

But more than sight or sound, what hit me was the smell—hovering close to the smell of bacon, then veering suddenly into the unmistakable stench of shit. The hogs bolted and reconvened as we walked, their hooves clicking anxiously on the slotted wooden floors; their waste, some still fresh and moist, was spread on the floor and smeared over their haunches and feet, slowly working its way down through the slats into the enormous underground pit. Still more waste had dried and turned powdery, a choking haze swirling in the dim light. And it carried with it a hot, fleshy stink—not just a smell but an astringent, chemical burn. It sears so deeply into your nostrils that it seems terrifyingly foreign and uncannily familiar all at once, as if your senses are somehow living the smell and the memory of the smell at the same time. On the back wall, giant fans did their best to vent the gases that rose from the pit below us.

It was hard not to be awed by the sheer scale and ruthless efficiency of the operation. By the time these pigs had reached this finishing barn, they had been through almost the entire modern hog-farming process: conceived via artificial insemination in sows held in gestation crates; transferred briefly to farrowing crates for milk-feeding; then, at three weeks old, trucked to this wean-to-finish operation, where they had been raised on genetically modified corn and soybeans delivered by automatic feeders. And when those young pigs eventually hit target weight, at about three months old, they were scheduled to be trucked to slaughter at the Hormel plant in Austin. Every part of the system, from temperature and amount of light to time and quantity of feed, was plotted on a rigid schedule and so completely computerized and mechanized that all three thousands hogs, held in the three connected barns, were overseen by a single manager, who checked on the hogs just twice a day.

Despite what industry advocates say, none of this is the traditional way of things. As recently as the 1950s, the process from birth to slaughter would have been much more time-consuming and labor-intensive, and the quick communicability of hog illnesses would have made trying to raise so many animals in such close confinement a disaster. All of which is why hogs were customarily raised in small groups with plenty of room to move, in lean-to shelters exposed to the elements—to let hogs forage and to let the winter's cold naturally kill off many bacterial illnesses. But this modern method of raising hogs is the farthest thing from natural; in fact, it is only made possible by massive amounts of antibiotics—used to prevent illness, to promote growth, and to increase fertility in ever increasing dosages as bacteria develop resistance and mutate into new, stronger strains. Many medical researchers and public health advocates now caution that the widespread use of antibiotics has grown reckless and potentially dangerous.

In the fall of 2013, the CDC and the Center for Science in the Public Interest (CSPI) issued a report raising fears that the bacteria in CAFO waste pits might be breeding grounds for antibiotic-resistant bacteria. "Because of the link between antibiotic use in food-producing animals and the occurrence of antibiotic-resistant infections in humans," the report said, "antibiotics should be used in food-producing animals only under veterinary oversight and only to manage and treat infectious diseases, not to promote growth." Food safety activists applauded the recommendation, but worried that its voluntary enforcement didn't go far enough. They warn that the increasing numbers of superbugs in our food when combined with our growing tolerance of critical antibiotics may be setting the stage for livestock illnesses to make the leap to human hosts, causing a severe and deadly outbreak.

New Fashion Pork's herd manager assured me that the company does not use antibiotics to promote growth and that none of its courses of antibiotics feature drugs critical to treating human illnesses. However, the company's last published set of instructions for barn managers to follow in reducing medications before slaughter listed eight injectable antibiotics, ten water-soluble antibiotics, and five feed-additive antibiotics that New Fashion Pork regularly administered to its pigs. Among those most commonly used were penicillin, amoxicillin, and neomycin—some of the most widely prescribed antibiotic treatments for human patients in the United States and around the world. Their hogs were also frequently given Chlortetracycline (CTC) and Oxytetracycline (OTC), marketed under the names Aureomycin and Terramycin. Not only are these antibiotics the most common drugs used by the hog industry to speed growth among piglets; they were first mass-produced and marketed after World War II by Hormel scientists for precisely that purpose.

In the fall of 1941, Jay C. Hormel invited a group of medical researchers at the University of Minnesota to his estate outside Austin. He wanted to share an idea. There was a large horse barn on the grounds, which he believed might be converted into a laboratory space. The scientists agreed and consulted on the creation of a 400-square-foot lab. A year later, the Hormel Foundation, the company's charitable wing, announced a partnership with the University of Minnesota to create the Hormel Institute—a facility officially founded to study "the relation of animal products to disease and to the treatment of disease," but, in reality, intended to search for ways of improving hog production. The university would supply the researchers, both professors and gifted graduate students, and Hormel would provide the space and funding. Because their research might have medical application, they also agreed that the supervisory board should include a permanent spot for a representative from the Mayo Clinic.

At first, the institute was little more than one chief laboratory technologist, Jacques R. Chipault, a doctoral student at the University of Minnesota, still sharing space in the barn with the stable of horses. But in 1945, with the war ended and demand for cheap meat soaring, the institute's staff was expanded to eight, including Lawrence E. Carpenter, a newly minted Ph.D. from the University of Wisconsin. That same year, Carpenter's former professor, Benjamin Duggar, a botanist who studied fungal infections in plants, reached mandatory retirement age at Wisconsin and took a job at the Lederle Laboratories Division of American Cyanamid in Pearl River, New York. Merck, a chief competitor for American Cyanamid, had saved the lives of countless wounded GIs by the mass production of the wonder drug penicillin before the invasion of Normandy and had recently begun manufacturing streptomycin to combat tuberculosis. American Cyanamid was hoping that Duggar would discover the next antibiotic marvel.

Duggar started by trying to solve an old farmyard mystery: why did chickens raised where they could peck through manure experience lower mortality rates and higher egg production than pullets raised in "cleaner" environments? He suspected the chick-

ens were benefiting from antibiotic fungi living in the soil and
fed by manure. Duggar ordered soil samples from research farms
across the country, eventually testing more than 3,500 vials of
dirt before a sample from the University of Missouri yielded an
unusual gold-colored mold with miraculous benefits. Duggar discovered that the drug which he named aureomycin from the
Latin for gold ("aureus") and fungus ("mykes")—had antibiotic
effects against 90 percent of the most common forms of bacterial
infection in humans. Doctors who began testing the drug in hospitals reported its effectiveness against everything from whooping
cough to typhus, but they found that it was especially effective
against amoebic dysentery and other intestinal infections. And the
drug not only halted life-threatening diarrhea but had an interesting side effect: the patients actually put on weight.

Thomas H. Jukes, a biochemist in the agricultural division
at Lederle who had been searching for an effective animal feed
additive, wondered if aureomycin would have the same effect on
livestock. Knowing its origins as a natural defense among chickens, Jukes gave baby chicks feed mixed with aureomycin, culled
surreptitiously from Duggar's lab waste, and found that the test
chicks grew as much as 50 percent larger than the control group.
He published his results and immediately set out to find if similar outcomes could be achieved with hogs—and young Lawrence
Carpenter at the Hormel Institute was eager, too, to test this new
application of his former professor's discovery.

So, in early 1950, Lederle Laboratories provided a supply of
aureomycin for Carpenter to test at the horse barn in Austin. By
April, he had conclusive evidence that supplementing the normal
diet of a weaned piglet with a daily dose of the antibiotic could
more than double feed efficiency. Carpenter announced the results in the *Hormel Farmer*, the free newsletter sent out to all of the
company's hog suppliers. By June, small town newspapers across
Iowa and Minnesota were running advertisements touting aureo-

mycin as "the most important advancement in Swine Nutrition in the last 25 years." Soon, even the *Wall Street Journal* was reporting that 85 percent of runts "given aureo in their feed survived and grew up into self-respecting hogs." Lester E. Corson of Lyle, Minnesota, told the reporter that he had decided to try the supplement with his runts. "Now they actually look like they are going to make good market hogs."

By the end of 1951, Jay Hormel told shareholders that the Austin plant was nearing its capacity in terms of animals it could process in a day, but he foresaw continued growth in the number of pounds of pork they could produce each year, thanks to antibiotics. Not only was aureomycin allowing hogs to be "brought to marketable weight more quickly," but now Hormel scientists were experimenting with weaning piglets sooner—and even feeding them artificial milk laced with antibiotics, which could replace the natural immunity built up by breastfeeding. Jay envisioned a future where sows could give birth and go directly back into breeding. "This could mean that they might immediately be put back to work producing another litter," Hormel said, "instead of consuming eight pounds of feed a day for fifty-six days, performing no other service than can be performed by the milking machine at the nearest dairy."

Best of all, the Hormel Institute, which had seen devastating mortality rates among their barn-raised test herd due to the rapid spread of illness, was seeing those losses almost entirely eliminated. Being able to keep hogs safely indoors through the winter—and even breed them during that time—would mean tremendous gains in the number of piglets Hormel's farmers could raise each year.

Amid all the good news, researchers sounded one note of caution. Carpenter himself recorded that aureomycin was believed to bring about weight gain by wiping out intestinal flora that might otherwise constitute competition for nutrients in the hog's digestive tract. Because the uptake of the antibiotic was focused on the gut, he wondered if the aureomycin might be passing through the hogs and into the manure that farmers were being encouraged to use as natural fertilizer. To mitigate this effect, he experimented with injected antibiotics but found "that aureomycin, administered either orally or by injection, is excreted in the feces of pigs."

Researchers hoped that this might not pose a problem; if aureomycin wiped out all bacteria in a hog's digestive tract, then the feces might actually emerge as a safer manure. It might even produce hogs free from disease. But scientists at the University of Illinois soon discovered just the opposite to be true: for the first nine days of receiving the antibiotic, they found, there was "a marked decrease in the coliform organisms in the feces of the pigs," but after that the levels began to equalize until at sixteen days "this difference had disappeared." This data sequence suggested that antibiotic-resistant *E. coli* were breeding inside the pigs' intestinal tracts, yielding a manure laced with super bacteria. And already three physicians at the University of Illinois College of Medicine reported: "Although aureomycin has been in general use for only three years, there is evidence that resistant strains of staphylococci are appearing in hospitalized patients."

Despite this early concern, the problem was kept in relative check for decades. In the 1950s and 1960s, few hogs were raised in year-round confinement, so their manure was rarely concentrated enough to pose a public health risk. Then, in the 1970s, with the passage of the Family Farm Protection Act in states across the Midwest, there were decades in which the ban on vertical integration kept large-scale hog confinements from being economically viable. But when the bans on corporate backing of concentrated animal feeding operations began to fall, thousands of mega-barns sprang up, bringing their massive lagoons and enormous concrete waste pits along with them.

In 2002, just as the CAFO building boom in Iowa was beginning, the University of Iowa and Iowa State University published a joint report investigating complaints of a litany of illnesses, particularly eye lesions and chronic respiratory problems, among people living near CAFOs. The investigators concluded that air pollutants in the form of hazardous gases from hog confinements were a plausible source of the illnesses. Large-scale confinements, they wrote, "may constitute a public health hazard"—and explained that the problem did not arise primarily from the containment of manure in waste pits but from its application aboveground as fertilizer, attributing fully 80 percent of air exposure to the first six hours after it was spread.

In response, the Iowa DNR announced new air-quality regulations. But state lawmakers overruled those standards within days. While they were eager to keep out-of-state meatpackers from crowding into Iowa, they didn't want to hamstring potential development for local hog producers. So, in place of more stringent air quality constraints, stopgap guidelines were established requiring liquid manure to be immediately knifed into the topsoil or directly injected into the subsoil, preventing harmful gases from escaping into the air. Soon after, Iowa adopted a more elaborate scheme known as the Master Matrix Plan—a scoring system, to be implemented and enforced by the DNR, that would evaluate the siting and manure management practices of proposed large-scale operations.

Critics say that the Matrix is both a virtual rubber stamp for industry and intentionally byzantine to make it hard for watchdog groups to monitor compliance. The system determines permitting based on forty-four factors—covering air quality, water quality, and community impact—each assigned a maximum value of twenty points. The Environmental Protection Commission decided that a passing grade would be 440 points—or half of those available. Steve Roe, president of the Raccoon River Watershed Association, bitterly denounced the system one night at a potluck dinner of landowners opposing new construction of hog confinements. "Whoever heard of passing a test with a score of fifty percent?" Roe pointed out that the test is really a self-exam with results submitted for certification and approval. In most cases, counties and municipalities have no means to check Matrix submissions for compliance. One DNR inspector told me that many county supervisors do not attend visits of potential sites when they are offered by the department. And even in cases where a county does object, the builders can appeal directly to the political appointees who head the DNR. Roe said he didn't know of a single instance in which the department had denied a permit request.

As the building of CAFOs boomed and the state's hog inventory tripled in a few short years, the quantity of waste grew too. David Goodner, a spokesman for the watchdog group Iowa Citizens for Community Improvement, told me that the state's factory farms now produce well over five billion gallons of liquid manure a year. He said the volume of applied fertilizer is now so high that the ground simply can't hold all the manure being produced, especially in recent years as spring rains have sheeted off drought-hardened fields. The daily loads of antibiotics, drug-resistant bacteria, and nitrates began regularly violating levels allowed under the Clean Water Act, leading to renewed worries about the immense number of antibiotics being administered to livestock and the potential impact on humans.

When a rash of MRSA was reported in 2008, health officials worried that the illness, which was already prevalent among hogs in Europe and other parts of North America, had spread to herds in the United States and was now jumping to human hosts. A representative for the National Pork Producers Council told a reporter for the *Seattle Post-Intelligencer* that there was "nothing to worry about." No cases of MRSA had been found among pigs on "this side of the border," he said, claiming that the USDA and CDC had issued "our pigs a clean bill of health." But the CDC immediately denied having ever made any such statement.

In fact, Tara Smith, an assistant professor in the University of Iowa Department of Epidemiology, was in the midst of conducting the first scientific test of hogs for MRSA in the United States—and the findings were not nearly as reassuring as the Pork Council had suggested. Members of Smith's team had swabbed the noses of 209 pigs from ten hog barns in Iowa and Illinois and found MRSA present in 70 percent of the animals. More disturbingly, two of Smith's graduate students also took swabs from twenty workers at several Iowa farms and found that 45 percent of the workers were also culture positive.

Because the bacteria live primarily in the nose and respiratory system, Smith undertook another study—this time in partnership with Margaret Carrel, a specialist in the geography of infectious disease at the University of Iowa—to investigate whether MRSA might be spreading to people beyond the confines of the hog barns. The team gathered the records of more than a thousand patients from rural Iowa who had been admitted to the Iowa Veterans' Affairs Hospital with respiratory complaints in 2010 and 2011. In all, they found that 119 of the patients were suffering from MRSA. That rate in itself was distressingly high, but the greatest shock came when the home addresses for those patients were overlaid onto the Iowa DNR's map of CAFOs. The overwhelming number of patients with MRSA lived within one mile of a hog confinement. They were three times more likely to have the antibiotic-resistant bacteria than other residents of rural Iowa—and nearly ten times more likely than someone living in an urban area.

The researchers were unable to say exactly how MRSA was making the jump from the confined hogs to the workers in the barns and the nearby residents, but they noted that manure from

CAFOs is typically spread as fertilizer on the corn and soybean fields surrounding the barns. "MRSA can be aerosolized from this manure to human food or water sources," they concluded. "The increasing populations of swine raised in densely populated CAFOs and exposed to antibiotics presents opportunities for drug-resistant pathogens to be transmitted among human populations."

Brad Freking at New Fashion Pork told me that he simply didn't believe that antibiotics could be passing through his hogs and producing resistant bacteria in his waste pits. "A lot of those antibiotics are broken down within the pig by the time it goes through the liver and the kidney. What the pig is actually urinating into the pit is a changed molecule. You see where I'm going?" he asked rhetorically. "If I put tetracycline into the pig, what is that molecule that comes out? Then, it sits in an active pit. Does it get broken down or changed again? I don't know." But recent research indicates that as much as 80 to 90 percent of tetracyclines and other common antibiotics are still in active form when excreted by hogs. And far from hostile environments to bacterial growth, waste pits have been shown to be an ideal breeding ground for antibiotic-resistant strains of *E. coli* and *S. aureus*. Officials from the Des Moines Water Works assured me that their filtration systems, and those used in most local municipal water treatment plants, do an excellent job of removing antibiotics and bacteria from the water supply. But those downstream systems do nothing for people taking their water from wells near hog confinements or who live in homes neighboring fields where the application of manure releases antibiotic-resistant bacteria—and other contaminants—into the air and soil.

The University of Iowa researchers were unequivocal: "Our study indicates that residential proximity to large numbers of swine in CAFOs in Iowa is associated with increased risk."

Chapter 14

LAY OF THE LAND

Jay Lausen parked his pickup on the side of the gravel road and walked out to the edge of the field. This was the quarter section of land he had wanted me to see, and he stood quietly, letting me take it all in. But this 160-acre plot, just north of Estherville, Iowa, and only a few miles from the Minnesota border, didn't look much different from any number of cornfields stretching away in all directions—not to my eye, anyway. It was November now, and I could see that the rows had been harvested, the brown stalks chopped to stubble, and someone had recently applied rich, dark fertilizer, ahead of the hard frost that would be coming soon. But, beyond that, I didn't see what was so special about this particular parcel of land.

Lausen smiled. He had spent twenty years farming this field for a neighbor and had mastered its every contour. He lifted his finger and traced the spinelike ridge that divides the acreage, then the serpentine gully that winds toward the southwest fence corner where runoff pools and swells into a culvert. That west side of the property, he explained, is sloped enough that in the early 1990s he had enrolled some fifty acres of it into the Conservation Reserve Program (CRP), an initiative by the U.S. Department of Agriculture to take environmentally sensitive land out of crop production by paying farmers to instead plant native grasses, tall deciduous trees as windbreaks along property lines, and evergreens to hold soil along waterways.

Even with the improved ground cover, this property drained so directly into the West Fork of the Des Moines River in the near distance that, when his landlord decided to put the acreage up for auction, Lausen fully expected that the Iowa Department of Natural Resources would snap it up. After all, he said, turning and pointing to the west and south, they already owned adjacent property on two sides and even paid to undercut the dirt road to reestablish the gully's direct flow to the river as part of a wetland restoration program. But when the auction came around after Thanksgiving of that year, the DNR was nowhere to be found. Instead, the high bid came from New Fashion Pork. "I knew right away what the intentions were," Lausen told me.

Lausen is soft-spoken with wispy blond hair and a shy smile. He doesn't seem like the kind of guy who goes looking for trouble, but his roots run deep around Estherville. His family's Century Farm is just five miles away from where we stood, and a mile to the east, he and his wife are homeschooling their four children, in the same house where Lausen grew up with his four older siblings. He'd never had any great love for New Fashion Pork, as they erected confinements all around the outskirts of town, but now they were planning to build less than a mile upwind from his family's home and uphill from where they drew their water, bringing Lausen's concerns about modern hog farming right to his front door.

When Jay was young, Estherville was a community of eight thousand people, supported almost entirely by agriculture. But in the late 1970s, as the economy stumbled and then fell into the worst agricultural recession since the Great Depression, Estherville, like so many farm communities, began to empty out. Struggling families sold off their ancestral land and moved away to find jobs, and the forces of agribusiness, from seed companies to harvester dealers, moved in—encouraging farmers to buy more land, plant more crops, invest in more equipment. They could do more with less, they said, by using modern techniques.

By the time Lausen began farming with his father, some 1,500 people had left Estherville, and more and more acres were owned by or mortgaged to out-of-state interests. To prevent further encroachment, Iowa had strictly enforced the prohibition on meat-packers owning livestock or feed crops, but the big packers were always searching for loopholes. In 2000, the legislature tightened language, prohibiting packers from contracting for the care and feeding of hogs in the state. Two years later, lawmakers banned packers from financing the construction of confinements or receiving a percentage of profits from a hog operation.

In 2002, Virginia-based hog producer Smithfield, by far the nation's largest producer, had had enough; they sued, accusing the state of Iowa of engaging in discriminatory business practices. Fearing an all-out repeal of the bans, Iowa attorney general Tom Miller instead brokered specific exemptions for Smithfield, Hormel, and Cargill. Some counties in northern Iowa, like the Interstate 35 corridor to the east of Estherville, which had almost no hog confinements during the years of the vertical integration ban, soon had hundreds, each housing thousands of hogs.

New Fashion Pork has been a major player in the boom. The company not only raises 1.2 million hogs per year—about half of those in more than fifty wean-to-finish facilities across northern Iowa—but also owns hundreds of thousands of acres of farmland, dozens of feed mills, and produces so much manure that it has developed and marketed its own line of fertilizer injectors. The company has been recognized by Hormel Foods as one of its top suppliers. Lausen understood that the whole goal of such vertical integration, controlling every link in the supply chain, was to reduce costs by establishing seed-to-slaughter monopolies. New

Fashion already owned five other hog barns within a few miles of Estherville and had purchased a feed mill just south of town, so Lausen knew the best thing for the company would be putting the land surrounding this new barn into corn production to feed the hogs inside—and, in turn, he said, "I knew as their source of fertilizer, they'd like to use hog manure."

The practice has become so widespread—especially along Iowa's northern border, where even seemingly remote communities like Estherville are less than twenty miles from Minnesota's Interstate 90 into Austin—that the impact on Iowa's waterways has been almost too massive to comprehend. Of ninety test stations established across the state, only two now rate water quality as good. None rate as excellent. The Raccoon River and Des Moines River watersheds, which together supply most of the drinking water for the city of Des Moines and converge just east of the capital, have the highest and second-highest nitrate loads of the forty-two major tributaries to the Mississippi River. The Iowa DNR estimates that the level of *E. coli* in the Raccoon River needs to be reduced by 99 percent.

Lausen said he knew that putting up a hog confinement at the high point on the quarter section near his home would virtually ensure that the land would be taken out of the Conservation Reserve Program, that twenty years of plantings would be torn out, and that the erosive hillside would be planted with corn and fertilized with hog manure. "I knew firsthand how the farm laid and when we got a heavy rain where the water went," Lausen told me. "There's an open ditch that starts right at the edge of that property and leads roughly three-quarters of a mile directly to the Des Moines River." If New Fashion Pork were allowed to put up a hog barn there, he feared it could pump contaminants straight into the whole town's drinking water.

At the height of the Dust Bowl, when deep plowing and uprooting of native grasses on the Great Plains during a period of historic drought created enormous storms of lost topsoil, dubbed "black blizzards," and put the future of the entire nation's food supply in doubt, FDR's secretary of agriculture, Henry A. Wallace, initiated a series of projects aimed at stopping soil loss and discouraging the overproduction of crops that had created wide swaths of erosible earth in the first place. Though the era is often remembered as the Dirty Thirties, it was also a moment of revolutionary advances in agricultural methods—and perhaps the greatest focused environmental effort the country has ever undertaken.

First, at Wallace's urging, FDR signed the Soil Conservation Act, establishing subsidies for farmers to restore native grasses and trees, rather than planting commercial row crops that reduced ground-cover and depleted soil nutrients. At virtually the same time, FDR authorized employing federal foresters to plant more than 200 million trees at the perimeters of farm fields in a hundred-mile-wide zone from the Canadian border to the Brazos River. The idea was to create a national windbreak—what was termed the Great Plains Shelterbelt—to reduce the velocity of dust storms and the loss of moisture due to evaporation from windswept soil.

Second, to mitigate crop overproduction, Wallace proposed the "ever-normal granary." The mechanisms were often complex, but the concept was simple: when grain supplies went too high and drove down prices, the government would pay farmers to take portions of their land out of production. During these peak times, the government would also stockpile grain, then release it during years when supply dropped due to crop loss. Just as Wallace predicted, the steady flow of key commodities normalized supply and stabilized prices in ways that benefited farmers, meat producers, and ultimately the consumer. And, in combination with soil conservation efforts, soil loss had been reduced by 80 percent by the time the United States entered World War II.

But the whole system was dismantled when Earl Butz became Richard Nixon's secretary of agriculture in 1971—an appointment opposed by family farmers and congressional Democrats right from the start. Butz had grown up on a dairy farm in Indiana, taken a doctorate in agricultural economics from Purdue in 1937, and spent the next thirty years on the faculty there, becoming dean of agriculture. But he also served as the key voice for turning small-scale farming into big business. At his appointment hearing, the president of the National Farmers Organization warned Senate leaders that Butz, as assistant secretary of agriculture under Eisenhower, had pushed for policies that favored agribusiness and earned a reputation among farmers "for his callous lack of concern about their welfare." His refrain for them, famously, was: "Get big or get out."

Almost as soon as Butz's appointment won approval, the worst fears of small farmers were realized. In a reversal of thirty-five years of farm policy, he canceled payments for fallow land and exhorted farmers to "plant fencerow to fencerow," promising to use the emerging global economy as a bulwark against low prices. If our supply threatened futures, we would simply go to the world market and use our size and economic might to meet the demand and forge foreign dependence on American food in the bargain. To illustrate his philosophy—and shore up reelection support for Nixon among farmers—Butz pulled off the remarkable sale of our grain reserve to the Soviets in 1972. With supply now low, prices climbed internationally but remained low at home. And America was sold on a future where we could economically dominate the world and feed it at the same time.

To take advantage of the new policies, farmers acquired more land, put fallow land back into production, invested in new and more advanced equipment, and bought more fertilizers and pesticides and engineered seeds. Interest rates were low, so farmers without capital could afford massive loans, using their land as collateral. Those growers who felt nervous about so much overhead often "got out," as Butz had instructed, keeping a ready supply of land available at bargain prices for still further expansion.

"People used to have an eighty-acre farm and raise a family," one farmer who used to raise corn and hogs in Nebraska told me. "Now you've got eight-*thousand*-acre farms. It's just like a corporation. But pretty soon you get too big for your britches—and that acreage rears up and bites you." And in the late 1970s, that's exactly what happened. The economy slowed, interest rates rose, and foreign markets declined. When the Soviets invaded Afghanistan, President Jimmy Carter attempted to use American grain as a political tool. But the USSR simply established new supply sources in South America and Europe, and American commodity prices plummeted. Instead of making the world dependent on our grain supplies, we had grown reliant on their demand. In an attempt to undo the damage, Carter convinced Congress to pass the Federal Crop Insurance Act of 1980. But this policy had serious unintended consequences.

First, it kicked production into overdrive. The high-density and high-volume planting encouraged by Earl Butz was possible at new levels by the 1990s. Emerging technology—everything from the GPS-mapped furrows to computer-controlled irrigation systems—made it possible to plant crops (especially corn) in places no farmer would have dared waste seed, much less water, a generation earlier. The more farmers planted, the more they stood to profit, and crop insurance removed the element of risk.

But after a period of sustaining heavy losses, the insurance companies began taking a stronger hand in determining what was planted—the second consequence of the policy change. Initially, insurance companies simply decided which crops were insurable and set variable payouts, making certain crops more attractive than others. But in recent years, they have taken to telling tenant farmers what to grow on land acquired through foreclosure. Big companies, with lots of resources, can afford to irrigate and fertilize and spray against pests; their yield increases—and drives down prices for their smaller competitors. Everyone gets locked into a system where farms carry outrageous overhead and need outsized grosses just to show a profit. Insurers and loan agents alike insist on the crop most likely to produce profits: corn.

Ironically, the problem was exacerbated by U. S. Environmental Protection Agency (EPA) efforts to reduce carbon emissions and improve air quality. Approval of the first Renewable Fuel Standard in 2005, requiring the production of at least 7.5 billion gallons of renewable transportation fuels within seven years, created runaway demand for ethanol. The market price quadrupled, encouraging farmers to plant more rows into already overplanted fields. The steep jump in feed prices tipped many struggling hog operations toward bankruptcy, but the increased planting also drove up demand for fertilizer and spurred farmers to consider lower-cost manure over industrial anhydrous ammonia. Manure sales soon helped stabilize hog profit margins and lowered input costs for row crops, driving still more corn production—which, in turn, tempered steep feed prices and encouraged still more hog production.

To make this self-perpetuating cycle viable, however, the industry needed buyers, which is why Iowa's Republican Governor Terry Branstad and other Midwestern governors have made repeated overtures to Japan, China, and South Korea. (The three countries collectively import more than $3 billion worth of American pork each year.) The industry also argued that it needed greater control over its supply chain and demanded the end to decades-old legislation aimed at keeping meatpackers from becoming major players on the feed commodities market. Desperate farmers didn't complain. If packers wanted to build large confinement barns filled with hogs eating their corn and producing waste that could be used as a cheaper alternative to commercial fertilizer, it seemed like a win for everyone.

Soon, however, the impact on Iowa's water became obvious. In 2009, the Washington, D.C.–based Environmental Integrity Project, joined by the Iowa Chapter of the Sierra Club and Iowa Citizens for Community Improvement, filed a petition with the EPA, informing the agency of the dire water quality problem in Iowa and calling on them to take over enforcement of the Clean Water Act in the state. The EPA never responded.

In the spring of 2012, just as the ground was beginning to thaw, Jay Lausen spotted markers on the hillside across from his property, a sure sign that New Fashion Pork was preparing to dig a pit for a hog confinement. He called the DNR to get a copy of the blueprints and the application to build and soon learned that New Fashion was intending to erect a 2,400-head wean-to-finish operation. But under the Master Matrix Plan, the state of Iowa doesn't count livestock according to heads. Instead, they count by "animal units"—using weight equivalence to standard-size slaughter cattle. A hog is considered 0.4 animal units; thus the operation was proposed to hold 960 units, just below the 1,000-unit size that requires a public hearing under DNR rules. There would be no official opportunity for Lausen and his neighbors to oppose the construction. And, just as he suspected, the manure management plan submitted to the DNR called for injecting the contents of the facility's waste pit into the surrounding fields as fertilizer— including the fifty acres that empty directly into the Des Moines River. So he started digging through USDA data, DNR reports, and Iowa Department of Public Health records, researching all of the laws governing the permitting of concentrated animal feeding operations (CAFOs). What he found was even more troubling than he'd imagined.

In spring 2011, Republican governor Terry Branstad, newly re-elected after more than a decade out of office, announced the elimination of one hundred positions at the DNR, including fourteen unfilled vacancies in CAFO inspection and enforcement. Branstad also appointed Roger Lande as the new director of the Iowa DNR. A former chairman of the Iowa Association of Business and Industry, Lande is an attorney whose law firm represented the Iowa Farm Bureau, Monsanto, and other agribusiness interests. Wayne Gieselman, then head of the agency's environmental compliance division, told the Associated Press that the cuts would hurt enforcement. "If we could be on site on a more regular basis, producers would know we're watching," he said. Shortly after those comments hit the newspaper, Gieselman was removed.

The governor also announced four appointments to the nine-member Iowa Environmental Protection Commission: Eugene Ver Steeg, owner of Sunnycrest Inc., a wean-to-finish operation that markets 20,000 hogs per year, and past president of the Iowa Pork Producers Association; Brent Rastetter, the owner and CEO of Quality Ag Builders, a company that has built hundreds of hog confinement facilities in Iowa; Dolores Mertz, recently retired from the Iowa House, where she had sponsored and fast-tracked a bill that gutted an existing state law banning the spreading of confinement pit manure on frozen and snow-covered ground; and Mary Boote, who served as agriculture adviser to Governor Branstad from 1997 to 1999 and, at the time of her EPC appointment, was the CEO and managing partner of Policy Management Interests LLC, a private fund-raising firm founded by Branstad. The appointments were a clear message: the governor wanted to attract agricultural dollars to Iowa, and if he couldn't do that through deregulation, he would accomplish the same goal through lax enforcement.

Soon after, Branstad's allies in the statehouse went one step further; they proposed transferring all EPA Clean Water Act programs from the DNR to the Iowa Department of Agriculture and Land Stewardship, formally putting environmental enforcement in the hands of a department with no environmental mandate. Watchdog groups alleged that these moves were payback from the governor. They pointed out that Branstad Farms, a cattle operation with capacity for 2,500 animals, owned and operated by the governor's brother Monroe Branstad, was at that very moment under investigation by the Iowa DNR, accused of letting 900,000 gallons of manure removed from a basin run into a drainage tile that emptied into the Winnebago River. And it wasn't the first offense for Branstad Farms. In 2010, the business had been ordered to pay civil penalties for a contaminated water spill that allegedly killed 31,200 fish in the same river.

In August 2011, just before the sale of the land near Estherville, the Environmental Integrity Group and its Iowa partners grew tired of being ignored by the EPA. They filed notice of their intent to sue the agency for failing to answer its earlier petition. In their letter of notice, they again urged the agency to "de-delegate" the state of Iowa from all water quality enforcement and instead assume direct control themselves. The DNR responded by issuing plans for reducing contaminants in the state's waterways—but cautioned that the challenge had grown enormous. Their report estimated that nitrate levels in the Raccoon River and Des Moines River watershed needed to be reduced by a shocking 60 percent and *E. coli* by 99 percent just to come into compliance with federal standards.

In advance of the April 2012 meeting of the county supervisors at which New Fashion's building proposal would come to a vote, Jay Lausen asked for an exception to the rules so that they might be allowed to address the board. He shared everything he had uncovered about lax inspection of hog confinements and distributed USDA data showing that 60 percent of the property lay on the Des Moines River Watershed, classified by the DNR as an endangered waterway. But Jay Moore, New Fashion Pork's environmental construction manager, was also in attendance, and he had come armed with statistics of his own. He passed out flyers showing that the company supported seventeen full-time employees in Emmet County and tallying the tax dollars and other economic benefits paid into the local economy. "We have invested in Emmet County," Moore said, and he assured the board that his company understood small agricultural communities. New Fashion Pork started as a family farm just across the border in Minnesota, he told them. "It's still run as a family operation."

Lausen said that he had done his research on New Fashion Pork, too. "How many family-run operations have three hundred and twenty employees?" he asked Moore. Lausen admitted to me later that he was flushed with anger when turned back to address the board. "This is corporate farming," he said.

Nothing gets under Brad Freking's skin quite so much as when people in northern Iowa call him a corporate farmer. "Like we're these big guys from out of state," he said to me ruefully. New Fashion's headquarters are barely twenty miles from Estherville, just across the divide onto the Minnesota River watershed but otherwise indistinguishable from the rolling hills of Iowa, so Freking still views himself as a local farmer and veterinarian whose business grew simply as a way of staying in the game. The expansion of his operation, to his mind, is evidence of sound decision-making and careful planning in a rapidly changing industry. As I sat across the New Fashion conference table from him, I found it hard to peg Freking as some corporate suit. He was a wiry man in his forties, dressed in a blue Oxford shirt and jeans, soft-spoken and careful in choosing his words; but he also made no effort to conceal his corporate ties. Hormel Spirit of Excellence plaques stood lined up on the mantel above a wide fireplace, and Freking sipped from a Hormel mug. He freely admitted that he had been advised against our meeting, but he said there was nothing to hide so he wasn't going to duck my questions. "Call us a little bit unique in that," he said. And that openness, he hoped, would show that New Fashion Pork was not some faceless corporation.

Freking grew up on a small farm in Jackson County, Minnesota, with just two hundred head of hogs raised on pasture during warmer months and housed in a barn during the winter. Graduating from the local high school in 1986, at the very height of the worst agricultural downturn since the Great Depression, Freking had no prospects for farming at the time. So he went first to South Dakota State University, where he got a degree in animal science, then continued on to veterinary school at the University of Minnesota. In 1994, he came home with his wife, Meg, to found New Fashion.

"It started extremely small," he told me, "producing about sixteen thousand pigs a year." But, having grown slower and more strategically than his competitors, Freking was presented with an opportunity when the downturn in the hog industry arrived in 1998. "We were, financially, in a very good position at that time," he said. "So we started acquiring distressed sow farms." That's why New Fashion's operation is so geographically diverse. From the Rockies to the Great Lakes, he acquired failing breeding barns, building what he calls a "sow base."

In 2004, just as this period of acquisition was ending, Iowa began exempting big packers from its vertical integration laws. New Fashion Pork, with its sow base expanded from fewer than 1,000 to more than 50,000, joined in the boom, building as fast as it could and aggressively investing in every link on the supply chain. A decade later, New Fashion Pork not only raises 1.2 million hogs per year but also owns hundreds of thousands of acres of farmland from Indiana to Wyoming, and its Triumph Foods packing plant in St. Joseph, Missouri, now processes 24,000 hogs per day, making it the second-largest hog kill in the United States. The result of all this integration, Freking told me, is that "we're not only producing pigs. Now we're producing pork."

The whole process is fed—and made possible—by injecting waste pits into cornfields as cheap manure, but Freking doesn't make any apologies for that fact. "It is a great model, if you think about it," he said. "Here's my farm, and I put my pig barn on my farm and then I take the organic nutrients out of that pig and put it on the farm to grow the corn to feed the pig. It's very sustainable."

Freking allowed that not every one of his competitors lives up to the standard he expects from his facilities, especially during cash-strapped times. "When I think about the acquisitions I did of failing farms," he said, "most of them had environmental issues. That's true." Still, given the construction standards imposed on hog waste pits and the piles of paperwork that must be completed to stay in compliance with the DNR, Freking said he didn't believe that hog confinements could be contributing more to water contamination than corroding pipes and leaky septic systems in old farmhouses or small town water-treatment plants that flush their systems during flooding.

And if manure was being overapplied and making its way into surface water, that was the fault of corn farmers, not him. While the manure was under his control, he assured me, he made certain it was confined in well-built and well-maintained waste pits. After it was pumped out and sold as manure, it was up to farmers to apply it responsibly and to safeguard their own local water supplies.

A few weeks after the county supervisors meeting at which he had spoken out against New Fashion Pork, Jay Lausen gathered a group of his neighbors to attend a meeting of the Estherville City Council and lobby for passage of a resolution opposing the proposed facility. Everyone knew that such a gesture was merely symbolic and nonbinding, but they wanted the council to send a message to Brad Freking. The resolution was read and unanimously approved, and a week later the Emmet County Board of Supervisors approved a similar Good Neighbor motion. The second vote came just hours before a public meeting at the Regional Wellness Center, called by an upstart group calling itself the Concerned Citizens of Emmet County. More than a hundred people were gathered in the gymnasium as Joe Fitzgibbons, a local attorney and de facto leader of the group, rose to explain concerns about impact on air quality and on the Des Moines River.

Fitzgibbons read from a letter he had sent to Freking, outlining the steps the group intended to pursue: petitioning for mediation, seeking preemptive injunctive relief, and, if necessary, filing suit. He conceded that these legal avenues were "somewhat limited," but the motions would at least temporarily stave off building and would draw media attention, giving the group time and a platform to make their case. "We've taken our fight to the court of public opinion," he said.

Fitzgibbons then asked if anyone from New Fashion Pork was present in the audience. No one had yet met Freking in person, so they didn't know he had been in the gymnasium from the very start of the evening. He waited in the audience for a long moment, wondering if anyone had done homework on him and recognized him as he came through the door and sat through the meeting. When no one's eyes fell on him, Freking finally rose and walked to the front of the room. "Joe, it's your party," he said. "What do you want to do here?" Fitzgibbons handed him the mic, and Freking took an hour and a half of questions.

"We are pretty comfortable with the site," Freking told the crowd at the outset, but by the end of the evening he could see the strength of the opposition. He made the group a promise: "We're going to pursue an alternative location if possible." And, in the end, that's exactly what they did.

"We don't want to be in a place that we're not wanted," Freking told me later. "We honor those in the communities that we work in."

After the battle in Estherville (and a similar outcry from citizens in Dickinson County in 2006), Freking said he had gained "tremendous respect" for the Iowa Great Lakes Watershed and the rivers they feed. He had learned to consider those concerns before purchasing property or applying for a permit to build. "I actually have a map on my desk of the Iowa Great Lakes Watershed," he said. "We just avoid issues. You understand the watersheds, and you just stay out of them. That's our approach."

Later, I recounted that conversation to Lausen. I asked him if this might represent a ray of hope—and a way forward. Sure, the EPA appeared cowed by political pressure and, yes, the Iowa Department of Natural Resources, hamstrung by the governor and legislature, seemed unlikely to carry out more than minimal enforcement of the Clean Water Act. But maybe direct public pressure was enough to appeal to the conscience of these businesses. Maybe it was still possible to have a one-on-one conversation and find the best solution for everyone involved.

Lausen broke out in a broad, characteristic smile. "You haven't seen where they built instead, have you?" he asked.

By the time we arrived, the sun had burned through the morning rains. The cold of weeks before had turned into a brief, unseasonable warm-up. The sun was so bright, in fact, that we could actually see light glinting on the water running off the newly fertilized fields toward Brown Creek, right where it passes under a bridge and bends into a stand of trees, on its way to the Des Moines River. Steam rose off the blacktop, casting the whole scene in a slight haze. But you could still plainly see: the fields surrounding the New Fashion Pork facility, bright white on the hill above, drained directly into a DNR-maintained wetland restoration site.

The spot where New Fashion Pork had built swung deftly to the east of drainage points affecting local water supplies and therefore avoided Estherville and opposition from townspeople and the city council. But what about everyone downstream in Emmetsburg or Fort Dodge or the half million people who depend on the river in Des Moines? What about all the other Iowans who go to the tap expecting to find clean, safe water?

Chapter 15

WATER WORKS

The soaring, vaulted ceiling and complete quiet can make the filter building of the Des Moines Water Works (DMWW) feel like a cathedral. Tucked into sheltered niches on either side of the tiled gallery, the filters themselves look like nothing more than soaking pools at some long-forgotten Turkish bath, but their green-hued waters are pumped in from the Raccoon and Des Moines rivers, then slow-filtered, up to 50,000 gallons at a time, through 100 tons of gravel and 130 tons of sand. Linda Kinman, the policy analyst and watershed advocate at the DMWW, explained that this building had been in use since the 1940s, but the process it employs is ancient in its simplicity and has worked as effectively as ever—until recently.

Scientists at the water works have been tracking steady increases in levels of nitrates and *E. coli* in the contributing watersheds since the 1970s, when industrial agriculture first started to hit its stride. But in the last decade those levels have started to assume a predictable pattern: spikes track with periods of peak manure application with noticeable increases each November and then vertiginous leaps to dangerously high concentrations in late spring and early summer. And in the past decade those nitrate levels have started to pose greater and greater threats to public health—an even broader source of concern than the spread of antibiotic-resistant bacteria. And in 2013, the situation finally reached a crisis.

For three months straight, between the end of April and the end of July, as spring thaw then heavy downpours ran off drought-parched fields, scientists at the DMWW measured record nitrate loads coming into their treatment plant. Their public health officials issued alerts to warn parents on days when it was unsafe to let children drink from the tap, reminding them of the risk of "blue baby" syndrome. (Nitrate impairs the oxygen capacity of the bloodstream; in babies and toddlers the syndrome can effectively cut off their air supply, rendering them a deathly blue.) The Raccoon levels at one point reached 24.39 milligrams per liter, more than double the 10 mg/L required by the EPA for safe drinking water under the Clean Water Act.

The situation eventually grew so dire that the DMWW turned off its intakes from the Raccoon and Des Moines rivers and began drawing from alternative sources—lakes under its control, an aquifer storage system, the utility's underground filtration and storage hold. But as the months wore on and the backup sources began to run dry, the DMWW had no choice but to pull high-nitrate water from the Des Moines River, treat it, and mix it with what remained in the utility stores. By late July, the water flowing through the pipes was registering at 9.65 milligrams per liter. Kinman was granted a face-to-face meeting with the EPA and the Iowa DNR to discuss ways of reducing nitrate loads but came away without any promises. "The political scene in Iowa right now is almost over-the-top supportive of agriculture," Kinman told me.

After the Iowa environmental groups filed their suit in 2011, asking the EPA to take control of Clean Water Act enforcement, the federal agency had finally been forced to respond. In July 2012, it issued a scathing critique of the DNR's handling of the state's CAFOs, finding that the agency had failed to properly issue required permits for operating such a facility, to administer inspections of facilities, to respond to manure spills and other environmental violations, or to assess adequate fines and penalties when violations did occur. But nearly a year after the EPA report, the state of Iowa had still failed to take any action. Seeing the dangerous levels of nitrates—and the overall trend line of water contamination—the DMWW leadership decided they had to speak out publicly. "We didn't think we could afford to have that happening over and over, year after year," Kinman told me. "At some point, we will violate."

Apparently fearing that the crisis would give the EPA leverage to intercede, Governor Branstad stepped in. On May 20, 2013, he sent a letter to Acting EPA Administrator Bob Perciasepe and Assistant Administrator Gina McCarthy, whom President Barack Obama had nominated to lead the agency. Branstad denounced the CAFO compliance inspections as "the 'gotcha' approach." He insisted that "the majority of discharges into Iowa's waters are accidental spills" and claimed that runoff was unavoidable because it was "caused by Mother Nature." He demanded that McCarthy come to Iowa and meet with livestock industry leaders before recommending any new corse of action.

In August 2013, McCarthy, who had just been confirmed by the U.S. Senate, gave in; she met with the Farm Bureau members under the picnic shelter at the Iowa State Fairgrounds, pledging to establish a "more trusting relationship between EPA and the agriculture community." Jay Moore at New Fashion Pork told me, "It was just refreshing to hear her talk." But many rural residents felt betrayed; Barb Kalbach, a fourth-generation family farmer from Dexter, Iowa, questioned, "Whose side is McCarthy on? Corporate ag polluters or everyday people and the environment?" Within weeks, the EPA and Iowa had struck a deal: the state would reopen hiring for seven of the fourteen positions eliminated by the governor since 2011 and would allocate roughly $30 million to water quality initiatives.

Scientists at the Des Moines Water Works point out that the DNR's own report on the Raccoon River Watershed, issued in 2008, estimated that 98 percent of overall contamination in Iowa's waterways originates from manure. A second report, released in late 2011, estimated that "hog manure overall contributes about 63 percent of the bacteria load in the North Raccoon Watershed." The $30 million allocation, they say, is just too little to address the enormity of the problem, especially when the official stance of everyone involved—from the governor to the Environmental Protection Council to the Farm Bureau—is that excessive manure and soil erosion are not the root causes of the issue.

"I have four little grandkids," Kinman told me. She tells her daughter, who lives in a rural community, not to give her children tap water. "There are companies that make special bottled water for infants. I said, 'You buy that in the spring and the fall.'"

I told Dennis Hill, the microbiologist at the DMWW, that everyone at New Fashion Pork had insisted that high nitrate levels were the fault of commercial fertilizers and bacterial loads were the result of aging pipes and poor waste treatment in small towns along the rivers. Hill asked me to simply consider the numbers. There are now nearly 22 million hogs in Iowa and, according to a study conducted by Mark D. Sobsey, director of the University of North Carolina's Environmental and Virology and Microbiology Laboratory, each one produces about ten times the fecal matter of an average human. Human waste now accounts for roughly 1 percent of all fecal matter generated each year in Iowa. Are we really to believe *that* is the source of the state's water problem?

"Those little towns might as well straight-pipe their sewage to the river," Hill told me. "Compared to what comes in from agriculture, it wouldn't make any difference."

Gordon Brand, senior chemist at the DMWW, agreed with Dennis Hill's assessment. Brand explained that the drought in 2012 had set the stage for a disastrous convergence. Nitrogen-rich fertilizers applied that spring were never dissolved by the usual rains and remained near the surface. Also, with so many crops failing, there were fewer corn and soybean plants uptaking nitrogen, so it all remained in the soil. (In 2012, researchers from the Louisiana Universities Marine Consortium found that the lack of runoff that year had created one of the smallest hypoxic zones in the Mississippi River Delta since scientists began measuring in 1985.) By spring 2013, the ground was extremely hard and supersaturated with nitrogen. But farmers, concerned about the prospect of losing a second year's crops, spread more fertilizer. "The farmers like to apply a little bit more on the surface," Brand explained, "to give their corn plant a kick-start." But almost as soon as they had completed this fresh application, a series of heavy thunderstorms hit Iowa. "And the water's now really going through the soil," said Brand, "and that's not only this year's nitrate, but some of last year's."

Brand is the first to concede that nitrate problems are not exactly new in Iowa. In the 1980s, as the farm crisis led to consolidation and the rise of industrial agriculture, DMWW chemists began recording substantial increases in nitrate levels in the Raccoon River. That's when the DMWW built its intake at the Des Moines River, but soon the Des Moines was experiencing similar problems. In 1991, the DMWW built the world's largest nitrate removal plant, a massive negative-ionic system adjacent to the filter building, at a cost of nearly $4 million. The system was intended as an emergency backup, to be turned on in cases of spikes in nitrate levels. A decade later, the system was in operation for 106 days—and nitrate levels in the Raccoon River were continuing to rise. Finally, a comprehensive study of nitrate levels in relation to fertilizer application on the Des Moines River Watershed found that a combination of subsurface tile drainage and annual cropping that left soil exposed throughout the winter were miner-alizing the nitrogen from fertilizers, which then leached into the soil and ran off into waterways.

In response, the USDA provided nearly $40 million in fund-ing to restore buffers and maintain wetlands in the thirty-seven tile-drained counties of north-central Iowa on the Raccoon River Watershed. At the same time, a number of commercial fertilizer producers, led by Dow AgroSciences, banded together to create Agriculture's Clean Water Alliance in hope of encouraging farm-ers to embrace responsible application methods and avoid new regulations governing use of nitrogen fertilizers. Yet, even as meth-ods improved—enough for DMWW to take the nitrate filtration system off-line in 2007—more and more incentives were being created to take croplands out of conservation programs and put them back into production. Worse still, a significant shift in Iowa's law governing the vertical integration of livestock production en-couraged grand-scale construction of massive hog barns—and use of manure as a replacement for commercial fertilizers.

Brand said that the problem has grown too large for the Des Moines Water Works to engineer a technological solution. If the systemic pollution of Iowa's waterways is to be reduced, it will fall upon politicians—and the ordinary citizens who elect them—to demand that the row crop farms and livestock producers of the state comply with federal law. "The agricultural community says, 'We have to produce food. That's the core of who we are,'" Brand told me. "But the Des Moines Water Works says, 'We produce *water*. That's the core of who *we* are.' And do you know anybody who can get by without either food or water? There are better agri-cultural practices available, but the industry is resistant to change, to adopting something that they're not familiar with. We have to demand better practices. They are out there."

In April 2013, Jay Moore appeared again before the Emmet County Board of Supervisors to propose building another confinement on the east side of town. The tone was quite different from the year before. Supervisor Joe Neary pointed out that the county, in adopting a Good Neighbor policy, had asked that anyone undertaking a major construction project—including erecting a hog confinement—provide evidence that he had first sought out the approval of his neighbors. Neary said that two of farmers with land adjoining the proposed property had come to him to express their opposition to the project.

Supervisor Linus Solberg couldn't stand any more. His grandfather had come to Iowa from Norway more than a century before, and Solberg's father had bought a parcel of land near Estherville and farmed it until he was eighty-two years old. Now Solberg farmed that same land, raising a small herd of hogs. "Teddy Roosevelt broke up all those corporations and packing plants way back in the early 1900s," he had reminded a documentary film crew a few years before, but thanks to "high-priced lawyers in Washington, D.C.," the laws against vertical integration and monopolies were no longer enforced against meatpackers. "And it's just been a rat race trying to make a living and support yourself off the land," he said.

Now Solberg had a simple question for Moore.

"Why don't you guys build up in Minnesota?"

"The last thing we want to do is break any rules here," Moore said in reply. "We want to work with you."

"We want *you* to have the same respect for our people that you do for your pigs," Solberg replied, and moved that the supervisors bring the application to a vote. The permit was unanimously denied.

Despite the increasing contentious climate around Estherville— or maybe *because* of it—Brad Freking surprised me yet again in

November 2013. I asked if I could attend the inspection of a New
Fashion Pork facility near Estherville, and Freking agreed, re-
questing only that I check in with Jay Moore when I arrived at
the site and follow all biosafety protocols. By then, the porcine
diarrhea virus that had been ripping through herds earlier in the
fall had turned into an outright epidemic that would eventually
put a sizable dent in the national pork supply. I had quickly agreed
and soon after found myself waiting outside another New Fashion
Pork wean-to-finish operation, known officially as the Booth Site.

Moore arrived in the lot not long after I did, accompanied by
a large team from New Fashion, and a few minutes later the Iowa
DNR inspection team, led by environmental specialist Don Cunningham, pulled into the gravel parking area. Even before shaking
hands with Moore, Cunningham slipped plastic covers over his
boots and cinched them at the top. Cunningham is young, still in
his thirties, with a hawkish expression and by-the-book demeanor,
but he is one of the seniormost inspectors now at the DNR, one of
the few to elude the waves of departures under Governor Branstad.
He chatted briefly with Moore, then laid open the thick binder of
paperwork related to the site across the bed of his truck and went
point by point through the specifics of the manure management
plan. New Fashion Pork was preparing to pump the pit under
the confinement in a matter of days, applying that manure to the
tilled fields all around us. It was Cunningham's job to make sure
that the pit wasn't leaking, adding more manure to the soil than
the management plan allowed.

We walked around the outside of the facility—the pea gravel
crunching underfoot, pit fans roaring as they vented methane
off-gassing from the underground waste. "Primarily we're looking
for the integrity of the concrete. Is it cracking, or is it fresh and
sound?" Cunningham explained. "The pit fan is a direct port to
the manure that's underneath in that pit, so we look for any leak-
age coming from around those pit fan ports. Are there manure

leaks?" At every key spot, Cunningham squatted and snapped photos with his handheld digital camera. On this day, one of the seven newly hired inspectors followed along, observing the inspection from a cautious distance.

Later, I asked Cunningham to explain the seeming contradiction: here he was checking to make sure there were no minor leaks in the concrete or around the access ports, when in a matter of days nearly 300,000 gallons—by Moore's own estimation—of that same manure would be applied to these very fields. "We're really looking for accountability for the manure," Cunningham said. During periods of containment, the manure was supposed to be in the pit. During periods of application, the manure was supposed to be on the fields in the quantities and distribution approved by the DNR's manure management plan.

Cunningham paused a moment. He understood what I was driving at—but he wanted to be careful what he said. He told me that when he came out of South Dakota State University with a degree in wildlife and fisheries science, he had expected to get a job in biology and wildlife management. When those jobs weren't available, he worked in Farm Bill programs, encouraging farmers to put acres into CRP and instructing them on replanting native grasses and trees. When that funding dried up, he took his current job. He emphasized how much he generally enjoyed being outside and "working with livestock producers to keep the streams clean and keep soil where it should be," he said. "At the end of the day, we're still achieving some great things for natural resource management."

I told Cunningham that he seemed to be describing a series of compromises—perhaps even a regret that instead of working with wildlife, he was now expected to ensure the safety of massive confinements without ever even seeing the hogs inside. It wasn't that exactly, he told me. He said that when he was just out of college he'd worked in a breed barn near Emmetsburg, Iowa, not twenty-five miles from Estherville—a large farrowing facility very much like those run by New Fashion Pork. And he'd learned one thing: "Concentrated animal feeding operations are designed, really by definition, to house as many animals in as small a space as possible for maximum production. I think they do that very well—in terms of temperature and the amount of feed that they have and the amount of water that they have. Their barest essential needs are being met—but any animal has needs, and wants, beyond food, water, and shelter."

What bothered him, he said, was the knowledge that the behaviors that define these animals in the wild—rooting for food, wallowing in mud—were impossible in large-scale livestock production. "Any animal, I think, should have the opportunity to have dirt under their feet and the sun on their backs," he said. "But, of course, they can't have those things. There's no way that you could raise as many hogs and feed as many people if you were to put hogs on pasture for farrowing and feeding, thereby sacrificing millions of acres of row crop production." When I said that he seemed to be holding back, Cunningham paused again, longer this time, then sighed. He said he stuck to his job description: inspecting manure management plans, ensuring compliance with existing regulations, and reporting problems when they were observed.

At the end of the walk around the New Fashion Pork facility, Cunningham reviewed his observations with Jay Moore. He told Moore that the soil samples were out of date and noted that the well seemed to be closer to the confinement than entered on the Matrix application. (Moore later conceded that the well was only half the distance claimed on the original permit.) He informed Moore that there would be a formal notice of violation—the site's second in eighteen months. New paperwork would need to be submitted, and everything would proceed as before. He shook hands with Moore again and stripped off the plastic covers for his boots.

Within days, the confinement's pit was pumped dry and the fields injected with hundreds of thousands of gallons of manure.

And what became of Jay Lausen, who had expressed such concern for his family in the face of this endless cycle? Brad Freking sent me an e-mail in early 2014. "I thought you might be interested to know," he wrote, "Jay Lausen is now one of our growers."

Part Six

Chapter 16

THE CITY OF NO

The wind in Fremont seems always to be blowing—not just blowing but whipping.

When I reached the railroad tracks on the south edge of town, just past the corner of Union and Factory, in March 2012, the gate arm bobbed and crossbuck flapped, as the Union Pacific cars clacked and squealed into the headwind. Big flat-bottomed, billowy clouds—dark, ready for rain—trucked across the sky, over the Golden Sun Seeds silo, the Fremont Beef grain elevator, the twin Spam towers of the Hormel plant, and onward, shadowing the Platte Valley toward West Omaha. As I drove down the brick-laid boulevards, old oaks pitched and swayed overhead; American flags, anchored to the porch beams of neatly lined Victorians, snapped in the wind.

The gales were gusting so hard as I reached the Ostrom household on East Sixth Street that when Kristin unlatched the handle, the storm door flew open, slapping on its hinges, and she hustled me over the threshold. Inside, the house was an empty shell—all the furniture moved out, ghost trails worn on the wood floor where everything used to be—and the wind fluting through the leaded windows echoed down the halls. Kristin invited me to sit on the marble lip of the fireplace, joking that it was the only chair she had left. She sat in the middle of the floor, cross-legged, and marveled at the timing—that she and her husband would be closing on their house the next day, handing over their keys to new owners on the very day the anti-immigration ordinance she had so vehemently opposed officially was scheduled to go on the books.

Ostrom had scoffed at the housing portion of the ordinance when it was first proposed; it was simply unprecedented, she said, and she had never imagined it would hold up in superior court. So when the ordinance passed, Ostrom continued her efforts. When the ACLU, together with the Mexican American Legal Defense and Educational Fund (MALDEF), filed suit against the city of Fremont, they hired Ostrom full-time—and, initially, the legal team assumed that the courts would strike down the ordinance, just as they had with previous measures in other small towns, and that would mark an end to the long battle in Nebraska, too.

Instead, with former pro-ordinance councilman Charlie Janssen now in the legislature, the anti-immigration movement pressed its advantage. In January 2011, he introduced LB48—a bill clearly modeled after Arizona's LB1070, authored by Kris Kobach. But Janssen bristled at the suggestion of outside influence. "I've always said this is Nebraska-style," he said. But the legislation stalled at the hearing in March over language assigning the power to any peace officer to take steps to determine the immigration status of a person "when reasonable suspicion exists that the person is unlawfully present in the United States." In particular, other senators wanted clarification on what would constitute "reasonable suspicion."

In a public hearing, Senator Steve Lathrop, representative of the Twelfth District in Omaha, asked, "Can you think of anything besides skin color and a command of the English language that would provide a reasonable suspicion?" Janssen stumbled. "If you . . . you know, one scenario would be perhaps if you pulled somebody over in an unlicensed vehicle. Nobody knew exactly where they were going. There were way too many people in the vehicle as far as . . ." Video of the hearing shows that the gallery let out a collective gasp, then a disgruntled murmur passed up and down the rows until the sergeant at arms called for order. But Janssen proceeded. "There are ten people in a vehicle," he said, "that could be . . . reasonable suspicion." Ostrom thought the obvious racial profiling inherent in Janssen's comment would not only sink LB48 (as it did) but also the city of Fremont's legal defense, argued by Kobach, that there was no evidence of racial bias underlying the city ordinance.

But, then, in May 2011, the U.S. Supreme Court handed down a ruling in *Chamber of Commerce v. Whiting* that upheld Arizona's right to "suspend or revoke business licenses of employers who knowingly or intentionally hire unauthorized aliens." Two weeks later, the Court voided a lower court ruling on the ordinance in Hazleton, Pennsylvania, which, like the one in Fremont, not only sought to crack down on businesses that hire undocumented workers but also targeted the landlords who house them. Judge Laurie Smith Camp of the U.S. District Court for the District of Nebraska issued a declaratory judgment on the Fremont ordinance—a ruling that slapped the ACLU for arguing racial bias when they had pointed to no precedent cases in which "such scant evidence and conjecture has been found sufficient to support a conclusion that unlawful discrimination was a motivating factor in the enactment of the statute." Smith Camp struck down provisions of the ordinance that sought to bar the harboring of illegal aliens, revoke occupancy licenses if renters were found in violation, and impose fines on violators. However, she not only upheld the E-Verify provision, in keeping with the recent Arizona ruling, but also upheld the portion of the ordinance that empowered the city to require occupancy licenses in the first place.

Smith Camp's equivocating ruling appeared a marginal victory for anti-ordinance advocates (and the ACLU was quick to claim the win), but the judgment effectively closed a loophole in existing Nebraska law. With the advent of these housing permits, people would either have to lie on their application forms—an act that would likely violate laws for document fraud and Social Security fraud in Nebraska—or willingly acknowledge their illegal status on a form submitted at the Fremont Police Department that could then be entered into the FBI database, which, thanks to the Secure Communities program, was now linked automatically to U.S. Immigration and Customs Enforcement. For would-be renters who had entered the country without legal documentation, it was a classic catch-22: either admit to violating federal law, or lie and, in so doing, violate state laws. Many undocumented immigrants said they would simply pick up and move out of town—exactly as the architects of the ordinance had hoped they would. For Ostrom, the development was enough to convince her and her husband that Fremont was no longer their home.

"They're a lot smarter than I gave them credit for," Ostrom conceded. She rocked up and wrapped her arms around her knees, ruefully. The bare walls of her empty house creaked against the lashing wind outside. "I just found myself thinking, I can't live here anymore."

The couple that bought the Ostroms' home, Rafael del Jesus and his partner of thirteen years, April Wadleigh, got their keys to the house on the very day the ordinance went on the books. Their two children, Eleyanna and Audrek, went bellowing through the empty house, charging up and down the stairs with wild excitement, as April and Rafael stood outside with me—still marveling that this beautiful Victorian, with its wraparound porch looking out onto the boulevard, was really theirs.

The family had lived at Conestoga Crossing Apartments for two years, then moved to a snug duplex near the YMCA for the next six. All the while, Rafael had worked at Hormel, starting out droving animals through the chutes to the kill floor and eventually working his way up to running the spice mixer, a computerized system that chills and blends 9,000 pounds of sausage at a time. Rafael is disarmingly baby-faced, with Cabbage Patch cheeks and sad eyes; his emotions are just barely under the surface, and he had no qualms about working through his thoughts in front of a relative stranger. He freely admitted that he supported the ordinance when it was first proposed and only slowly came to oppose it.

We stepped into the new kitchen of their home, empty except for the two bar stools the Ostroms left at the island in the kitchen. Rafael paced while he talked, searching for the words to explain the source of his ambivalence. When he was eleven years old, he came to the United States with his brother from the Dominican Republic. By then, the boys had been separated from their mother for seven years while she worked to save up enough money and thread the bureaucracy of the immigration system to bring them to be with her in Brooklyn, New York. "Being honest with you," he said, "I did not want to come here." He could barely remember his real mother, and his grandmother was the only mother he knew.

But one day, after school, his grandmother told him, "You're going somewhere."

"I want to stay here with you," Rafael protested.

A black car pulled up to the curb, Rafael's brother already inside. "I jumped in," Rafael told me, "going I-don't-know-where, and we just went to the airport."

His eyes turned toward the ceiling and then toward the sidewalk out the kitchen window, as he struggled to regain his composure, but he couldn't do it. He broke into a quiet sob. "Let me tell it," April said gently, and Rafael went outside. She explained that Rafael had never been able to get over the double loss—first of his real mother when he was four, and then of his grandmother when he was eleven. He blamed the glacial pace of the immigration process and couldn't help but think that his wait might not have been so long, so painful, if there hadn't been so many illegal immigrants flooding into the country ahead of him. When the ordinance was proposed, Rafael thought, "Good," he told me later, "they should have to play by the same rules as me."

But then, Rafael started to notice a change in Fremont. After a night of drinking and dancing, a friend of his from work was stopped by a sheriff's deputy; he failed a field sobriety test and was put on probation for driving under the influence. Cruisers were always positioned at the western edge of town, picking up cars as they came in from the Mexican dance hall there—never outside the bars frequented by white Fremonters in town. Later that same friend's Habitat for Humanity home was one of those vandalized before the immigration vote in 2010. Most importantly, when Rafael and April applied for a home loan, they were initially denied because they didn't have any credit history. To build credit fast, Rafael bought a BMW sedan, but driving around Fremont in 2011 he had been repeatedly stopped by police demanding to see proof of ownership. When he was stopped a third time—this time on the pretext that his tinted windows were too dark—and police officers again asked to see proof of ownership, Rafael objected. He began "yelling and swearing at the officer," according to the Fremont deputy chief, and was arrested for disorderly conduct.

Rafael had grown quiet and withdrawn after that, but in the weeks after taking possession of the house, he was back to his old self. For Easter Sunday, April invited Rafael's friend from work and his family to come over for an egg hunt in the grass. April conceded that she wondered what the neighbors were thinking, watching a group of Hispanics out in the yard, grilling and playing with their children, but suddenly a thought occurred to her: "This was exactly what Kristin was fighting for."

At the end of October 2013, a daylong fog turned to light rain as the city council in Fremont convened for its monthly meeting. In chambers, a crowd packed into tight rows of folding chairs or stood at the back of the room, spilling out into the hallways. They'd been drawn by news that council member Todd Hoppe had asked the city attorney to draft an amendment repealing sections of Ordinance 5165, requiring renters to prove their citizenship in order to acquire occupancy licenses, and making it a crime for landlords to rent to undocumented immigrants. Hoppe, a manager at All Metals Market who also holds multiple rental properties in Fremont, was visibly wary as he took his seat. Craig Corn, an unsuccessful candidate for mayor in 2012, couldn't resist needling him. "You sure know how to draw a crowd, Todd," Corn called from the front row. Hoppe managed only a cautious smile.

The tone soon turned from tense to contentious. As Mayor Scott Getzschman opened with a pro forma resolution to thank third-grade students at Washington Elementary School on Fremont's largely Hispanic south side for inviting him to their classroom, Cindy Hart, the sister of petitioner Jerry Hart, called out from the second row, "How could you understand them?" (Later, at the lectern, she explained unapologetically, "I don't want Spanish in my schools.") It was the recommencing of a now-familiar refrain: that Fremont has been overrun by Hispanic immigration, that those immigrants are overwhelmingly in the country illegally, and that they create a drain on the city's resources—by requiring it to provide instruction in schools for English as a second language, by failing to pay for emergency care at the local hospital, or by collecting public assistance for food and housing.

But the facts about the Hispanic presence in Fremont were less cut-and-dried than the rhetoric. Proponents of the ordinance point to Washington Elementary as evidence that overwhelming numbers of Fremont preschoolers arrive unable to speak English, but the school's former principal told me that by the time those students are fifth graders, they score highest among the city's elementary schools on statewide reading comprehension exams. Similarly, the CEO of the Fremont Area Medical Center said that while it's true Hispanics account for roughly half a million dollars in unpaid medical bills each year, uninsured Hispanics actually pay up at a higher rate than uninsured white patients. By now, these well-worn points were less about mounting an argument than giving vent to the outrage at having to revisit a battle ordinance backers thought they had already won with 57 percent of the vote—and seen upheld despite repeated legal challenges.

In June 2013, a three-judge panel from the Eighth U.S. Circuit Court of Appeals reversed Judge Smith Camp's finding that the housing portions of the ordinance violated federal fair-housing laws. Then, just weeks before the city council meeting, the court rejected a petition by the ACLU and MALDEF to have the full Eighth Circuit court rehear their challenges. With that loss, opponents of the law seemed to be left only with the possibility of an appeal to the U.S. Supreme Court, which all parties agreed was unlikely with Congress promising to take up the immigration issue itself.

However, in October, Tim Butz, assistant director of the Fair Housing Center of Iowa and Nebraska, warned the city that there was a high risk that enforcement of the ordinance could be viewed as a violation of the Fair Housing Act. If so, the U.S. Department of Housing and Urban Development (HUD) could deny future Community Development Block Grant funding—and even demand repayment of millions of dollars in federal grants awarded to the city for downtown revitalization since the passage of the ordinance in June 2010. "I'm here to tell you that you need to act," Butz told the city council. "You cannot ignore this thing. You've got to do something to counteract the effect of the ordinance on the Hispanic population of this city." Following this meeting, Hoppe requested that an amendment be drafted to remove the potentially problematic sections of the ordinance. Supporters of the law, who had been celebrating their court victory and now expected the occupancy licensing provisions to be enacted at last, were enraged to learn that the council was instead exploring the possibility of repealing those sections.

As he opened the public-comment period of the meeting, Mayor Getzschman emphasized that the council had drafted the amendment so that it could better weigh its options and solicit the opinions of Fremont's citizens. Bob Warner stood at the lectern breathing impatiently into the microphone as the city clerk read the text of the amendment. By the time the clerk was done, Warner could barely contain his anger. "You already know what the people's wish was because they told you in a voting booth," he said, his voice so loud that his words were distorted by the speakers.

John Wiegert echoed Warner's outrage. "You're totally going against the will of the people and the decisions of the courts," he said to the council. "To think that you would use one of the best lawyers in the nation to represent us—and he's won every court decision—and then turn around and you stick it to him and the citizens of Fremont who voted for this, it's despicable." Wiegert went so far as to speculate that council members were "in cahoots" with attorneys from the ACLU and MALDEF. "We have a crooked government," he said. "You guys should be ashamed of yourselves."

But the most pointed criticism of the night came from Jerry Hart. "When you talk about the HUD grants," he started calmly, "what you forget to take into account is that the courts have already looked at this ordinance." He explained that the courts had ruled that the ordinance did not conflict with federal law and did not constitute discriminatory practice; if it came down to a struggle between HUD and the courts, Hart predicted, the courts "would have more say-so." He then straightened his papers on the lectern and turned to address Hoppe directly. "My opinion, based on the houses that you have: you're nothing but a slum landlord." Others, too, had asserted that Hoppe was pushing to repeal the housing provisions in order to keep his low-rent tenants, but Hart was more explicit. "You've got a house down on South Pierce that's inhabited by multiple families of Hispanics," he said. "Most of those, I understand, are illegal." The amendment, he added, was "underhanded, unscrupulous, backroom, immoral, unethical, Chicago-style politics."

Charlie Janssen, who was now seeking the Republican nomination for governor of Nebraska, rose to suggest a compromise. "This, to me, at this point isn't about illegal immigration anymore," he said. "It's about listening to your constituents." Repealing an ordinance that voters in sixteen of twenty precincts had approved was "just not right," he said. "If you want to do something, throw it back to the people. See where they're at."

It was after nine o'clock by the time the crowd spilled out onto the side streets along Military Avenue. The rain was picking up, but many people lingered, still talking under the streetlights, heedless of the shower and the cold. Most were loudly complaining about "illegals on food stamps" or "José in his lowrider." I stopped Hoppe as he was coming out of the building. He seemed circumspect, even shaken, by the anger he had unleashed. "That's just emotions, and I understand it; it's an emotional issue," he said. "It may seem that we're at opposite ends, but we're not. We want to take care of the illegal-alien issue in this community, and I believe everybody, when they voted, voted to take care of the illegal aliens. But sometimes they don't know what price tag is attached to that."

After seeing what he called "the ferocity" in chambers, he said he was inclined to heed Janssen's advice and put the issue to a ballot measure. "Honestly, I couldn't feel right passing it through the council," he said. "We need to look at a special election, making sure everybody can vote on whether they want to keep this part in the ordinance—asking everybody, before we go ahead, 'Are you sure you want to pull these purse strings?' "

A month later, the Fremont City Council met for a second reading of the amendment. But before the reading could even begin, council member Jennifer Bixby introduced a resolution to call a special election that would put the decision before voters. Another heated public-comment period followed, in which ordinance supporters pointed out that four thousand citizens had already cast their ballots in favor of it in 2010. Former council member Bob Warner demanded of Mayor Getzschman, "Do you represent the four thousand? Or do you represent Hormel?"

After comments closed, Bixby's resolution passed by a vote of 7–1. There would be a special election on February 11, 2014, to decide if the citizens of Fremont still wanted to implement the ordinance.

In the weeks before the vote, everything looked positive for ordinance opponents. An anti-ordinance group, called Fremont YES, raised $71,000 for signs and advertising compared to just $8,000 brought in by ordinance supporters. In the run-up to the special election, Mayor Getzschman appeared in a pro-repeal TV commercial. A slate of ads ran on local radio. The editors of the *Fremont Tribune* endorsed the yes vote. The owner of a billboard at the far end of the overpass crossing the Union Pacific tracks—the most visible spot in town—donated the space to Fremont YES.

By the day of the special election, old tensions were again nearing a boil. Poll workers at the Precinct 3C voting station—relocated to the frozen foods section of Brady's Meats & Foods just before the election, because it was the only handicapped-accessible building on Fremont's poor south side—told me that they had been forced to ask several people to leave. One woman, upon discovering that her home was technically outside the city limits, disqualifying her from voting, pointed at lined-up Hispanic voters waiting to cast ballots and demanded to know, "Why do *they* get to vote, and I don't?"

But by the time the polls were set to close, the wind had picked up outside and temperatures plummeted, cooling tempers and reducing the flow of voters to a trickle. Bryan Lopez, who worked gutting cattle on the kill floor at Cargill Meat Solutions in Schuyler, filled out his ballot at a table next to refrigerator cases filled with ice cream, then dropped the form into the locked box. "I voted yes," he told me, but he wasn't optimistic about the vote's outcome. "People who want this, I hope they're making an educated decision, instead of just being on the bandwagon."

His hope echoed the message pushed by Mayor Getzschman and several city council members: that the ordinance would do considerable financial damage to the city but resolve none of the underlying problems. Before the 2010 ballot measure many people didn't know that the Hormel Foods plant and the Regency II trailer park both fell outside the city limits and therefore would be exempt from employment and housing portions of the ordinance. People didn't know that the city would have to lay off employees and raise taxes to fill coffers for a $1.5 million legal defense fund. They didn't know the potential threat to federal block grants being used to redevelop the downtown. Now, with benefit of hindsight and knowledge of these factors, the majority of the city leaders hoped Fremonters would vote to repeal the ordinance. Instead, as soon as the polling stations closed, early results showed not only that voters had upheld the ordinance, but that the margin of victory had actually widened.

Blake Harper, the landlord who had joined the ACLU suit, was disappointed by the outcome but not surprised. "I'm embarrassed and ashamed, but I'm not shocked that Fremont has enough closet bigots to carry the vote," Harper told me when I reached him by phone in Pennsylvania, not long after the election results were posted. Then he sighed. "Well, maybe not so closeted."

In fact, on the east side of town, pro-ordinance group Our Votes Should Count, founded by John Wiegert, held a loud celebration at the Gathering Place, complete with an impassioned address by Charlie Janssen. There were cheers and applause as the final tally—60 percent opposed to the repeal, 40 percent in favor—was held up on poster-board signs. A big band struck up, and people started dancing. Janssen slipped into the icy quiet outside to field a few phone calls from reporters. "It is pretty rocking inside," he told one. "They're enjoying an evening that culminated several years of hard work." Emboldened ordinance supporters were vowing to ride the momentum of their victory into efforts to recall Mayor Getzschman and all of the city council members who had brought the repeal to the ballot.

Harper didn't dismiss that possibility, but he said that the problem in Fremont would only grow now—as more and more young people move away to Omaha and Lincoln and more and more immigrants arrived in Fremont to work. "As long as Hormel is processing thirteen hundred hogs per hour," he said, "there will continue to be high demand for low-wage, unskilled labor. This is a demand that cannot be filled by the local workforce and cannot be stymied by silly ordinances." I asked Harper what his next move would be. He paused a moment, then laughed. "You want to buy some duplexes in Fremont?"

Later that same evening, Jonathan Chavez, one of Harper's renters at those duplexes, returned home from a twelve-hour shift at Midwest Manufacturing in Valley, Nebraska, about ten miles down the highway from Fremont. His girlfriend, Kayla Jacquart, patted and burped their five-week-old son, Jameson. The previous July, when Jacquart found out she was pregnant, they started looking for a larger apartment. She spotted the FOR RENT sign here, and after Chavez talked to Harper at length, they were convinced that this was the place for them. "It's two bedrooms—so he has his own room," Jacquart said, bouncing Jameson on her knee. "It's perfect for us right now."

They were both hoping to return to school in the fall. Jacquart was completing a degree at Metropolitan Community College in Omaha, and Chavez, who had recently graduated from Midland College, was hoping to pursue a master's in business management. He worked as a shift manager for the moment and figured that an advanced degree would help his chances of becoming a plant manager one day. When that happens, he said, breaking into a broad smile, "we can get out of here, and get our own place. Get out of Fremont." He hoped eventually to buy a home in Omaha where they could settle down.

It's a far cry from Chavez's beginnings in Guerrero, Mexico. Like so many people in Fremont and Schuyler, he was born in the mountain town of Chichihualco and came to the United States when he was still a toddler. After his parents split, his mother bought a trailer in Regency II and went to work on the line at Hormel. It was a hard life, he said. His mother had recently had her whole arm crushed by a machine at work, requiring multiple surgeries, and he wasn't sure how she was paying the doctor's bills. But he took issue with the way that the trailer park has become a stand-in for Fremont's ills. "If you come here and don't have documents and only Hormel is going to hire you, that's all you can get," he said. "Obviously, it's trailers. It's not nice fancy homes. But people are people." He said that he had a happy childhood there, held down a 3.75 grade point average in high school, and received academic and soccer scholarships to Midland. "I lived there, and I'm okay," Chavez said with a smile.

Affirming the passage of the ordinance, even if it means costing the city millions of dollars, won't stop the influx of immigrants who are willing to make that journey and work jobs at Hormel in return for giving their kids a better life. All it means, Chavez said, is that young people like him, once they've received their education and are ready to work and start families, get as far away from Fremont as possible. That was certainly his plan. But, for now, he had to get some rest. Jameson was finally ready for bed, and Jonathan had to be back up and on the road to work by 5 a.m.

He smiled again, but a little wearily this time. "It's a lot—having a kid and working," he said. "But I got to pay the rent, right?"

It's four o'clock in the morning when Raul Vazquez rises from bed in Schuyler and begins readying for another day's shift at Hormel. He puts the coffee on and gets dressed—always in a sweater to keep off the chill of the refrigerated ham department. He fills his thermos and then starts out on his predawn rounds, checking in on his wife's cousins, picking up another cousin who works on the kill floor. The streets in Schuyler are still dark—but they are anything but abandoned. Headlights hunt down the side streets and out onto Colfax; they crawl across the overpass—the grain elevators and the city water tower floodlit from below—and then jog east onto Sixteenth Street. Most mornings, when Raul reaches Highway 30, the clock on his dash reads just 4:50 a.m., but already a phalanx of cars stretches out before him, snaking toward Fremont.

This sunrise exodus, uninterrupted by the passage of the ordinance, is daily proof of just how completely the immigrant workforce brought in to work on the line at Hormel—and other plants in the area like it—has changed the face of rural Nebraska. In May 2014, the U.S. Supreme Court declined to hear the ACLU's appeal of the ruling handed down by the 8th Circuit U.S. Court of Appeals, thus allowing both the E-Verify portion of the ordinance and the housing permit portion of Fremont's ordinance to stand. "It's final now, and Fremont's victory is complete," Kobach said. More than that, he said, the decision gave a "bright green light" for other cities to pass similar measures. Soon, he predicted, there could be similar ordinances introduced in other towns in Nebraska, or in Minnesota and Iowa, or in Arkansas, Missouri, and the Dakotas. "It is beyond question that every city in the 8th Circuit has the ability to adopt the Fremont ordinance, word for word."

But unresolved are rather potent and polarizing questions: Who will determine the face of small-town America? Will it be a de facto decision made by the unstoppable tide of changing demographics or will it be preordained and enforced by decree? Will ordinances sprout up, as Jim Crow laws did across the rural south, to forestall the inevitable? Whatever happens, Raul Vazquez hopes to stay in Schuyler, to one day have his business loan paid off and be making enough to quit his job on the line and spend his days with Miguela behind the counter at the liquor store. But for now he still has to rise before dawn to make the journey each morning to the south edge of Fremont and trim the fat from bins of hams at Hormel for another employee to gather for cans of Spam. It's awful work, but his family depends on the job to pay the bills, and he doesn't want to be late.

Chapter 17

INSPECTION

In May 2013, the USDA's Office of the Inspector General (OIG) released a report with the decidedly bland title "Inspection and Enforcement Activities at Swine Slaughter Plants." But the findings of the report proved a flashpoint for the agency. OIG concluded that, after more than a decade, enforcement by FSIS of food safety protocols in pork processing plants participating in the experimental HIMP project was so lax that, between 2008 and 2011, three of the plants included in the pilot program were among the ten that had received the most noncompliance records of any plant. That's out of 616 nationwide.

The identities of the plants were not included in the report— but several could be matched to their violation history from the descriptions provided. Most noticeably, one of the worst offenders was described as "a plant in Nebraska that slaughtered about 10,600 swine per day." Only two plants in Nebraska—the Farmland plant in Crete and the Hormel plant in Fremont— fit that general description. And the only location in Nebraska listed among "all sites visited" in preparing the audit report was Fremont. Still, all branches of the USDA steadfastly declined to confirm—or deny—that identification, even after Dan Hoppes, president of the United Food and Commercial Workers Local 293 in Fremont, told me, "Yeah, that's us."

But denials didn't change the stark facts: FSIS recorded a total of 607 violations at that plant, roughly three per workweek, including 50 repeat violations for "yellow fibrous fecal material" on hog carcasses bound for processing and another 39 repeat violations for "yellowish colored residue" and a scum of flesh and fat inside storage vats. A line worker told me he had so often seen "chunks of stinky, rotting meat" inside sausage grinders at the Fremont plant that he had instructed his wife not to buy anything containing Hormel ground meat at the supermarket.

The inspector general felt that these violations should have resulted in a written warning or even a plant shutdown—something the USDA does only about seven times a year in the entire country—but no such actions were taken. Worse still, the report notes an instance where an inspector in Nebraska spotted fecal matter on the hind foot of a carcass that had moved past the plant's quality control employees "without being detected"—which is considered a "more serious violation" because it "would impact food safety of the product." The report concluded that investigation "revealed a systemic failure and not a sporadic problem, including recurring zero-tolerance violations."

The report also never provided any identifying information about the plant that incurred the most violations nationwide from 2008 to 2011—other than to say it was a HIMP plant. However, noncompliance records for 2012, obtained by a Freedom of Information Act request by the nonprofit watchdog group Food & Water Watch, revealed that the Quality Pork Processing plant in Austin had far and away the most violations of any HIMP plant. And the portrayal of conditions inside the plant, as collectively created by those records, is sometimes harrowing.

During 2012 alone, QPP received more than 225 noncompliance records, including 60 violations for meat contaminated by fecal matter or intestinal contents. More disturbingly, FSIS inspectors noted eight separate instances where carcasses had to be condemned for disease after having been approved for butchering by plant quality assurance auditors. In March, inspectors found an undetected four-inch cancerous tumor. In April, they found full-body inflammation from bacterial infection in one hog, lesions from tuberculosis in another, malignant lymphoma in a third. In June, another carcass with a "grossly enlarged thymic gland" was determined to be cancerous. In August, one hog showed signs of muscle degeneration; in September, another was determined to have septic arthritis after a bloody fluid was noted discharging from its joints. Several of these were classified as "stumble-on" records—that is, chance findings past critical control points, which should therefore be considered zero-tolerance violations. In many cases, these violations were discovered so late in the process that the reports conclude with some variation of the same comment: "Had the inspector failed to retain this carcass, it would have entered commerce."

The inspector general warned: "Since there are no substantial consequences for plants that repeatedly violate the same food safety regulations, the plants have little incentive to improve their slaughter processes. It is critical that plants work towards preventing violations from occurring in the first place because recurring, severe violations may jeopardize public health." Stricter enforcement, the report concluded, is necessary to ensure that "the nation's commercial supply of pork is safe and wholesome."

When the inspector general's report was released, Philip Derfler, deputy administrator of the FSIS, told me there was no cause for alarm, that the additional violations were only evidence that inspectors in HIMP plants were conducting more thorough checks in the kill area. "Given the fact that we're looking at it a lot more intensely," he said, "it's not surprising that we find more of it." And inspectors spotting cancerous growths and lymph nodes swollen with tuberculosis only proved, he said, that visual inspection, followed up by microbiological testing, is an adequate tool for identifying disease.

But I couldn't help wondering: if the HIMP model of inspection is truly superior, why then has the public been kept largely uninformed of the results of this decade-long government study on food safety—and blocked from knowing the identities of the participating plants? Even leaders at Local 293 in Fremont were unaware of the OIG report—and, after I asked about the inspection record at the Hormel plant there, national UFCW leadership hastened to provide me with data showing that meatpacking plants under union control generally have better records of worker and food safety.

They pointed to statistics showing that the Hormel plant in Fremont has tracked at or below industry-wide numbers for rates of injury and illness since the advent of the HIMP inspection model. But the overall statistics conceal the fact that plant workers still suffer major lacerations and amputations at a rate of 1 percent per year—slightly more than one major injury per month. For workers who work at any meatpacking plant for five years, their chances of suffering a serious injury are nearly fifty-fifty. And an extensive study of packinghouse workers conducted by the University of Iowa in 2008 suggested that the actual number of injuries may be significantly underreported. In the last decade, the large numbers of undocumented workers hired by the industry have demonstrated a reluctance to report injuries or file workers' compensation claims. The Iowa study revealed that Hispanic workers are almost half as likely to report an injury as their white counterparts; one would assume that the rate of reporting is even lower among undocumented Hispanic workers, who often underreport for fear of firing or deportation. "The speed of work is causing an epidemic of quietly crippling injuries," Darcy Tromanhauser, program director for Immigrants & Communities at Nebraska Appleseed, told me. "People who work in meat and poultry make tens of thousands of repetitive motions each shift that cause permanent damage to their nerves, tendons, and bones, often leading to multiple surgeries and chronic pain."

Mark Lauritsen, director of the UFCW Food Processing, Packing, and Manufacturing Division, said, "It's not so much the speed; it's how many people are put on that job." Today, he said, it was no longer plant supervisors who monitored production speed with a watch. Now every plant has a union-hired industrial engineer, who walks the plant floor with a stopwatch around his neck, counting the cogs in the chain to monitor the number of carcasses per minute. If the speed starts to creep up, the union is pushing for additional workers on the line.

In Fremont, for example, Hormel bought property adjacent to the plant and, in May 2011, announced that they would be expanding the Spam facility and adding more jobs. Industry critics such as Tony Corbo at Food & Water Watch complain that Hormel has simply been rewarded for running one of the most unsafe plants in the country and now intends to shift more of its production there, but Lauritsen countered that the expansion is a positive development for workers and consumers alike. It not only creates additional jobs but also ensures that there are more hands to keep pace with the line, reducing the likelihood of accidents and increasing the cleanliness of the process. Workers in pork processing plants should be grateful, union officials say. While other industries have been fighting slow sales since the recession, Hormel has seen soaring earnings on the strength of sales of Spam. Meeting that demand through government-sanctioned increases in their line speeds and increasing market share means job security and opportunities to advance.

Tromanhauser told me she understood why the union didn't want to discourage anything that created jobs but cautioned that line speeds in meatpacking plants are now "dangerously fast." And rather than improving job opportunities, "what we hear from people across Nebraska and the country is that line speeds are increasing while staffing ratios are decreasing." The Hormel plant in Fremont, for example, has increased the speed of its lines by roughly 50 percent in the last decade—while their workforce has increased by about 20 percent.

Derfler said that FSIS doesn't have time to watch out for—much less document—risks to worker safety. If a violation is observed, he said, inspectors will report it to OSHA, but "the focus is on the safety of the food." Hany Sidrak, director of FSIS's Recall Management Staff, underscored this point by conceding that injuries and amputations are inevitable—that, in fact, he had personally witnessed such incidents while conducting site inspections—but his attention remained solely focused on food safety. "In such an incident, FSIS will deal with it as a sanitary issue and will stop operations to make sure that all human blood is completely cleaned off and that all product is protected," he said. "FSIS will not release the area or the line unless all products are identified as protected and cleaned—or whatever needs to be condemned is condemned because it cannot be made clean."

The reassurances of FSIS officials hark back to a famed passage from *The Jungle*. Sinclair vividly described the government inspector of hogs, "who sat in the doorway and felt of the glands in the neck for tuberculosis." He showed no signs of worry or fear that diseased carcasses might slip past his examination. In fact, if you struck up a conversation with this inspector, Sinclair wrote, he was only too glad "to explain to you the deadly nature of the ptomaines which are found in tubercular pork; and while he was talking with you could hardly be so ungrateful as to notice that a dozen carcasses were passing him untouched."

Likewise, today, it seems that we are not so much concerned with safety as promoting an illusion of safety. We feel assured that we are protected from illness, when, in fact, the real illness is the pretense we, as Americans, must collectively agree upon—In order to maintain the mirage of safe food, a safe workplace, well-treated livestock, a healthy environment, a strong economy, and a cohesive and equitable culture. In the case of Hormel, the disconnect is only so stark because the goal, producing greater and greater quantities of Spam, seems so absurd.

One late afternoon at the Labor Center office in Austin, I asked Dale Chidester if he ever stepped back and marveled at all this—the unyielding forward motion of production, all the people injured in the name of constant growth and increased output.

Chidester smiled and asked if I knew the formula for Spam. I shook my head.

By volume, he said, Spam is more than 27 percent fat. Two slices equals roughly half of your recommended intake of saturated fat for the entire day. The formula established by Julius Zillgitt in the 1930s as a way of getting rid of trimmings was now difficult to meet, because specially bred and genetically engineered hogs were getting leaner and leaner to satisfy buyers of pork chops and hams. "Do you know they have to truck in fat from other plants?" he asked. "Think about that."

Every day, all across the Midwest, hogs were—and are—being herded up ramps and shipped to the loading docks at QPP and Hormel in Fremont to match the relentless pace required to process 5 million hogs a year. Still more trimmings from millions more animals are loaded and brought in. And why? All because seventy-five years ago, the company established a corner on a niche market for cheap canned meat, and they have been holding on for dear life ever since. And to keep the whole production structure in place for times of prosperity when people are buying pork chops and hams, Chidester told me, in lean times like these when there's high demand for Spam, the company gives away those quality fresh cuts to the United Way and as part of international aid packages, just for the tax break.

I slumped back in my chair at the thought of this. "How do you go to work in the morning?" I asked. Chidester just laughed. You don't think about such things while you're working on the line, he explained; mostly you try not to think about anything at all. Your muscles remember and repeat. "It's like tying your shoes," he said, and that was that. You do what you're told, and at the end of the day, you go home to your family.

In January 2014, Hormel announced that the company would be shifting production of its bacon bits from the Tony Downs Foods plant in St. James, Minnesota, to the relatively new plant that Hormel had built in Dubuque, Iowa. Industry insiders were unsurprised; Hormel had been complaining for some time that the overhead in maintaining a specialized plant was too high, while the Dubuque plant, operated under the name Progressive Processing and originally designed to expand Hormel's line of microwaveable dinners, had been running below capacity because of flagging sales of high-cost, ready-made meals. Even at the plant's grand opening in 2010, CEO Jeffrey Ettinger acknowledged that the recession had caused sales to dip, so initial plans for two microwave meal production lines had been ditched in favor of turning one of the lines into a meat canning line. This meant that the Dubuque plant was well positioned to take over any of Hormel's high-demand canned meat lines, including bacon bits.

So company executives had approached Dubuque's economic development team to see if the city would offer incentives for expanding and adding as many as one hundred new jobs. City and state officials approved a $4.1 million incentives package, including state tax benefits, the extension of an existing tax increment financing agreement with the city of Dubuque, and a jobs-training partnership with Northeast Iowa Community College. Hormel accepted the offer and soon announced the expansion, but the press statements included an intriguing mystery. The city said that the bacon bits line was just the first of "two new production lines sought for the plant." Mark Seckman, vice president of national marketing for Greater Dubuque Development Corporation, would only elaborate by saying that he felt the deal "favorably positions us for Phase 2."

When Hormel submitted the blueprints for the nearly $30 million building permit application, a reporter for the *Dubuque Telegraph Herald* discovered that most of the design schematics were labeled "Bacon Bits Relocation"—but one was labeled "Spam." Upon closer inspection, he found that several of the bacon bits documents also contained production equipment and structural elements for the "Spam project." Rick Williamson, Hormel's manager of external communications, confirmed that Phase 2 of the project would be a Spam production line and that the product would join "the plant's exports." The news spread instantly. Hormel had not expanded Spam production into a new facility since the acquisition of the Fremont plant in 1947; this development indicated that the brand was continuing to thrive despite the downturn and showed that export demands were growing too rapidly for Fremont and Austin to keep up.

More than that, the shift of production to Dubuque may signal a new era of plant design—one where the linear design demanded by traditional meat inspection is no longer required. Mark Zelle, the plant manager at Progressive Processing, has been with Hormel for thirty years, running the Stockton, California, plant before taking over in Dubuque. But most of Zelle's experience has been in Hormel's labs and serving as a quality control manager, both in Stockton and at the plant in Beloit, Wisconsin. In that time, he had begun to imagine a production model where the cut line was replaced by a modular system of interconnected but independent rooms, where independent processes could be sped up according to demand. "By separating operations," he told an industry magazine, "the plant can potentially run 24/7," without having to shut the entire production line down for cleaning.

But decentralizing production also implied something significant. It meant that production at the Dubuque plant would be too spread out to be covered by traditional inspection by the USDA. Did Hormel know something they weren't saying publicly? Were the elevated line speeds that had confined production of Spam to two plants about to be implemented more broadly?

In an emailed statement to reporters, Hormel's spokesman Williamson would only say, "The timing for the Spam operation is still in process, and we anticipate production to begin in early 2015." A USDA spokeswoman, meanwhile, said the department would not comment until completion of its evaluation of HIMP for pork was made public in March 2014. When that deadline came and went, I filed a FOIA request for materials used to prepare the report. I got a letter from the USDA approving the request, but I never received any materials. Another spokeswoman said I could sue if I was dissatisfied, bit I was advised against it by Adina H. Rosenbaum, part of the litigation group at the watchdog group Public Citizen in Washington, D.C. She said Public Citizen had successfully sued FSIS in the past and still not gotten access to the documents they had requested. "If the USDA is committed to keeping documents from you," she said, "you won't be able to get them."

My last morning in Austin, I parked across the road from the plant and rolled down the windows. It was still cold, the snow piled along the sidewalks turning gray and pitted. As the day shift started up, the smell was unmistakable: fresh pig shit and baking ham. Along the access road, marked Hormel Drive, eighteen-wheelers came barreling in, pulling livestock trailers. They took the corner through the chain-link gate and reversed into the loading docks, all but concealed by the barrier wall. But as each new truck arrived, I could hear the beeping of the backup warning, then the rattle of rear doors opening. And then there was the sound of sizzling electric prods, the clatter of cloven hooves on metal grating, and the guttural, almost human, screeching of hogs.

I saw the QPP security guard trundle out to his pickup truck and begin circling the block, driving by again and again. But he couldn't touch me. I was on a public street, next to Horace Austin Park with its clear view of the Cedar River. I sat and watched as evidence of our national industry and know-how arrived by the truckload. Our whole history of conquering the West, industrializing agriculture, and turning hog slaughter into a "custom meat operation" arrived right there at QPP's door. And, in that moment, an illness like PIN and all the other social ills brought on by Hormel in their quest for increased output seemed an inevitable by-product of an industry that has grown too large and gained too much momentum to ever stop or even slow down.

I rolled up the windows and turned the key in the ignition. More than nineteen thousand hogs were processed at QPP that day. It was a day like any other.

ACKNOWLEDGMENTS

Portions of this book originally appeared as:

"Cut and Kill," *Mother Jones*, July–August 2011

"Why Big Ag Loves the Drought," onearth.org, December 10, 2012

"This Land Is Not Your Land," *Harper's*, February 2013

"Spam's Shame," slate.com, May 31, 2013

"Gagged by Big Ag," *Mother Jones*, July–August 2013

"Who Belongs in Fremont, Nebraska?" harpers.org, November 1, 2013

"The Truth about This Pork Chop and How America Feeds Itself," *Bloomberg Businessweek*, December 5, 2013

"The City of No," harpers.org, February 14, 2014

"Hog Wild," *OnEarth*, Spring 2014

An excerpt in *The Nation*, September 2014.

Grateful acknowledgment is made to Brad Wieners, Christopher Cox, Jeremy Keehn, George Black, Scott Dodd, Betsy Reed, and John Swansburg for their editorial input. Special thanks to Clara Jeffery for her early support—giving tough feedback but also ample room within the pages of *Mother Jones*. Thanks to Ryann Liebenthal, Maddie Oatman, Zaineb Mohammed, and especially Joe Kloc for their fact-checking, research, and additional reporting. Particular gratitude to Don Fehr at Trident Media Group, for seeing a book here from the start, to Tim Duggan at Harper-Collins for making it happen, and to Calvert D. Morgan Jr., Emily Cunningham, and Kathleen Baumer for getting me across the finish line. Last but not least, my thanks to Mary Anne Andrei for her co-reporting and her photographs.

NOTES

PROLOGUE

xi   *Maria Lopez will never forget that day*: Interview with "Maria and Fernando Lopez" (not their real names) was conducted in Fremont, Nebraska, November 2013.

xi   *the line had jumped recently, from 1,000 hogs per hour to more than 1,100*: Line speeds throughout the book are derived from a variety of sources; they come, most often, from worker recollection and have been verified against union records whenever possible.

xiii   *"reduce the speed of the processing line to minimize the severe and systemic risks"*: Petition filed on September 3, 2013, http://www.splcenter.org/sites/default/files/splc_osha_poultry_worker_safety_petition.pdf.

xiii   *an extensive study of packinghouse employees conducted by Nebraska Appleseed in 2009*: "'The Speed that Kills You': The Voice of Nebraska's Meatpacking Workers," Nebraska Appleseed, 2009, http://boldnebraska.org/uploaded/pdf/the_speed_kills_you_030910.pdf.

PART I

1: The Brain Machine

3   *Matthew Garcia felt feverish and chilled*: Interviews with "Matthew Garcia" (not his real name) were conducted in Austin, Minnesota, and via telephone throughout 2010 and 2011.

4   *a J-shaped, steel-encased bench called the "head table"*: Line speeds and working conditions at QPP between 2000 and 2006 are well documented. A map of

the cut line and detailed descriptions of the plant operations, as prepared by the Minnesota Department of Health, were published in Stacy M. Holzbauer, Aaron S. DeVries, et al., "Epidemiologic Investigation of Immune-Mediated Polyradic-uloneuropathy Among Abattoir Workers Exposed to Porcine Brain," *PLoS ONE*, March 2010, e9782.

5   *On December 11, Garcia awoke to find he couldn't walk*: Garcia provided access to his medical file, maintained by his caseworker Roxanne Tarrant at Employee Development Corporation in St. Paul. All medical records are derived from Tarrant's monthly reports.

7   *"They are state-of-the-art facilities (nothing to be squeamish about!) but media tours are not available"*: Email communication from Julie Henderson Craven, Vice President, Corporate Communications, Hormel Foods, February 26, 2010.

7   *Litchfield Building on Mill Street in November 1891*: Details of Hormel's early years of operation derive from Richard Dougherty, *In Quest of Quality: Hormel's First 75 Years* (St. Paul: North Central, 1966).

8   *By the turn of the century, the plant was processing 120 hogs per day*: From 1948 to 1952, socialist Fred H. Blum conducted groundbreaking work in Austin, Minnesota, studying how Jay C. Hormel's Guaranteed Annual Wage Plan affected company productivity and worker satisfaction. His findings, from which I have taken numerous details, were published in Fred H. Blum, *Guaranteed Annual Wages: A Case Study* (Berkeley: University of California Press, 1952); and Fred H. Blum, *Toward a Democratic Work Process: The Hormel-Packinghouse Workers' Experiment* (New York: Harper & Brothers, 1953).

9   *"benevolent dictatorship"*: Blum, *Toward a Democratic Work Process*, 4.

10   *six hundred Hormel workers to sign up on the spot*: Roger Horowitz, *Negro and White, Unite and Fight! A Social History of Industrial Unionism in Meatpacking, 1930–90* (Champaign: University of Illinois Press, 1997), 42.

10   *"I am not going to get mixed up in a fight in my hometown"*: *Austin Daily Herald*, September 23, 1933, 1, quoted in Blum, *Toward a Democratic Work Process*, 10.

10   *"He suggested that we go out and organize"*: Horowitz, *Negro and White, Unite and Fight!*, 42.

10   *"I couldn't lick you, so I joined you"*: Frances Levison, "Hormel: The Spam Man," *Life*, March 11, 1946, 63.

10   *"red capitalist"*: "The Name Is HOR-mel," *Fortune*, October 1937, 138. A decade later, Frances Levison wrote that Hormel had been "labeled everything from pale pink to red." Levison, "Hormel: The Spam Man," 63.

11   *Just as Emiliano Ballesta's shift at QPP was ending*: Interviews with "Emiliano Ballesta" (not his real name) were conducted in Austin, Minnesota, throughout 2010 and 2011.

12   *Hormel employees told the* New York Times: Andrew Martin, "Spam Turns Serious and Hormel Turns Out More," *New York Times*, November 15, 2008, B1.

14   *Julius A. Zillgitt went to the Square Deal Grocery on Main Street in Austin*: Carolyn Wyman, *Spam: A Biography* (New York: Harcourt Brace, 1999), 7.

14   *"the can, the solder, the seam, the fill, the mix"*: Wyman, *Spam: A Biography*, 7.

15   *"along about the fourth or fifth drink they began showing some imagination"*. Dan Armstrong and Dustin Black, *The Book of Spam: A Most Glorious and Definitive Compendium of the World's Favorite Canned Meat* (New York: Atria Books, 2008), 63.

15   *To launch the product, Hormel's marketing team*: Description of the marketing strategies derive from Dougherty, *In Quest of Quality: Hormel's First 75 Years*, 163.

15   *"If they think Spam is terrible"*: Brendan Gill, "The Talk of the Town: Spam Man," *New Yorker*, August 11, 1945, 15.

15   *"I ate my share of Spam along with millions of other soldiers"*: Dwight D. Eisenhower's signed letter of June 29, 1966, to H. H. "Tim" Corey, president of George A. Hormel & Company, is on display at the Spam Museum in Austin, Minnesota. An unsigned file copy, retained by his staff, is at the Eisenhower Presidential Library and Museum (Post-Presidential Papers, 1961–1969: 1966 Principal File, Box 27) in Abilene, Kansas.

17   *Richard Schindler, a family care physician*: Interview with Daniel Lachance was conducted at the Mayo Clinic, Rochester, Minnesota, February 2010. See also Howard Bell, "Inspector Lachance," *Minnesota Medicine*, November 2008, 22–27.

17   *Schwartz and Hidalgo noticed the similarity of symptoms*: Interview with Walter Schwartz was conducted in Austin, Minnesota, April 2010.

17   *Carole Bower, the plant's occupational nurse, who reported that she had been noticing*: Interview with Carole Bower was conducted in Austin, Minnesota, February 2010.

19   *"The line speed, the line speed"*: Chris Williams, "Mayo Confirms Cause of Slaughterhouse Illnesses," Associated Press, November 30, 2009.

2: Have a Cup of Coffee and Pray

21   *"not because the public cared anything about the workers"*: More than a decade after the publication of *The Jungle*, Upton Sinclair published a detailed—and typically scathing—account of the "condemned meat industry" and his "adventure with Roosevelt" as part of his diagnosis of all that was wrong with American newspapers and magazines. Upton Sinclair, *The Brass Check: A Study of American Journalism* (Pasadena, CA: Author, 1920), 47.

21   *"the specific evils you point out shall, if their existence be proved"*: Theodore Roosevelt to Upton Sinclair, March 15, 1906, in Elting E. Morison, ed., *The Letters*

of Theodore Roosevelt, vol. 5 (Cambridge, MA: Harvard University Press, 1952), 178–80.

22   *"the laws regulating the inspection of meat"*: Upton Sinclair, "The Condemned-Meat Industry: A Reply to Mr. J. Ogden Armour," *Everybody's Magazine*, May 1906, 613.

22   *"determined by clockwork"*: Upton Sinclair, *The Jungle*, introduction by Eric Schlosser (New York: Penguin Classics, 2006), 123.

23   *"I aimed at the public's heart, but by accident I hit it in the stomach"*: Sinclair, *The Brass Check*, 47.

23   *"I grew up in a Hormel family"*: Richard L. Knowlton with Ron Beyma, *Points of Difference: Transforming Hormel* (Garden City, NY: Morgan James, 2010), 27.

24   *"Especially in the fall of the year, I remember him"*: Knowlton, *Points of Difference*, 153.

24   *"I showed up at 5 a.m. at the employment office"*: Knowlton, *Points of Difference*, 28.

24   *"I was rushing through the side door"*: Knowlton, *Points of Difference*: 28.

25   *"Hormel's labor practices continued pretty much as he established them"*: Knowlton, *Points of Difference*, 35.

25   *"resulting bone-free pork shoulder along with boneless ham"*: Knowlton, *Points of Difference*, 65.

26   *"wholesale retrenchment in hourly wages"*: Knowlton, *Points of Difference*, 151.

26   *The outbreak was soon traced back to tainted hamburgers*: In January and February 2013, online publication *Food Safety News* ran an outstanding series of articles reconstructing the events of the Jack in the Box case and its impact. Attorney Bill Marler, publisher of *Food Safety News*, represented one of the plaintiffs in a lawsuit brought against Jack in the Box.

27   *Boyle petitioned the Department of Agriculture*: On February 10, 1994, J. Patrick Boyle, testifying before the U.S. Senate, stated, "Today, AMI has formally petitioned Secretary [Mike] Espy to initiate similar rulemaking to mandate HACCP programs in all meat and poultry plants in the United States, and I would like to submit for the record a copy of the letter, that I sent to Secretary Espy today, urging him to go forward immediately, and make this proven system a mandatory part of our Nation's meat and poultry inspection requirements." *The Federal Meat Inspection Program: Hearings Before the Subcommittee on Agricultural Research, Conservation, Forestry, and General Legislation of the Committee on Agriculture, Nutrition, and Forestry, United States Senate, One Hundred Third Congress, Second Session* (Washington, DC: U.S. Government Printing Office, 1994), 11.

28   *"Have a Cup of Coffee and Pray"*: This was the back-derivation that caught on among meat inspectors across the country, but trade magazines in the 1990s

also suggested "Hard, Agonizing, Complicated, Confusing Paperwork" and "Hire a Consultant and Confuse People."

28 *Instrumental in that victory was a man named Joel W. Johnson*: In 2004, when Joel W. Johnson was awarded the Richard L. Knowlton Award, industry magazine *Meatingplace* conducted an interview with Johnson and quoted from interviews with colleagues, including Richard L. Knowlton and J. Patrick Boyle. "The Spam Master," *Meatingplace*, December 2004, 19–33, http://www.meatingplace.com/ Print/Archives/Details/2877.

28 *"Like heck it will"*: Knowlton, *Points of Difference*, 98.

30 *The National Joint Council of Food Inspection Locals filed a complaint*: United States, Department of Agriculture, Food Safety and Inspection Service, Washington, D.C. (Respondent) and American Federation of Government Employees, AFL-CIO and National Joint Council of Food Inspection, Locals, AFGE (Charging Parties), August 29, 2003, https://www.flra.gov/decisions/v59/59-013ad.html.

31 *Nick Rinaker vowed never to work at Hormel Foods*: Due to illness, Nick Rinaker preferred to conduct our interviews by email. His quotations are taken from an extensive correspondence in February and March 2014.

33 *"all animal tissue has some commercial value"*: George A. Hormel & Company, Patent for Apparatus for Splitting Animal Heads (US 4662028 A), http:// www.google.com/patents/US4662028

34 *in 2004, Excel and Hatfield achieved*: "Pork Processors Boost Capacity," National Pork Producers Council, September 30, 1994, http://www.porknetwork .com/pork-news/pork-processors-boost-capacity-114010229.html.

35 *"There are the obvious things we read about over and over"*: Interview with Joel W. Johnson, "The Spam Master," *Meatingplace*.

36 *Between 2006 and 2013, Hormel increased*: Adam Harringa, "Skippy Leads the Way at Shareholders Meeting," *Austin Daily Herald*, January 30, 2013.

36 *Pablo Ruiz speaks with a heavy accent*: Interviews with Pablo Ruiz (his real name) were conducted in Austin, Minnesota, and via telephone throughout 2010, 2011, and 2012.

3: Alter Egos

39 *Aaron DeVries, an epidemiologist at the Minnesota Department of Health (MDH) in St. Paul*: Interview with Aaron DeVries, Stacy Holzbauer, and Ruth Lynfield was conducted at the Minnesota Department of Health, St. Paul, Minnesota, April 2010.

41 *"Let's stop harvesting brains"*: When I interviewed Lynfield in April 2010, she was reluctant to reconstruct the exact exchange she had with Wadding. More than two years earlier, however, she recounted these when speaking to the *New York Times*. Denise Grady, "A Medical Mystery Unfolds in Minnesota," *New York Times*, February 5, 2008.

41   *QPP quietly sold an 80 percent interest in itself*: Articles of Incorporation of Quality Pork Processors Inc. (including the November 2007 transfer to the Blaine Jay Corporation), obtained through the Office of the Secretary of State of Texas. I have placed these documents online at https://www.documentcloud.org/documents/207645-qpp-papers.html.

41   *The buyer, Blaine Jay Corporation, had incorporated in 2004*: Articles of Incorporation of Blaine Jay Corporation, also obtained through the Office of the Secretary of State of Texas. I have placed these documents online at https://www.documentcloud.org/documents/207644-blainejaypubdocs.html.

42   *"That simply did not happen"*: Interview with Kelly B. Wadding was conducted via telephone, June 2010.

42   *Dale Chidester, the longtime office coordinator of the United Food and Commercial Workers Local 9*: Interviews with Dale Chidester were conducted in Austin, Minnesota, and via telephone throughout 2010 and 2011.

42   *the 1985–86 strike that so harshly divided the town*: There are several outstanding histories of the Hormel strike in Austin, and upon which I have relied for historical details, most notably: Dave Hage and Paul Klauda, *No Retreat, No Surrender: Labor's War at Hormel* (New York: William Morrow, 1989); Hardy S. Green, *On Strike at Hormel: The Struggle for a Democratic Labor Movement* (Philadelphia: Temple University Press, 1990); and Peter Rachleff, *Hard-Pressed in the Heartland: The Hormel Strike and the Future of the Labor Movement* (Boston: South End Press, 1993).

42   *The Wilson Foods pork-processing plant in neighboring Albert Lea filed for bankruptcy in 1983*: Winston Williams, "Wilson Foods Fights Back," *New York Times*, December 3, 1983.

43   *"There was automated batching in the dry sausage, prepared sausage, and canned meat departments"*: Rachleff, *Hard-Pressed in the Heartland*, 49.

45   *Carole Bower arrived and ushered me toward the entrance*: Interview with Carol Bower was conducted in Quality Pork Processors Inc., Austin, Minnesota, February 2010.

48   *"What good is a union contract if the company can avoid the contract"*: Scott Carlson, "Hormel Loses Right to Lease Austin Plant, Ruling Closes Slaughterhouse," *St. Paul Pioneer Press*, June 9, 1988, Metro, 1A.

49   *Angeles spoke to me at Austin's Centro Campesino*: Interview with Miriam Angeles (her real name) was conducted in Austin, Minnesota, February and April 2010. For more on Angeles, see Elizabeth Baier, "Workers Sickened at Pork Plant Still Wait for Compensation," Minnesota Public Radio News, March 31, 2010, http://www.mprnews.org/story/2010/03/31/pork-illness-compensation.

51   *Dyck had some good news for Garcia*: Interview with Lachance, February 2010. See also Daniel H. Lachance et al., "An outbreak of neurological autoimmunity with polyradiculoneuropathy in workers exposed to aerosolised porcine

neural tissue: A descriptive study," *Lancet*, November 30, 2009, http://www
.thelancet.com/journals/laneur/article/PIIS1474-4422(09)70296-0/fulltext.

PART II

4: Little Mexico

55   *Raul Vazquez walks out of the Hormel plant on the outskirts of Fremont*: Interviews with Raul Vazquez (his real name) were conducted at San Miguel Liquor,
Schuyler, Nebraska, throughout 2012, 2013, and 2014.

57   *Ben Nelson, who was in the midst of a reelection campaign*: See David Welna,
"Nebraska Senator Takes Tough Stand on Immigration," NPR *Morning Edition*,
April 24, 2006, http://www.npr.org/templates/story/story.php?storyId=5358608.

57   *Kris Kobach, who had cut his teeth under Attorney General John Ashcroft*: See
"When Mr. Kobach Comes to Town: Nativist Laws & the Communities They
Damage," Southern Poverty Law Center, January 2011, http://www.splcenter.org/
sites/default/files/downloads/publication/Kobach_Comes_to_Town.pdf.

59   *"Americans are meat-hungry"*: Hugh A. Fogarty, "Cattle Men Out West See
No Meat Shortage," *New York Times*, June 29, 1947, E9.

60   *major packinghouses in Omaha were in the grip of a walkout by striking stockyard
workers*: "Stockyards Shut by Omaha Strike," *New York Times*, June 25, 1947, 3.

60   *the arrival of five hundred new jobs (which, on average, paid $3,000 each)*: For
discussion of Hormel annual salaries, see E. J. McCarthy, "Guaranties and Annual
Earnings: A Case Study of George A. Hormel and Company," *Journal of Business*,
January 1956, 41–51.

61   *"Most Hormel workers"*: Jack H. Pollack, "Revolution in Wages," *Los Angeles
Times*, March 16, 1947, E12.

62   *Harold Harper was working the night shift*: Interview with Harold and Linda
Harper was conducted in Fremont, Nebraska, January 2014.

64   *They sent out roving pickets*: For an excellent contemporary account of the
roving pickets, see Steve Boyce, Jake Edwards, and Tom Wetzel, "Slaughterhouse
Fight: A Look at the Hormel Strike," *ideas & action*, Summer 1986, http://www.
uncanny.net/~wetzel/hormel.htm.

64   *"poor profit margins"*: "Hormel Plans Layoffs," *Los Angeles Times*, September
3, 1988, CSD2.

65   *Between 1983 and 1993, sales doubled on increased output*: Jim Rasmussen,
"Hormel's Changes Lead to Expansion," *Omaha World-Herald*, January 31, 1993, 1M.

67   *"After a rest and once their supplies are set"*: Michael O'Boyle, "From Guerrero to Nebraska," *Business Mexico*, July 1, 2003.

67   *Chichihualco's mayor Leopoldo Cabrera estimated*: Michael O'Boyle, "Migrants Changing Nebraska Town," *Herald Mexico*, February 14, 2005.

70   *"When they find out that Fremont"*: Don Bowen, "Landlords Oppose Immigration Ordinance," *Fremont Tribune*, July 16, 2008.

5: They Threw Me Away Like Trash

71   *"worker exposure to aerosolized pig neural protein"*: "Investigation of Progressive Inflammatory Neuropathy Among Swine Slaughterhouse Workers—Minnesota, 2007–2008," U.S. Centers for Disease Control and Prevention, Morbidity and Mortality Weekly Report, January 31, 2008, 1–3.

72   *QPP as policyholder had $600,000 of liability for "Each Accident or each Person for Disease"*: For further details of QPP's dispute with American Home Assurance, see the eventual lawsuit: *State of Minnesota in Court of Appeals A10-1443, Quality Pork Processors, Inc., v. The American Home Assurance Company*. I have placed these documents online at https://www.documentcloud.org/documents/210076-qppvamericanhomeassurance.html.

72   *Susan Kruse, retained attorney*: Interview with Susan Kruse was conducted in Austin, Minnesota, February 2010.

72   *"a substantial contributing factor"*: Mia Simpson, "Former QPP Worker Fights for Workers' Compensation," *Austin Daily Herald*, April 3, 2008.

73   *"Something is out of sorts"*: Grady, "A Medical Mystery Unfolds in Minnesota."

73   *"Not once did any of the nurses tell me"*: Helen Meyers, "Workers Disabled at Minnesota Plant Demand Answers," *Militant*, January 21, 2008.

73   *"Once it's determined that they've contracted the illness at work"*: Simpson, "Former QPP Worker Fights for Workers' Compensation."

73   *"They're really scared"*: Ibid.

74   *Miriam Angeles was told to report to Human Resources*: Interview with Miriam Angeles, Austin, Minnesota, February 2010.

75   *"How could a person"*: Interview with Bob Warner, John Wiegert, and Jerry Hart was conducted in Fremont, Nebraska, March 2012.

76   *"I'm not telling you this can't be done"*: Don Bowen, "Warner Introduces Illegal Immigration Proposal," *Fremont Tribune*, May 14, 2008.

76   *a draft of the ordinance was scheduled for its first public reading*: My account of this meeting is drawn from interviews with Bob Warner; from Cindy Gonzalez and Judith Nygren, "Proposed Ban on Illegal Immigrants Stirs Uproar in Fremont," *Omaha World-Herald*, July 11, 2008; and from Don Bowen, "Landlords Oppose Immigration Ordinance," *Fremont Tribune*, July 16, 2008.

77   *When Roxanne Tarrant*: Ruiz provided access to his medical file, maintained by his caseworker Roxanne Tarrant at Employee Development Corporation in St. Paul. All medical records, including this account of Tarrant's initial consultation, are derived from her monthly reports.

79   *"I most worry about my leg"*: Interview with Pablo Ruiz, Austin, Minnesota, April 2010.

79   *opposition group One Fremont, One Future*: Bertha Valenzuela, Leslie Velez, and Kristin Ostrom, "Fremont's First Costs: Statement of One Fremont One Future," September 8, 2010, http://www.neappleseed.org/wp-content/uploads/downloads/2013/08/One-Fremont-One-Future-US-Civil-Rights-NE-Sept-2010.pdf.

79   *Maggie Zarate turned away a salesman*: Zarate testified about this incident at the October 29, 2013, meeting of the Fremont City Council.

79   *"We're in a battle right now"*: Schnatz sent this same email to numerous individuals over a period of years. See, for example, Fred Knapp, "We Will Shed Blood Again," *NET News*, January 11, 2011, http://www.kvnonews.com/2011/01/we-will-shed-blood-again/.

80   *Alfredo Velez, owner of Tienda Mexicana Guerrero*: Interviews with Alfredo Velez were conducted in March 2012 and November 2013.

81   *Velez received an anonymous letter*: The letter was supplied to me by Kristin Ostrom of One Fremont, One Future.

82   *"Racism has nothing to do with this ordinance"*: John Ferak and Cindy Gonzalez, "Immigration Problem Is Bigger than Fremont, Mayor Says," *Omaha World-Herald*, July 30, 2008.

82   *"This has weighed very heavy on me"*: Don Bowen, "Immigration Issue Continues to Simmer in Fremont," *Fremont Tribune*, July 25, 2009.

82   *"Control of illegal immigration is a federal issue"*: "Starting at the Beginning: A Look at How Fremont Got to June 21 Election," *Fremont Tribune*, June 11, 2010.

6: This Land Is Not Your Land

83   *"Who was doing these jobs before?"*: "Immigration Debate Hot," *Austin Daily Herald*, August 19, 2008, http://www.austindailyherald.com/2008/08/video-immigration-debate-hot/.

83   *Hendrycks had launched MinnSIR with her husband*: For more background on Ruthie Hendrycks, see Jean Hopfensperger, "Standing Firm in Opposition to Illegals," *Minneapolis Star-Tribune*, April 28, 2006.

85   *"Three times raids were scheduled"*: "Immigration Debate Hot," *Austin Daily Herald*, August 19, 2008.

85   *"We've sat down with ICE"*: Amanda Lillie, "Sheriff: Illegal Immigration Process Is out of Our Hands," *Austin Daily Herald*, January 31, 2011.

85   *"We're having to build a new jail for a reason"*: Judy Keen, "Immigration Debate Grips Minn. City," *USA Today*, August 27, 2008.

85   *"It's like us against them"*: "Immigration Debate Hot," *Austin Daily Herald*, August 19, 2008.

86   *"We had people that lived in tar paper shacks"*: Marie Casey and Casper Winkels, quoted in Horowitz, *Negro and White, Unite and Fight!*, 39.

87   *"Hormel hired 40 niggers"*: Roger Horowitz's remarkable interview with John Winkels is extensively quoted in James W. Loewen, *Sundown Towns: A Hidden Dimension of American Racism* (New York: New Press, 2005), 207.

89   *"I'm pretty upset"*: Interview with Bob Warner, John Wiegert, and Jerry Hart, Fremont, Nebraska, March 2012.

90   *"The more that I look around Fremont"*: Jerry A. Hart, "This City Is Being Destroyed by Greed," *Fremont Tribune*, February 4, 2009.

91   *Over burgers and fries, Kobach offered to represent them pro bono*: Interview with Bob Warner, John Wiegert, and Jerry Hart, Fremont, Nebraska, March 2012, and interview and subsequent email correspondence with Kris Kobach, Topeka, Kansas, May 2012.

92   *"People are scared"*: "Workers Picket QPP," *Austin Daily Herald*, December 1, 2008.

92   *"They made a lot of accusations"*: "Workers to Demonstrate at QPP," *Rochester Post-Bulletin*, November 27, 2008.

93   *"When was I last in Mexico?"*: Interview with Pablo Ruiz, Austin, Minnesota, November 2012.

PART III

7: From Seed to Slaughter

97   *Lynn Becker got the phone call every hog farmer fears*: Interview with Lynn Becker was conducted in Fairmont, Minnesota, in September 2012.

99   *when the Associated Press released*: The AP story ran in newspapers nationwide. See, for example, Frederic J. Frommer, "Video Shows Abuse of Pigs," *Boston Globe,* September 17, 2008, http://www.boston.com/news/nation/articles/2008/09/17/video_shows_abuse_of_pigs/.

102   *The epicenter of the boom was in North Carolina*: See "North Carolina in the Global Economy: Hog Farming," http://www.soc.duke.edu/NC_Global Economy/hog/overview.shtml.

102   *"Feces and urine"*: Peter T. Kilborn, "Hurricane Reveals Flaws in Farm Law," *New York Times*, October 17, 1999, http://www.nytimes.com/library/national/101799floyd-environment.html.

102   *Smithfield, joined by livestock subsidiaries*: For an excellent, detailed account of Smithfield's challenge to the packer ban in Iowa, see Christopher Leonard, *The Meat Racket: The Secret Takeover of America's Food Business* (New York: Simon & Schuster, 2014), 240–56.

103   *Hormel and Cargill had negotiated exemptions*: The official announcements and particular conditions of the exemptions are available at http://www.state.ia.us/government/ag/latest_news/releases/jan_2006/cargill.html and http://www.state.ia.us/government/ag/latest_news/releases/apr_2006/hormel.html.

104   *increasing production at the Fremont plant*: A particularly telling item appeared in the *Lincoln Journal-Star*: "Hormel Food Corp.'s hog slaughter plant in Fremont can increase production, thanks to a court agreement reached with Iowa officials.... The Fremont plant employs about 1,350 people and slaughters about 9,000 hogs a day. Hormel plans to increase production to 10,500 hogs a day, with some of the production coming from hogs raised in Iowa. No significant increase in jobs was expected." "Business Briefs," April 7, 2006.

105   *top-scoring hog was 49.7 percent lean meat and 21.3 percent fat*: J. L. Anderson, "Lard to Lean: Making the Meat-Type Hog in Post-World War II America" in Warren Belasco and Roger Horowitz, eds., *Food Chains: From Farmyard to Shopping Cart* (Philadelphia: University of Pennsylvania Press, 2009), 29–46

106   *"red box"*: Much background information on Hormel's "red box" comes from conversations with herd managers at New Fashion Pork, one of Hormel's top suppliers in Jackson, Minnesota. Special thanks to Steve Larson, head of marketing for NFP.

106   *hot-weight carcasses of between 174 and 222 pounds, with less than 1.1 inches of backfat*: Debra Neutkens, "Sorting for the Perfect Weight," *National Hog Farmer*, November 15, 2002, http://nationalhogfarmer.com/mag/farming_sorting_perfect_weight.

106   *about 105 percent of base price*: "Hormel Foods' Exec Make the Case for Uniformity," *Progressive Pork* (newsletter of Farmweld), 2011, http://www.farmweld.com/progressivepork/november_2004/carcass-uniformity.htm.

109   *years working with large corporations like Pepsi, Procter & Gamble, and Monsanto*: Many details of Weihs's biography come from a phone interview with Weihs in April 2013 and from a marketing letter sent to potential investors, http://www.docstoc.com/docs/28457175/Create-opportunities-for-rural-families-and-communities-by-developing.

109   *"We flat price everything"*: Joe Vansickle, "Farrow-to-Wean Business Booms," *National Hog Farmer*, January 15, 2005, http://nationalhogfarmer.com/mag/farming_farrowtowean_business_booms.

110   *"raise 800,000 hogs a year and pollute less than my dad used to"*: Ibid.

110   *"We put them in separate crates"*: Jeff Caldwell, "Family Hog Operation Proactively Realizes Environmental Husbandry Despite Critics," *Midwest Ag Journal*, October 4, 2004, http://www.supportfarmers.com/news-articles/family-hog-operation-proactively-realizes-environmental-husbandry-despite-critics.

110   *thirty-eight applications statewide to build confinements*: Numbers of applications to the Iowa DNR and the number of hogs in confinement from Deb Nicklay,

"The Smell of Money? Profitability Drives Iowa's Pork Boom," *Mason City (Iowa) Globe Gazette,* January 14, 2007.

111 *"you have daydreams—or nightmares—of that $5 mark":* "The Price of Corn," *New York Times,* February 6, 2007, http://www.nytimes.com/2007/02/06/opinion/06tue4.html?_r=0.

111 *"When corn started going from two dollars to four dollars":* Weihs, phone interview, April 2013.

112 *"as long as PETA don't find out":* This portion of the whistle-blower's letter to PETA was supplied by Dan Paden, PETA's spokesman and evidence analysis manager, via email, November 27, 2012.

112 *"This is cruel treatment of the animals":* Paden, email correspondence, November 27, 2012.

8: Don't Be Afraid to Hurt Them

113 *Ruderman showed up at Natural Pork Production II's sow barns:* Robert Ruderman's story is told from his daily logs, June 10, 2008, to September 8, 2008, and video footage supplied by PETA.

116 *Lynn's grandfather, Walter:* Andrea Johnson, "LB Pork Is Minnesota Pork Producers' Family of the Year," *Minnesota Farm Guide,* January 24, 2003, http://www.minnesotafarmguide.com/lb-pork-is-minnesota-pork-producers-family-of-the-year/article_2d5e8809-72b5-55b3-bb02-5d77c2aa5fe2.html.

117 *Walter's farm was still quite small when he passed it on:* Andrea Johnson, "Lynn and Julie Becker Tell This Winter's Story of Pork," *Minnesota Farm Guide,* November 23, 2005, http://www.minnesotafarmguide.com/news/producer_reports/lynn-and-julie-becker-tell-this-winter-s-story-of/article_2ada1329-3dcf-5c91-a022-bc1a3c07177c.html.

117 *When a spate of Methicillin-resistant* Staphyloccus aureus *(MRSA) tore through the barns in the winter of 1996–97:* Joe Vansickle, "New Large Pen Design for Wean-to-Finish Systems," *National Hog Farmer,* January 31, 1999, http://nationalhogfarmer.com/mag/farming_new_large_pen.

118 *there were more than 10,000 hog farms in Minnesota; by 2007 that number had fallen to 4,700:* Minnesota Pork Industry Profile, prepared by Su Ye, Agricultural Marketing Services, Minnesota Department of Agriculture, 2009, 5, http://www.mda.state.mn.us/food/business/~/media/Files/food/business/economics/porkindustryprofile.ashx.

118 *Martin went from turning out 240,000 hogs per year in 1990 to 790,000 in 2008:* United States Department of Agriculture. National Agricultural Statistics Service.

119 *"Calculated growth and modifications to our operation are how we've steadily maintained growth":* Tom Dodge, "Hogs, Corn and Baseball," *Progressive Farmer,* August 2010, http://www.dtn.com/ag/realfarmer/hogscorn.cfm.

119 *"Because of this agreement"*: Hormel Foods, Corporate Responsibility Report, 2007, 37, http://2011csr.hormelfoods.com/wp-content/themes/twentyeleven/pdf/HormelFoods2006-2007CSRReport.pdf.

120 *Michael Steinberg, the second PETA operative*: Michael Steinberg's story is told from his daily logs, July 23, 2008, to September 11, 2008, and video footage supplied by PETA.

123 *the secret audio recording*: Audio file and transcript of this recording supplied by Dan Paden of PETA in November 2012.

124 *Hallmark/Westland recalled more than 143 million pounds of beef*: Andrew Martin, "Agriculture Dept. Vows to Improve Animal Welfare," *New York Times*, February 29, 2008, http://www.nytimes.com/2008/02/29/business/29food. html?ref=westlandhallmarkmeatcompany&_r=0.

124 *a PETA investigator managed to get hired*: For a detailed account of PETA's investigation of Murphy Family Ventures, see Steven M. Wise, *An American Trilogy: Death, Slavery, and Dominion on the Banks of the Cape Fear River* (New York: Da Capo Press, 2009), 75–98.

125 *a piece of model legislation then called the Animal and Ecological Terrorism Act*: Full text of the model legislation is available at http://www.alec.org/model-legislation/the-animal-and-ecological-terrorism-act-acta/.

125 *"damaging or interfering with the operations of an animal enterprise"*: The full text of the Animal Enterprise Terrorism Act is available at http://www.gpo.gov/fdsys/pkg/BILLS-109s3880enr/pdf/BILLS-109s3880cnr.pdf.

126 *immortalized by* 60 Minutes *as "Dr. Evil"*: See the *60 Minutes* segment, "Dr. Evil," http://www.cbsnews.com/news/meet-rick-berman-aka-dr-evil/.

126 *Court filings in the suit revealed that Hormel*: Ian T. Shearn, "Investigative Report: Richard Berman," Humane Society of the United States, May 11, 2010, http://www.humanesociety.org/news/news/2010/05/investigative_report_berman_1.html.

126 *a canceled check for $50,000*: Mark Drajem and Brian Wingfield, "Union Busting by Profiting from Non-Profit May Breach IRS," Bloomberg News, November 1, 2012, http://www.bloomberg.com/news/2012-11-02/union-busting-by-profiting-from-non-profit-may-breach-irs.html.

126 *"have a chilling effect"*: *Congressional Record*, vol. 152, part 17, November 9, 2006–December 6, 2006, 21836.

126 *"The No. 1 domestic terrorism threat is the eco-terrorism, animal-rights movement"*: Henry Schuster, "Domestic Terror: Who's Most Dangerous?," CNN.com, August 24, 2005, http://www.cnn.com/2005/US/08/24/schuster.column/.

126 *The jury handed down convictions for seven*: Court filings relating to the case of *United States v. Stop Huntingdon Animal Cruelty* are available at http://ccrjustice.org/us-v-SHAC7.

127   *Jeff Kayser, the production manager at Suidae Health*: The account of the transition from Natural Pork Producers II to MowMar Farms is taken from the daily logs of Robert Ruderman and Michael Steinberg.

9: Ag Gag

131   *"Abuse and Neglect of Livestock at Sow Farm"*: Dan Paden at PETA supplied a copy of this report.

131   *"But in the environment"*: All quotes from police interviews come from Greene County Sheriff's Office Investigative Report, Case: 09-1591, Abuse and Neglect of Livestock at Sow Farm located at F Avenue and 330th St., submitted by Russell C. Hoffman, Chief Deputy Sheriff.

132   *Lyons acknowledged to the sheriff's deputy*: Interview with Shawn Lyons was conducted in Bayard, Iowa, November 2012.

134   *Authored by Himle and released through Cunningham's office*: In our interview, Lynn Becker was evasive about who authored the statement and managed other aspects of the pushback against PETA, saying only that he had worked with "a PR firm in the Twin Cities"; however, the electronic file of the statement issued by National Pork Board contained metadata indicating that the author of file was "John Himle." That PDF is still available at http://www.pork.org/filelibrary/features/MowMarFARMsept08statement.pdf.

134   *"shares our commitment to animal welfare and humane handling"*: Frommer, "Video Shows Abuse of Pigs."

134   *"One month later, the pigs at this farm"*: The Associated Press story by Steve Karnowski ran in numerous newspapers; see, for example, "PETA: Manager Still at Farm Where Pigs Were Abused," *Minneapolis Star-Tribune*, October 21, 2008, http://www.startribune.com/31706519.html.

135   *"We are appalled that PETA representatives"*: Ibid.

135   *"during an industry meeting almost nine years ago"*: Hormel Foods, Corporate Responsibility Report, 2007, 36.

136   *Lyons called his wife, Sherri*: The account of Lyons's arrest and booking comes from Chief Deputy Sheriff Russell C. Hoffman's reports and from the interview with Shawn Lyons in November 2012.

137   *"to represent the most vital interests"*: The mission of the Minnesota Agri-Growth Council is stated on their website: http://www.agrigrowth.org/who-we-are.html.

137   *Hormel's vice president for legislative affairs, Joe C. Swedberg*: Joe C. Swedberg's interview at Ag-Nite is available at http://agwired.com/2008/09/03/hormel-provides-protein-punch-for-hunger-relief/.

137   *"We raise a good, clean crop"*: John Rusling Block's interview at Ag-Nite is available at http://agwired.com/2008/09/03/former-ag-secretary-attends-agnite/.

137 *"this year providing media and strategic counsel"*: "Member in Focus," *Minnesota Agri-Growth Council Newsletter*, December 2008: 2, http://www.agrigrowth.org/pdf/MACGDecJan08.pdf.

138 *"economic arguments supportive of rational immigration"*: Minutes of the Legislative Coordinating Commission, Ethnic Heritage and New Americans Working Group, Thursday, September 18, 2008.

138 *The talk, according to the council's newsletter*: See the *Minnesota Agri-Growth Council Newsletter*, February 2011, 3, http://www.agrigrowth.org/Newsletters/Feb2011.pdf.

138 *"It's absurd"*: Interview with Amanda Hitt was conducted via telephone in April 2013.

139 *"an important deterrent tool in our toolbox"*: Bob Von Sternberg, "Bill Would Ban Video of Farming Operations," *Minneapolis Star-Tribune*, April 8, 2011, http://www.startribune.com/politics/statelocal/119516799.html.

139 *pushed the legislation in the Sunshine State*: Matthew Yglesias, "Florida Conservatives Standing Up For Liberty with New Law to Ban Farm Photo," thinkprogress.org, March 7, 2011, http://thinkprogress.org/yglesias/2011/03/07/200129/florida-conservatives-standing-up-for-liberty-with-new-law-to-ban-farm-photo/.

139 *Jack DeCoster was under a federal investigation*: The U.S. Food and Drug Administration's letter of warning to Decoster is available at http://www.fda.gov/ICECI/EnforcementActions/WarningLetters/2010/ucm229805.

139 *the Iowa Poultry Association freely admits*: A. G. Sulzberger, "States Look to Ban Efforts to Reveal Farm Abuse," *New York Times*, April 13, 2011, http://www.nytimes.com/2011/04/14/us/14video.html.

140 *supposedly composed around Sweeney's kitchen table*: This claim was made by Emily Meredith, communications director for the Animal Agriculture Alliance, during an interview with Amy Goodman on the radio show *Democracy Now!* Full transcript of the interview is available at http://www.democracynow.org/2013/4/9/debate_after_activists_covertly_expose_animal.

140 *"Was that House File 1369?"*: Interview with Rod Hamilton was conducted via telephone, October 2012.

140 *"At a time when a significant share of the consumer food market"*: Sally Jo Sorensen, "Consumers Are Stupid: Agri-Growth Council Touts Babe in a Blender Restoration Act," bluestemprairie.com, April 12, 2011, http://www.bluestemprairie.com/bluestemprairie/2011/04/consumers-are-stupid-agri-growth-council-touts-babe-in-a-blender-restoration-act.html#sthash.VdMQcOw0.dpuf.

141 *"On or about August 27, 2008, I did the following"*: Greene County Sheriff's Office Investigative Report, Case: 09-1591.

141 *"They completely snubbed him"*: Interview with Sherri Lyons in Bayard, Iowa, November 2012.

142 *"Who in their right mind"*: Interview with Dan Paden was conducted via telephone, November 2012.

142 *"We try to leave pigs home with Mom"*: Joe Vansickle, "Charting a Course for Day-One Pig Care," *National Hog Farmer*, August 17, 2010, http://nationalhogfarmer.com/mag/charting-course-pig-care-0815.

PART IV

10: I Thought It Was Fishy

147 *Roxanne Tarrant received a phone call*: Ruiz provided access to his medical file, maintained by his caseworker Roxanne Tarrant at Employee Development Corporation in St. Paul. All medical records are derived from Tarrant's monthly reports.

148 *"I was walking slowly"*: Interview with Pablo and Noelia Ruiz was conducted in Austin, Minnesota, March 2013.

149 *"For most patients that have gone on to have complaints"*: Interview with Lachance, Rochester, Minnesota, February 2010.

150 *In the early morning hours of June 12, 2009*: Except where otherwise noted, details of the case of Patricia Rodriguez-Sanchez derive from the unpublished opinion in *State of Minnesota v. Patricia Rodriguez-Sanchez*, Mower County District Court File No. 50-CR-09-1932, October 11, 2011, http://mn.gov/web/prod/static/lawlib/live/archive/ctapun/1110/opa102137-103111.pdf.

150 *"You're lucky to be alive"*: Paul McEnroe, "Protecting Illegal Immigrants to Catch Criminals," *Minneapolis Star-Tribune*, October 27, 2011, http://www.startribune.com/local/132387733.html.

151 *it didn't sit right with Detective Sergeant David McKichan*: Ibid.

152 *Johnson and fellow NSM member Robert Hester*: Mike Rose, "Immigration Protest Brings Out Two Sides," *Austin Daily Herald*, June 3, 2009, http://www.austindailyherald.com/2009/06/immigration-protest-brings-out-two-sides/.

152 *"You think America's going to let you get away with this?"*: Video of the protest is available at https://www.youtube.com/watch?v=obOaW_hnZbY.

152 *"Hitler is not dead; he's alive in our hearts"*: "Rally Heats Up, No Arrests," *Austin Daily Herald*, July 13, 2009, http://www.austindailyherald.com/2009/07/rally-heats-up-no-arrests/.

152 *"It didn't feel right morally"*: McEnroe, "Protecting Illegal Immigrants to Catch Criminals."

153 *Kelly Wadding and human resources director Dale Wicks agreed to speak*: Mike Rose, "QPP Weighs In on Forgeries," *Austin Daily Herald*, September 12, 2009, http://www.austindailyherald.com/2009/09/qpp-weighs-in-on-forgeries/.

155 *Ballesta was given work restrictions and assigned to other jobs*: Ballesta provided access to his medical file, maintained by his caseworker Roxanne Tarrant at

Employee Development Corporation in St. Paul. All medical records are derived from Tarrant's monthly reports.

156 *when I got Wadding on the line*: Interview with Wadding, June 2010.

159 *"It's a slaughterhouse"*: Interviews with Roxanne Tarrant were conducted in Minneapolis, Minnesota, and via telephone in March and April 2010.

11: You Are Not Welcome

161 *ICE agents . . . entered the Fremont Beef processing plant*: The account of the case of Rosaura Carrillo Velasquez comes from a phone interview and emails with her attorney, Bassel F. Kasaby, in August and September 2012 and court filings in *United States v. Rosaura Carrillo-Velasquez* in the U.S. District Court for the District of Nebraska, Case Number 8:10CR80. The best detail appears in Findings and Recommendation That the Motion to Suppress 35 Be Denied, September 21, 2010, http://www.gpo.gov/fdsys/pkg/USCOURTS-ned-8_10-cr-00080/pdf/USCOURTS-ned-8_10-cr-00080-5.pdf.

162 *"To those people who want proof"*: Jerry A. Hart, "We Shouldn't Have to Fight Our Leaders," *Fremont Tribune*, March 26, 2010, http://fremonttribune.com/news/opinion/mailbag/we-shouldn-t-have-to-fight-our-leaders/article_6cb-c03f2-38e5-11df-9ac8-001cc4c002e0.html.

162 *"This ordinance will not change the complexion"*: Monica Davey, "City in Nebraska Torn as Immigration Vote Nears," *New York Times*, June 17, 2010, http://www.nytimes.com/2010/06/18/us/18ncbraska.html.

163 *called out to the Hormel plant to investigate a bomb scare*: "Explosive Device Found at Hormel; Officials Have Suspect," *Fremont Tribune*, March 30, 2010, http://fremonttribune.com/news/local/explosive-device-found-at-hormel-officials-have-suspect/article_756b579a-3c15-11df-8034-001cc4c002e0.html.

163 *He advised former Fremont city councilman Charlie Janssen*: JoAnne Young, "Senators Hear Arguments on Repealing Nebraska Dream Act," *Lincoln Journal-Star*, February 1, 2010, http://journalstar.com/news/local/govt-and-politics/senators-hear-arguments-on-repealing-nebraska-dream-act/article_c1af210a-0f5a-11df-a0e1-001cc4c03286.html.

164 *called these local ordinances and state bills "field tests"*: Paul Reyes, "'It's Just Not Right': The Failures of Alabama's Self-Deportation Experiment," *Mother Jones*, March/April 2012, http://www.motherjones.com/politics/2012/03/alabama-anti-immigration-law-self-deportation-movement.

164 *Arizona governor Jan Brewer signed the Kobach-authored SB1070*: For an excellent discussion of the legal issues surrounding Arizona's SB1070, see "Experts Go Over SB 1070's Key Points," *Arizona Daily Star*, May 2, 2010, http://azstarnet.com/news/experts-go-over-sb-s-key-points/article_a9006f6b-f9b6-59db-87b4-d54a09b4b786.html.

164 *"That's not it at all"*: Interview with Kobach, May 2012.

165   *Kristin Ostrom, a Fremont resident who held a law degree with certification as a master mediator*: Interviews with Kristin Ostrom were conducted in Fremont, Nebraska, and via telephone throughout 2011, 2012, 2013, and 2014.

167   *Hormel would dispatch Bill McLain*: In an email to me on October 1, 2012, Hormel spokesman Rick Williamson confirmed the events as described: "During the week of June 14, 2010, the Fremont Plant manager was out of town. Our plant locations do not have internal communications employees on site; as a result, Bill McLain, in the plant manager's absence, came to provide communications support for media inquiries that we had started to receive. As Chamber members, we also provided this support to the Chamber to help inform the community about the ordinance."

168   *refused to answer any questions*: I spoke to McLain via telephone during September 2012, but he directed all inquires to Hormel spokesman Rick Williamson.

169   *"There were a lot of tears in this room tonight"*: Monica Davey, "Nebraska Town Votes to Banish Illegal Immigrants," *New York Times*, June 21, 2010, http://www.nytimes.com/2010/06/22/us/22fremont.html.

170   *"I wasn't surprised that Fremont would bring up such a law"*: Interviews with Blake Harper were conducted via telephone and email during January and February 2014.

170   *"I am very concerned about the negative effect"*: Declaration of Blake Harper, July 28, 2010, *Martinez v. Fremont*.

12: Brother, Are You Okay?

173   *Not like the raid on the Agriprocessors plant*: For an outstanding account of the Postville raid and its effects, see Maggie Jones, "Postville, Iowa, Is Up for Grabs," *New York Times Magazine*, July 11, 2012, http://www.nytimes.com/2012/07/15/magazine/postville-iowa-is-up-for-grabs.html.

173   *"The raids resulted in the arrest"*: The full text of Franken's statement, "Effect of ICE Raids on Children," is available at http://www.franken.senate.gov/?p=issue&id=215.

174   *Patrick Neilon, the president of Local 6 in Albert Lea*: Interviews with Patrick Neilon were conducted in Albert Lea, Minnesota, in March 2013, and via email throughout 2013.

176   *Albert Lea was founded on meatpacking*: Cheri Register, *Packinghouse Daughter: A Memoir* (St. Paul: Minnesota Historical Society Press, 2000), 53–62.

178   *switched off the main sprinkler system*: Sarah Stultz, "Farmland: Ten Years Later," *Albert Lea Tribune,* July 8, 2011, http://www.albertleatribune.com/2011/07/farmland-10-years-later/.

179   *"We felt like the big losers"*: Erin Galbally, "Albert Lea Optimistic About Jobs Picture," Minnesota Public Radio, July 1, 2004, http://news.minnesota.publicradio.org/features/2004/07/01_galballye_aleaeconomy/,

179 *"We looked at a lot of sites"*: Ibid.

180 *Kelly Wadding rises*: Details of Wadding's daily schedule and biography come from Kevin Cross, "Serious About Swine," *Austin Daily Herald*, March 6, 2013, http://www.austindailyherald.com/2013/03/serious-about-swine/.

181 *"They see the problem"*: Rose, "QPP Weighs In on forgeries."

183 *The Karen Organization of Minnesota was officially formed in 2009*: History of the organization is available at http://www.mnkaren.org/about.htm.

184 *Tha Wah, at a meeting arranged by Patrick Neilon*: Interviews with Tha Wah were conducted in Albert Lea, Minnesota, in March 2013, and Des Moines, Iowa, in October 2013.

185 *On January 31, 2011, Local 6 filed a notice*: Copy of the NLRB petition (Case no. 18-RC-17746) was supplied by UFCW Local 6 in Albert Lea, Minnesota.

185 *"His hand was shaking when he was writing the numbers"*: Interview with Keh Moo was conducted in Des Moines, Iowa, in October 2013.

186 *"one-third to one-half of Karen-speaking employees"*: Employer's Exceptions to the Regional Director's Report on the Objections, *Albert Lea Select Foods v. UFCW Local 6*, Case 18-RC-17746, filed with the NLRB on April 29, 2011. Copy supplied by UFCW Local 6 in Albert Lea, Minnesota.

188 *Now he drove people from Minnesota back to Mexico*: For a more detailed account of Schwartz's changing business, see Trey Mewes, "Special Report: Are Hispanics Leaving?," *Austin Daily Herald*, November 10, 2011, http://www.austindailyherald.com/2011/11/why-are-hispanics-leaving-austin/

PART V

13: A Clean Bill of Health

193 *the gravel surrounding the New Fashion Pork*: The visit to the New Fashion Pork hog confinement near Jackson, Minnesota, was conducted during September 2013.

193 *would soon post record profits*: See Hormel's annual profits statement for 2013, http://www.hormelfoods.com/Newsroom/Press-Releases/2013/11/20131126-Earnings.

194 *Jim Snee, Hormel's head of international sales*: Adam Harringa, "Hormel: An Eye on China," *Austin Daily Herald*, July 29, 2013, http://www.austindailyherald.com/2013/07/an-eye-on-china/.

196 *CDC and the Center for Science in the Public Interest (CSPI) issued*: Antibiotic Resistance Threats in the United States, 2013 (Washington, D.C.: Department of Health and Human Services, Centers for Disease Control and Prevention), http://www.cdc.gov/drugresistance/threat-report-2013/.

197   *the company's last published set of instructions for barn managers*: "Food Safety Guidelines," *New Fashion Pork Vision*, Winter 2006. http://www.nfpinc.com/pdf/Winter06.pdf

197   *Jay C. Hormel invited a group of medical researchers*: Dougherty, *In Quest of Quality: Hormel's First 75 Years*, 306.

198   *"the relation of animal products to disease and to the treatment of disease"*: *Annual Report of the Hormel Insitute, 1955–1956* (St. Paul: University of Minnesota Press), 1.

198   *Benjamin Duggar, a botanist who studied fungal infections in plants*: For an outstanding overview of the work of Duggar and Jukes at the Lederle Laboratories, see Richard Conniff, "How did antibiotics become part of the food chain?" *Cosmos*, March 10, 2014, http://cosmosmagazine.com/features/antibiotics-become-part-food-chain/.

198   *Duggar started by trying to solve an old farmyard mystery*: Maureen Ogle, "Riots, Rage and Resistance: A Brief History of How Antibiotics Arrived on the Farm," *Scientific American*, September 3, 2013, http://blogs.scientificamerican.com/guest-blog/2013/09/03/riots-rage-and-resistance-a-brief-history-of-how-antibiotics-arrived-on-the-farm/.

200   *"the most important advancement in Swine Nutrition in the last 25 years"*: See, for example, *Sioux Center News*, June 19, 1950, 11.

200   *"given aureo in their feed survived and grew up into self-respecting hogs"*: Sydney B. Self, "Hospital & Hogpen: Antibiotic Germ Killers Conquer New Fields as Pig, Poultry Feed," *Wall Street Journal*, September 12, 1950, 1.

200   *"brought to marketable weight more quickly"*: "Antibiotics Used on Livestock by Hormel to Clear Bacteria for Full Effect of Fodder," *New York Times*, December 13, 1951, 53.

201   *"that aureomycin, administered either orally or by injection, is excreted in the feces of pigs"*: Nora L. Larson and Lawrence E. Carpenter, "The Fecal Excretion of Aureomycin by the Pig," *Archives of Biochemistry and Biophysics*, 36 (1952): 239–240.

201   *"a marked decrease in the coliform organisms in the feces of the pigs"*: R. C. Wahlstrom, Eva M. Cohn, S. W. Terrill, and B. Connor Johnson, "Growth Effect of Various Antibiotics on Baby Pigs Fed Synthetic Rations," *Journal of Animal Science* 11 (1952): 449–454.

201   *"Although aureomycin has been in general use for only three years"*: Harry F. Dowling, Mark H. Lepper, and George Gee Jackson, "Observations on the Epidemiological Spread of Antibiotic-Resistant Staphylococci, with Measurements of the Changes in Sensitivity to Penicillin and Aureomycin," *American Journal of Public Health* 43.7 (July 1953): 860–868, http://www.ncbi.nlm.nih.gov/pmc/articles/PMC1620328/.

202   *published a joint report*: "Iowa Concentrated Animal Feeding Operations Air Quality Study: Final Report," prepared by Iowa State University and the Uni-

versity of Iowa Study Group, February 2002, https://www.public-health.uiowa
.edu/ehsrc/CAFOstudy/CAFO_1.pdf.

202   *Master Matrix Plan*: The various versions of the Master Matrix Plan are
available on the Iowa DNR's website at http://www.iowadnr.gov/Environment/
LandStewardship/AnimalFeedingOperations/Confinements/Construction
Requirements/Permitted/MasterMatrix.aspx.

203   *"Whoever heard of passing a test with a score of fifty percent?"*: Interview with
Steve Roe was conducted near Jefferson, Iowa, at a potluck dinner hosted by the
Greene County Farmers and Neighbors, April 2013.

203   *David Goodner, a spokesman for the watchdog group Iowa Citizens for Community Improvement*: Interview with David Goodner was conducted via telephone
in January 2014.

203   *"nothing to worry about"*: Andrew Schneider, "Potentially Fatal Bacteria
Found in Pigs, Farmworkers," *Seattle Post-Intelligencer,* June 8, 2008, http://www
.seattlepi.com/local/article/Potentially-fatal-bacteria-found-in-pigs-1275922.php

204   *first scientific test of hogs for MRSA in the United States*: For an excellent overview and analysis of Smith's research, see Maryn McKenna, "A New Strain of
Drug-Resistant Staph Infection Found in U.S. Pigs," *Scientific American*, January 23,
2009, http://www.scientificamerican.com/article/new-drug-resistant-mrsa-in-pigs/.

204   *Smith undertook another study*: M. Carrel, M.L. Schweizer, M.V. Sarrazin,
T.C. Smith, E.N. Perencevich, "Residential Proximity to Large Numbers of Swine
in Feeding Operations Is Associated with Increased Risk of Methicillin-resistant
Staphylococcus aureus Colonization at Time of Hospital Admission in Rural Iowa
Veterans," *Infection Control and Hospital Epidemiology* 35.2 (February 2014):
190–3, http://www.ncbi.nlm.nih.gov/pubmed/24442084.

205   "A lot of those antibiotics are broken down": Interview with Brad Freking,
Jay Moore, and Emily Erickson was conducted at New Fashion Pork, Jackson,
Minnesota, September 2013.

14: Lay of the Land

207   *Jay Lausen parked his pickup*: Interview with Jay Lausen was conducted in
Estherville, Iowa, November 2013.

209   *New Fashion Pork has been a major player in the boom*: Data on New Fashion
Pork was supplied directly by the company.

210   *the highest and second-highest nitrate loads*: See You-Kuan Zhang and Keith
Schilling, "Temporal Variations and Scaling of Streamflow and Baseflow and
Their Nitrate-Nitrogen Concentrations and Loads," *Advances in Water Resources*
28 (2005): 701–710.

211   *FDR signed the Soil Conservation Act*: See John C. Culver and John Hyde,
American Dreamer: A Life of Henry A. Wallace (New York: Norton, 2001), 160–62.

211   *"ever-normal granary"*: See Culver and Hyde, *American Dreamer*, 178–79.

212   *whole system was dismantled when Earl Butz*: See Michael Pollan, *The Omnivore's Dilemma: A Natural History of Four Meals* (New York: Penguin Press, 2006), 51–53.

212   *"for his callous lack of concern about their welfare"*: See Shea Dean, "Children of the Corn Syrup," *Believer*, October 2003, http://www.believermag.com/issues/200310/?read=article_dean.

213   *"People used to have an eighty-acre farm and raise a family"*: Interview with Austin Genoways was conducted in Bayard, Nebraska, July 2012.

213   *Carter convinced Congress to pass the Federal Crop Insurance Act of 1980*: See "History of the Crop Insurance Program," USDA Risk Management Agency, http://www.rma.usda.gov/aboutrma/what/history.html.

214   *at least 7.5 billion gallons of renewable transportation fuels within seven years*: The EPA's Renewable Fuel Standard targets are available at http://www.epa.gov/otaq/fuels/renewablefuels/.

214   *collectively import more than $3 billion worth*: See the National Pork Producers Council, "Benefits of Expanding U.S. Pork Exports," http://www.nppc.org/issues/international-trade/benefits-of-expanding-u-s-pork-exports/.

215   *"animal units"*: The DNR's full calculation sheet for "animal units" is available at http://www.iowadnr.gov/portals/idnr/uploads/forms/5424021.pdf.

215   *announced the elimination of one hundred positions at the DNR*: See "Iowa DNR Eliminating More Than 100 Positions," KCRG (Cedar Rapids, Iowa), May 11, 2011, http://www.kcrg.com/news/local/Iowa-DNR-Eliminating-More-Than-100-Positions--121680249.html.

216   *"If we could be on site on a more regular basis"*: Kent Sievers, "Iowa DNR Cuts Mean Less Oversight," *Omaha World-Herald*, June 6, 2011, http://www.omaha.com/apps/pbcs.dll/article?AID=2011706069934&template=printart.

216   *The governor also announced four appointments*: For Branstad's 2011 appointees to the EPC, see the official list at http://governor.iowa.gov/2011/03/gov-branstad-announces-appointees-to-iowas-boards-and-commissions/?wpmp_switcher=mobile.

217   *was at that very moment under investigation*: Laura Millsaps, "Branstad's Brother Fined for Manure Spill in Winnebago River," *Ames Tribune*, November 17, 2011, http://iowa.amestrib.com/articles/2011/11/19/ames_tribune/news/doc4ec523ede1db9521609183.txt.

217   *nitrate levels in the Raccoon River and Des Moines River watershed*: Raccoon River Watershed Water Quality Master Plan, November 2011, prepared by Agren Inc., Carroll, Iowa, http://www.iowadnr.gov/Portals/idnr/uploads/water/watershed/files/raccoonmasterwmp13.PDF.

218   *"We have invested in Emmet County"*: Michael Tidemann, New Fashion Pork Finish Site Draws Strong Opposition," *Estherville Daily News*, April 24, 2012, http://www.esthervilledailynews.com/page/content.detail/id/515555/New-Fashion-Pork-finish-site-draws-strong-opposition.html?nav=5003.

218   "Like we're these big guys from out of state": Information for this section comes from my interview with Freking, September 2013.

221   *a public meeting at the Regional Wellness Center*: Account of the public meeting in Estherville come from my interview with Freking, September 2013, and Michael Tidemann, "Over 100 Attend Emmet Concerned Citizens Meeting," *Estherville Daily News*, May 15, 2013, http://www.esthervilledailynews.com/page/content.detail/id/515730/Over-100-attend-Emmet-Concerned-Citizens-meeting.html?nav=5003.

15: Water Works

225   *Linda Kinman, the policy analyst and watershed advocate*: Interview with Linda Kinman was conducted in Des Moines, Iowa, October 2013.

226   *a scathing critique of the DNR's handling of the state's CAFOs*: "Preliminary Results of an Informal Investigation of the National Pollutant Discharge Elimination System Program For Concentrated Animal Feeding Operations in the State of Iowa," Region 7, United States Environmental Protection Agency, July 2012, http://www.epa.gov/region7/water/pdf/ia_cafo_preliminary_report.pdf.

227   *"the 'gotcha' approach"*: Branstad's letter to Perciasepe is available at http://iowa.sierraclub.org/CAFOs/BranstadToEPA5-13.pdf.

227   *"more trusting relationship"*: See Gene Lucht, "EPA Chief Vows Cooperation," *Iowa Farmer Today*, August 21, 2013, http://www.iowafarmertoday.com/news/regional/epa-chief-vows-cooperation/article_0aee6e44-0a97-11e3-b2a5-0019bb2963f4.html.

228   *"hog manure overall contributes about 63 percent"*: Raccoon River Watershed Water Quality Master Plan, November 2011.

228   *Hill asked me to simply consider the numbers*: Interview with Dennis R. Hill was conducted in Des Moines, Iowa, October 2013.

228   *according to a study conducted by Mark D. Sobsey*: "Detecting Fecal Contamination and Its Sources in Water and Watersheds" was conducted with an EPA grant (R824782) from October 1, 1995, to October 31, 1998. Details of the grant, including reports, are available at http://cfpub.epa.gov/ncer_abstracts/index.cfm/fuseaction/display.abstractDetail/abstract/607/report/0.

229   *Gordon Brand, senior chemist at the DMWW*: Interview with Gordon Brand was conducted in Des Moines, Iowa, October 2013.

229   *In 2012, researchers from the Louisiana Universities Marine Consortium*: Kelly Slivka, "Big Drought Makes for a Small 'Dead Zone,'" nytimes.com, August 2, 2012, http://green.blogs.nytimes.com/2012/08/02/big-drought-makes-for-a-small-dead-zone/.

230   *banded together to create Agriculture's Clean Water Alliance*: See Tom Philpott, "House Republicans Aim Pitchfork at Food-System Reform," motherjones.com, June 23, 2011, http://www.motherjones.com/tom-philpott?page=40.

231   *In April 2013, Jay Moore appeared again*: This account of the county super-visors meeting comes from Dan Voigt, "Permit Applications Raise Questions," *Emmetsburg News,* April 4, 2013, http://www.emmetsburgnews.com/page/content .detail/id/511367/Permit-Applications-Raise-Questions.html?nav=5004.

231   *"Teddy Roosevelt broke up all those corporations and packing plants"*: See tran-script of interview with Linus Solberg for the film PRICELE$$, available at http:// www.pricelessmovie.org/interview-transcripts/farmers/linus-solberg/.

232   *"Primarily we're looking for the integrity of the concrete"*: Interview with Don Cunningham was conducted in Estherville, Iowa, and via telephone, November 2013.

PART VI

16: The City of No

240   *Kristin invited me to sit*: Interview with Kristin Ostrom, March 2012.

240   *"I've always said this is Nebraska-style"*: Transcript of the Public Hearing of on LB48, Judiciary Committee, Nebraska Legislature, State Capitol, Lincoln, Nebraska, March 2, 2011.

241   *"such scant evidence and conjecture"*: Art Hovey, "Immigration Ruling a Mixed Outcome," *Columbus (Nebraska) Telegram*, February 21, 2012, http:// columbustelegram.com/news/local/state-and-regional/fremont-immigration-ruling-a-mixed-outcome/article_e56a4d06-5c95-11e1-beef-0019bb2963f4.html.

242   *April and Rafael stood outside with me*: Interviews with April Wadleigh and Rafael del Jesus conducted in Fremont, Nebraska, throughout 2012 and 2013.

245   *as the city council in Fremont convened*: I covered this meeting for harpers .org. All details come from my notes and audio recording of the meeting.

246   *the school's former principal*: Interview with Mike Aerni was conducted in Fremont, Nebraska, May 2012.

246   *uninsured Hispanics actually pay up at a higher rate*: Quoted in Tammy Real-McKeighan, "Hospital Can't Tell Who's Illegal," *Fremont Tribune*, June 12, 2010, http://fremonttribune.com/article_90b670e6-75dd-11df-943f-001cc4c002e0.html.

247   *"I'm here to tell you that you need to act"*: Chris Zavadil, "Fair Housing Expert Says HUD Could Threaten Funding," *Fremont Tribune*, October 16, 2013, http://fremonttribune.com/news/local/fair-housing-expert-says-hud-could-threaten-funding/article_d71d546a-eed2-50ed-8e76-2b94ab325712.html.

249   *A month later, the Fremont City Council met*: I covered this meeting for harpers.org. All details come from my notes and audio recording of the meeting.

249   *By the day of the special election*: I covered the special election for harpers.org. All details come from my notes and audio recordings made that evening.

251   *"It is pretty rocking inside"*: Nicholas Bergin, "Fremont Voters Over-

whelmingly Affirm Anti-illegal Immigration Ordinance," *Lincoln Journal-Star*, February 11, 2014, http://journalstar.com/news/state-and-regional/nebraska/fremont-voters-overwhelmingly-affirm-anti-illegal-immigration-ordinance/article_91d84a16-e66b-5b30-8acc-bf741705f2b4.html.

251   *Jonathan Chavez, one of Harper's renters*: Interview with Jonathan Chavez and Kayla Jacquart was conducted in Fremont, Nebraska, February 2014.

254   *"It's final now, and Fremont's victory is complete"*: Joe Duggan, "U.S. Supreme Court Won't Weigh In on Fremont's Immigration Rules, but City Isn't Relaxing," *Omaha World-Herald*, May 5, 2014.

254   *"bright green light"*: Grant Schulte, "Court decision could open door to immigrant rules," Associated Press, May 5, 2014.

17: Inspection

255   *USDA's Office of the Inspector General (OIG) released a report*: The full text of USDA Office of the Inspector General, "Food Safety and Inspection Service—Inspection and Enforcement Activities at Swine Slaughter Plants," Audit Report 34601-0001-41, May 2013, is available at http://www.usda.gov/oig/webdocs/24601-0001-41.pdf.

256   *"Yeah, that's us"*: Interview with Dan Hoppes was conducted in Omaha, Nebraska, November 2013.

256   *noncompliance records for 2012*: These documents were supplied to me via email by Tony Corbo at Food & Water Watch.

258   *"Given the fact that we're looking at it a lot more intensely"*: Interview with Philip Derfler and Hany Sidrak, from the FSIS Office of Field Operations, was conducted via telephone, November 2013.

258   *Hormel plant in Fremont has tracked at or below*: Numbers supplied by Nicky Coolberth, Assistant Director of Communications at UFCW.

258   *that Hispanic workers are almost half as likely to report an injury*: Kenneth Culp, Mary Brooks, Kerri Rupe, and Craig Zwerling, "Traumatic Injury Rates in Meatpacking Plant Workers," *Journal of Agromedicine* 13, no. 1 (February 2008): 7–16. All authors of the study work in Occupational Health Nursing, College of Nursing, University of Iowa.

259   *"make tens of thousands of repetitive motions"*: Interview with Darcy Tromanhauser was conducted in Lincoln, Nebraska, and via email in November 2013.

259   *"It's not so much the speed"*: Interview with Mark Lauritsen was conducted in Omaha, Nebraska, November 2013.

260   *"In such an incident, FSIS will deal with it as a sanitary issue"*: Interview with Philip Derfler and Hany Sidrak, November 2013.

262   *Hormel announced that the company would be shifting production of its bacon bits*: Ben Jacobson, "Hormel Picks Dubuque Plant for Expansion," *Dubuque*

Telegraph Herald, January 14, 2014, http://www.thonline.com/news/breaking/article_8cf5bc66-7d52-11e3-b776-001a4bcf6878.html.

262   *at the plant's grand opening in 2010*: See Kevin T. Higgins, "Fabulous Food Plant: Hormel's Progressive Processing Plant Is Built for the Long Haul," *Food Engineering*, December 6, 2011, http://www.foodengineeringmag.com/articles/88936-fabulous-food-plant-hormels-progressive-processing-plant-is-built-for-the-long-haul-.

263   *"two new production lines sought for the plant"*: Jacobson, "Hormel Picks Dubuque Plant for Expansion."

263   *a reporter for the* Dubuque Telegraph Herald: Ben Jacobson, "Spam Production Coming to Hormel Plant in Dubuque," *Dubuque Telegraph Herald*, February 13, 2014, http://www.thonline.com/news/breaking/article_19a77b28-9508-11e3-8f05-0017a43b2370.html.

263   *Mark Zelle, the plant manager*: "Hormel Foods Celebrates Grand Opening of State-of-the-Art Production Facility in Dubuque, Iowa," Hormel Foods Corporation press release, March 30, 2010, http://www.hormelfoods.com/Newsroom/Press-Releases/2010/03/20100330.

264   *"By separating operations"*: Higgins, "Fabulous Food Plant."

264   *"The timing for the Spam operation is still in process"*: Jacobson, "Spam Production Coming to Hormel Plant in Dubuque."

INDEX

ABOUT THE AUTHOR

Ted Genoways served as the editor of the *Virginia Quarterly Review* from 2003 to 2012, during which time the magazine won six National Magazine Awards. He is a contributing editor at *Mother Jones* and editor-at-large at *OnEarth*, and his essays and poetry have appeared in *The Atlantic*, *Bloomberg BusinessWeek*, *Harper's*, *The Nation*, *The New Republic*, *Outside*, and *The Washington Post Book World*. He is a winner of a National Press Club Award, the James Aronson Award for Social Justice Journalism and the recipient of fellowships from the National Endowment for the Arts and the Guggenheim Foundation. He is a fourth-generation Nebraskan and currently lives in Lincoln.